This book belonged to
Sally Irish
1938-2003
Born in San Francisco,
served as a Peace Corps Volunteer
where she met and married Richard Irish,
later served as Private Secretary
to the Robert Kennedy family.
Moved to Five Points Road near Rectortown,
directed the Day Care Center at Upperville,
and then became a needlepoint rug designer
using abundantly colorful botanical themes.
Served as a member of the Vestry and
Altar Guild of Trinity Church, Upperville,
President of the
Fauquier Loudoun Garden Club,
served on Garden Club of America
Horticultural Committee
and as a flower show judge.
She loved Dick Irish,
their dogs Snowball and Roxie,
her garden and her friends,
whom she inspired
with her beautiful interpretations
of nature's bounty.

FERNS
ROGER GROUNDS

FERNS
ROGER GROUNDS

READERS UNION
Group of Book Clubs
Newton Abbot

This edition was published in 1975 by Readers Union
by arrangement with PELHAM BOOKS LTD

Copyright © Roger Grounds

Full particulars of RU are obtainable from
Readers Union Limited, PO Box 6, Newton Abbot, Devon

Printed in Great Britain
by BAS Printers Limited, Wallop, Hampshire
        for Readers Union

Dedication

For three super children
Xenny, Damian and Minky

Contents

Illustrations

Plus 61 black and white line drawings and nature prints in text.

Preface

Many people have helped me in the preparation of this book, a fairly major undertaking, and I should like to thank them all. In particular I should like to thank Jimmy Dyce, the Secretary of the British Pteridological Society, for the enormous amount of help and encouragement he has given me over the writing of this book, for his many valuable suggestions, particularly with regard to the varieties of British ferns, and for his so kindly writing a foreword.

I should also like to thank Henry Schollick, President of the British Pteridological Society who not only lent me a number of books on ferns which are difficult to obtain in this country, but also gave me the run of his exceptionally fine collection of ferns, showing me many plants that I have seen nowhere else. Another member of the British Pteridological Society whom I should like to thank is Jim Crabbe who gave me a great deal of help.

While this is the traditional place in which to thank one's wife 'without whom this book would never have been written', and one tends to feel that such thanks are obligatory, I really should like to thank my wife, Penny, because it really would have been impossible, against the pressures of a more than full-time job, to have written this book at all without her help. She tirelessly pursued Victorian fern books round the English countryside, where in some cases they were so hard to find we began to wonder whether they had ever actually been published, and spent many demanding, tedious and often frustrating hours in libraries searching for taxonomic details of some of the ferns mentioned in this book where such details do not yet appear to have been established.

Finally I should like to thank my three children, Xenny, Damian and Minky for contributing to the book in three ways: in kindly observing the rather vague rule in the garden that the lawn is for playing on, rather than the borders, when in fact borders are far more tempting to play in; for helping me to photograph and collect fern fronds and specimens from the branches of trees, from screes, cliffs and the tops of walls accessible to their nimbler feet but not to my bulkier frame; and for putting up with the months I spent tied to my typewriter writing the book rather than playing with them—something of a sacrifice on both sides.

Foreword

I was given the opportunity to read through the manuscript of this book and was able to make some suggestions, particularly concerning British ferns and their varieties, which have been my special interest for about forty years. Its content and presentation supplement the few—*very* few—good books on the subject which have been published in recent years, and I am therefore pleased to be invited to write a foreword.

Before the few twentieth-century fern books, the fern collector and grower had to rely very much on the spate published during the latter half of the nineteenth century. But, even though the information in them is as valuable and applicable today as ever it was, most of them—and this applies chiefly to the better ones—are now very difficult to obtain and costly to buy. On the other hand, the newer ones are easily available to interested readers, and this is where the present-day author is able to make an important contribution to the cult.

Roger Grounds covers a wide field in this book, dealing not only with our British ferns and their varieties, but also with a large number from other lands which can be grown in Britain and add immensely to the interest of the collection. It is a very readable book and the introductory chapters contain much useful information which will be readily understood by even the rawest beginner. It gives me great pleasure to recommend it to fern lovers and growers.

J W Dyce
SECRETARY, BRITISH PTERIDOLOGICAL SOCIETY

CHAPTER ONE

Introduction to Ferns

Ferns are indisputably the most beautiful of all non-flowering plants. They have a grace and charm that is uniquely their own. Whether they are grown in a shaded border along with hostas, hardy terrestial orchids and shrubs, in bottle gardens and Wardian cases, in the pampered environment of the greenhouse, or whether they are simply encountered in their native haunts in woodlands and hedgerows, it is the delicacy of their finely divided fronds and their flowing habit of growth that makes them so attractive.

Everyone knows a fern when he encounters one, though not everyone would be able to give a definition of what a fern is in terms that would be meaningful to a botanist. Many people are familiar with some of the commoner ferns by name without even realising that they are ferns—bracken and the hart's-tongue fern being examples. To anyone who has an eye for the countryside, the ferns form a clearly distinguished group of plants, and it is a group that holds a strange fascination, a fascination that increases the more one knows about them.

The ferns of the modern world could easily be taken at face value simply as a successful group of plants, like any other group of plants that has survived into the modern age. Yet things are not so simple. Ferns are indeed one of the most successful of all groups of plants, and yet they are plants of enormous antiquity. The ferns of today are but the diminutive relatives of the great forests of tree ferns that flourished together with giant clubmosses and giant horsetails in the Carboniferous Age some 350,000,000 years ago.

It was these giant ancestors of the modern ferns that laid down those rich seams of coal upon which not only the Industrial Revolution, but also the structure of modern society were to be founded. The ferns of those days were the most highly evolved form of vegetable life on earth—the dominant vegetation of a world of mists, swamps and quagmires. The tallest of the tree ferns reached as much as fifty feet in height, and many people believe that they had to evolve their finely cut leaves to offer the largest possible area of greenery to catch the sunlight to carry out the vital process of photosynthesis, because of competition from the giant clubmosses and horsetails that grew as tall or taller than themselves.

The dominance of the ferns has long since passed. Most of the species and many of the genera that made up those great coal forests have become extinct, displaced by the newly emergent group, the flowering plants. Yet even today ferns and their allies comprise a group of over 10,000 living species. Perhaps their antiquity and their ability to have survived into the modern world is part of their fascination.

The more one knows about ferns the more they intrigue one, and to appreciate them fully it is well worth examining in some detail their place in the plant kingdom and their evolutionary history.

THE PLACE OF FERNS IN THE PLANT KINGDOM

The plant kingdom is divided into two main groups, the flowering plants, known as *phanerogams*, and the non-flowering plants, known as *cryptogams*. Each of these two main sections is further sub-divided, the phanerogams into two sub-groups, known as classes, the conifers and the angiosperms, while the cryptogams are sub-divided into three sub-groups or classes detailed below. These classes themselves are further divided into orders, the orders into suborders, and those into families. The families are then divided into tribes and in some cases into subtribes. Finally, the tribes or subtribes are divided into genera, and these into species.

Working back up the scale to the two great subkingdoms, those species which bear a close botanical relationship are grouped together into genera; those genera which bear a close relationship to each other are grouped together into subtribes, and so on.

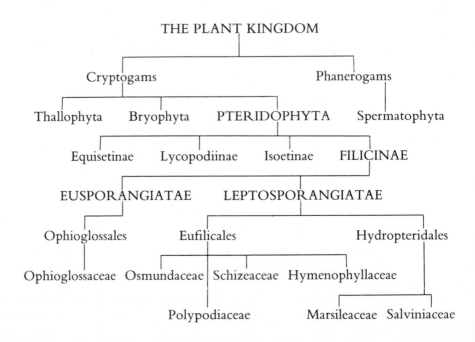

The point of all this seemingly unnecessary complication, apart of course from man's innate urge to classify, group and generally impose order onto what otherwise seems a disorderly universe, is to bring out the relationships between plants. Since all plants have developed from very primitive forms to highly complex forms, the system by which plants are classified reveals the evolutionary relationships between various groups of plants. Well, that's the theory, but different botanists suggest different evolutionary relationships between different groups of plants. These academic disputes, however, do not affect the broad outlines of the classifications of the plant kingdom. Certainly the subgroups with which we are dealing here are not in dispute. The following are the accepted three groups in the cryptogam subkingdom.

(1) *Thallophyta*　This is the most primitive of the four groups, and yet it is a remarkably diverse group, containing some 125,000 species of plants ranging in size from microscopic, single-celled organisms to the giant kelps (seaweeds) that can grow to a height of 100 feet. The group includes both aquatic and terrestrial plants, but it undoubtedly originated in the sea. It is divided into two classes (a) the algae and (b) the fungi. The seaweeds, including the green, red and brown algae are mainly aquatic, and the majority are capable of manufacturing chlorophyll. The fungi are mainly terrestrial and in general lack the ability to manufacture chlorophyll, having therefore to derive it from other sources, often as parasites but sometimes as symbionts. This class included the moulds, yeasts and those plants that are popularly known as fungi and mushrooms.

There is a third group that is occasionally given the status of a class, and that is the lichens, in which various individual species of alga and fungus live together in a symbiotic relationship (i.e. a relationship which is beneficial to both partners), the alga supplying the chlorophyll, the fungi the moisture necessary to sustain the alga. The combination is a formidable one—the group having colonised almost every remotely possible type of habitat on the face of the earth. The class is characterised by an almost total lack of organisation within the conglomerate of cells: the plants have no roots, no leaves and no stems.

(2) *Bryophyta*　A group of about 20,000 species of mainly terrestrial and invariably low-growing plants, needing very wet conditions for their existence. The mosses, liverworts and hornworts are typical of the class. Their cellular structure is somewhat more organised than in the case of the thallophyta. The majority attach themselves to the ground by means of hair-like appendages known as rhizoids, which are anchors but not true roots (i.e. they do not carry out the function of true roots which is, apart from anchoring the plant, to absorb moisture and nutrients from the soil to feed the above-soil part of the plant). The rhizoids can only absorb water, not

nutrients. The bryophytes have also made one further advance over the thallophytes: they have developed a thin cuticle over their surface, which prevents that surface from drying out as rapidly as in the case with the thallophytes.

(3) *Pteridophyta*   The ferns and so-called fern-allies comprise a class of about 10,000 species, all of them land plants. They are considerably more advanced than the bryophytes. They are, as it were, the first of the vertebrates of the plant kingdom. They are true vascular plants—that is, they contain bundles of veins. These bundles of veins serve two functions: firstly they enable the moisture and nutrients absorbed by the roots to be carried through the plant to the leaves and other parts of the plant while at the same time bearing the products of photosynthesis carried out in the leaves back to the roots and other parts of the plant; secondly, they give the plant a 'spine', so that for the first time in evolution plants were able to get up off the ground and grow erect. These were very major advances.

The next evolutionary advance was the seed-bearing plants, the conifers and the true flowering plants.

THE PLACE OF FERNS IN THE PTERIDOPHYTA
The class Pteridophyta includes a number of plants which, while closely related to the ferns, differ from them in a number of characteristics. All, however, have the one common characteristic of reproducing by means of spores. They are divided into four subclasses:

(a) the ferns proper, (Filicinae).
(b) the horse-tails (Equisetinae).
(c) the clubmosses (Lycopodiinae).
(d) the quillworts (Isoetinae).

Of these the clubmosses are the most primitive, followed by the horse-tails, with the ferns proper as the most advanced and most recently evolved of the group.

The ferns themselves (Filicinae) are divided into two subclasses, the Eusporangiatae and the Leptosporangiatae. The Eusporangiatae is the more primitive of the two subclasses, and includes the so-called succulent ferns, embracing the genera Ophioglossum and Botrychium, included in the Ophioglossaceae. The subclass Leptosporangiatae is subdivided into two orders, the Eufilicales and the Hydropteridales. Of the two, the Eufilicales are the true ferns, the plants that the great majority of people would recognise as ferns, and it is this group with which this book is primarily concerned. The other order, the Hydropteridales, the so-called water ferns, are a more recently evolved group, and are made up of only two genera.

THE PLACE OF FERNS IN THE EVOLUTION OF PLANT LIFE

In spite of the theories of scientists, in spite of their experiments—and some of them even claim to have created 'life' in test tubes—the reality is that we still do not know how life on earth began. A happy, and possibly chance, combination of chemicals and probably radioactivity seem the most likely explanation, but the form in which and the precise point in time at which life first appeared on earth still elude us. One thing is certain: life existed on earth for a long time before the earliest fossils known to man. The earliest fossil plants known are over 500,000,000 years old, but, since they are ill-preserved, little can be learned from them, especially regarding their function and structure. All that can be ascertained is that they are fossils of blue-green algae and bacteria—among the simplest of all known living things.

What is certain is that all life began in the sea, and that it began with very simple single-celled organisms, that are neither properly animals nor properly plants. Organisms very like them are found living today. They are classified in zoology textbooks as *Flagellata* and in botany textbooks as *Algae*, but they are the same creature. Considerable development had to take place before plants and animals could begin to develop their separate ways and that development—for such is the law of evolution—was towards greater and ever greater complexity. The simplest things are the most primitive: the most complex the most advanced.

Over a period of millions of years these original, simple, ambiguous single-celled organisms began to live together in colonies, and some of the cells began to carry out specialised functions.

The earliest organisations of cells were very simple structures. In the plant kingdom these were the algae. Although the largest of these can grow to a hundred feet in height (supported by the pressure of the surrounding sea), the cells have differentiated very little. Each cell still has to manufacture all the nutrients it needs to support itself: it does not exchange nutrients or other chemical products with its neighbours or with other parts of the plants. The giant kelps, in spite of their great size, have no stems, no leaves, no roots and no vascular system. They cement themselves to the sea floor, but this cement is not in any sense a root. Furthermore, these primitive algae have no 'skin', no cuticle to prevent them from drying out when exposed to the atmosphere. They evolved in the sea and there they had to stay until such a 'skin' evolved. Extraordinary though it may seem, for some 275,000,000 years plants and animals, some of them quite large, lived in the sea, and nothing at all inhabited the dry land.

That, however, may well have been because the land surface was uninhabitable. For millions of years the continents of the world were just vast expanses of bare dry rock upon which the sun beat down mercilessly, and in that bleak, desolate world there was not a blade of grass, not the wing of a bird to cast a shadow. But at the fringes of the continents there were great muddy swamps and estuaries, and it was via these that life, both animal and vegetable, first moved out of the seas and onto the land.

The next evolutionary step forward was taken by the Bryophyta, the mosses and liverworts. Both are plants that flourish in very wet conditions. The bryophyta have advanced in several ways. The cells of the parts of the plant that rest on the ground have specialised in their functions: they have formed rhizoids, which are not true roots, but thread-like anchors which can absorb water. They can do more than that: they can feed that water up into the higher parts of the plant, where it is transpired in the process of photo-synthesis. This, however, does not amount to a true vascular system, since the plants cannot pass the products of photosynthesis back down to the roots. The process is very much like holding a sheet of blotting paper vertically and dipping the bottom in water. Capillary action will cause the water to rise up the blotting paper, but on the high areas of the blotting paper the rate of evaporation will exceed the rate of absorption. However, it was a major advance: until then each cell had had to absorb all its own moisture require-ments.

The Bryophyta also made one other very important advance. They were the first plants to have leaves, though these were of a very rudimentary type: they were only one cell thick. Yet even that was very significant, for it in its turn could not have taken place without one other major evolutionary advance made by this group, the development of a 'cuticle' over the outer surface of the plant. This is a thin, waxy coating which slows down the rate at which the green parts of plants loose water. Though the least spectacular of the advances made by the Bryophyta, it was probably the most important.

The next group of plants to evolve were the Pteridophyta, the group to which the ferns belong. All are characterised by reproducing themselves by means of spores. Their major evolutionary advance is that they were all vascular plants, the group of plants known as tracheophytes. These have vascular bundles which give the plants a 'skeleton', which in turn gives them the structured rigidity necessary for them to grow stems and even trunks, and at the same time to carry the products of photosynthesis from the leaves to the roots and to all other parts of the plant. Today seventy-five per cent of all known species of plants are tracheophytes.

The first vascular plants emerged into the muddy swamplands of the Devonian Age, the Age of Fishes. The earliest of these vascular plants have been described from Canadian deposits but have since been found in many other parts of the world, including the U.S.A. and north-western Europe. They belong to the genus Psilophyton. This is an almost ridiculously simple vascular plant. It consists of a stem and little else. The stem crawls along in the mud, sending up vertical shoots at irregular intervals. At the tips of the shoots are spore-cases. Mostly they have no leaves and no roots, although one or two plants have been identified in which rudimentary leaves were present, and in a few instances plants are known in which the erect parts branched. The best preserved specimen of the whole group was of the simplest type and was found at Rhynie in Aberdeenshire in Scotland—in some of the oldest rocks in the world. Though originally included in the genus *Psilophyton*, it has now been transferred to the genus *Rhynia*. Although the Devonian period, which lasted for 100,000,000 years, ended some 350,000,000 years ago, plants like *Psilophyton* are still living today. One of them is the whisk-fern of Florida and Bermuda, *Psilotum nudum*.

The evolution of the Psilophytes was followed closely by that of the Pteridophytes, there being an obvious link between the Psilophytes and such primitive Pteridophytes as the quillworts and the horsetails. The earliest ferns known to have existed evolved only a little later than the Psilophytes, also during the Devonian period. These earliest of ferns, none of which has survived into the modern age, are often grouped together as Coenopteridinae. Many of them were shrubby plants, producing fronds very much like the fronds of some of the larger modern ferns, often three feet or more in length, and were dimorphic in character, that is, they produced fertile and barren fronds that were clearly distinguished from each other, as do some modern ferns.

The ferns, clubmosses and horsetails were coevals. They all flourished together during the Carboniferous Age, (which followed the Devonian period), and it is from fossils of that era that we have gained such accurate knowledge of these early ferns. Far from being small plants, and it is only natural that one should presume that larger plants have evolved from smaller plants and not the other way about, the earliest ferns were large plants—as were the earliest of the successful flowering plants. The clubmosses grew into trees 100 feet tall, the horsetails into trees sixty to ninety feet tall and the ferns into trees fifty feet or so tall. It seems likely that the ferns had to develop their very finely divided fronds in order to compete to the light with their taller-growing rivals. They had to evolve a highly efficient method of catching light to survive at all in such conditions.

Yet a curious anomaly exists in the fossil flora of the Carboniferous Age. A great many of the fern-like leaf fossils found do not belong to ferns at all, but to a now completely extinct and somewhat mysterious group of plants known as the seed-ferns or Pteridosperms—seed plants that had also had to evolve finely divided fronds in order to catch enough light to survive in those great primaeval forests.

It requires something of a leap of the imagination to grasp even remotely what those vast swamp-forests must have been like. We live today in a world dominated by the flowering plants, a world of herbs, trees, shrubs, grasses, of spring bulbs and autumn colours, and interrelated with this world is the whole complexity of the animal kingdom, including the birds with their brilliant colours and their songs as well as mammals and insects. In those great primaeval forests many of these elements were absent. There were only the tree horsetails, the tree clubmosses, the tree ferns and pteridosperms, growing in an atmosphere of extremely high humidity, their trunks and even fronds festooned with lichens, the forest floor thick with mosses, liverworts and algae. There was not a single flower to brighten up the whole of this gloomy, twilight world. No birds moved among the upper storey of the forest, no monkeys swung from trapeze to trapeze of tree-fern frond, no ungulates grazed the floor beneath. Only the great primitive reptiles came lumbering through the swamp-forests browsing on the vegetation.

Then quite abruptly—almost overnight in terms of geological time—the scene changed. The great dinosaurs and their relatives died out, and with them died out the great swamp-forests of the coal age. Many theories have been put forward for this abrupt change. It has been suggested that the dinosaurs died out because the vegetation changed: or simply because they were too stupid to go on surviving. But there are other abrupt changes in the pattern of the past. And there are inconsistencies in the pattern, breaks in the chain. The dinosaurs disappeared and in their place came the birds and the insects: suddenly the flowering plants appeared, and yet they seem to have no direct ancestors from which to have evolved, just as man himself cannot trace his origins back beyond a certain point. Always one goes back in time to find a break in the chain of continual evolutionary advance. If Darwin's theory of continual evolutionary advance is correct, then there should be no 'missing links'. Yet there are, and when these are linked with the sudden disappearance of the coal forests and the dinosaurs, then plainly further thought needs to be given to the subject.

Certainly continuous evolution in Darwin's sense is a reality. It can be seen going on in the world around us today, plants and animals adapting themselves to survive in new conditions. But to explain the record of the past a more violent form of evolution must also be put forward as a hypothesis. Modern plant breeders use the alkaloid substance colchicine to achieve new colour breaks with certain flowering plants. They also use radio isotopes. Observations of the effects of radioactivity on both flora and fauna following nuclear test explosions show that mutations not only occur but can be perpetuated if they offer a survival advantage.

More than twenty years ago Emmanuel Velikovsky, the American rabbinical scholar, put forward a theory suggesting that at certain irregular periods in its history the earth has been exposed to periods of extremely intense radioactivity brought about by comets or other errant stars coming too close to the earth (in *Worlds in Collision*, and elaborated in *The Day the Sun Stood Still*).

The theory has not been generally accepted, perhaps only because of man's innate desire to believe that behind the violence of man himself there lies a universe that is at heart a stable and organised system. More recently, and more acceptably, the theory has been put forward that at intervals of 120,000 to 150,000 years the earth's magnetism changes: it weakens, we lose our magnetic shield—the ionosphere—and are for relatively short periods exposed to the high energy particles from which the ionosphere normally protects us. Such exposure would produce mutations. It could for example, quite feasibly wipe out the dinosaurs and the swamp forests, and induce the mutations that produced flowering plants. Once the ionosphere returned these could stabilise themselves and the process of gradual, continual evolution continue again. This would certainly explain why there is no fossil record of a plant or group of plants intermediate between non-flowering and flowering plants, and why, in spite of the many learned arguments put forward, it still remains apparent that flowering plants did not evolve once and for all from a single plant or genus, but from several different plants in different places.

Theories such as these would also explain why it is that very few of the families of ferns of the coal age have survived into the present day. Most of the ferns of the modern world have evolved during the last 100,000,000 years—since the disappearance of the carboniferous forests.

Another point that is often overlooked is that the ferns of the primaeval forests belonged to a different fern group from those that survive today. It was the Eusporangiate group that was then dominant; this group is represented in the cool temperate world today only by the genera *Ophioglossum* and *Botrychium*. Today it is the Leptosporangiate group that is the more successful.

FERNS OF THE MODERN WORLD

The ferns have fared rather better as far as surviving into the modern world is concerned, than have their close relatives the clubmosses and the horsetails. Though the smallest class in the plant kingdom—so far as number of species is concerned—they still make a major contribution to the vegetation of the world we live in today.

It is perhaps the diversity—a diversity that is to be expected in any group of plants that had been evolving for a long time—that has enabled them to compete with the more modern flowering plants. Ferns can be found almost everywhere from the ice-caps to the equator, at altitudes ranging from sea-level to as much or perhaps more than 10,000 feet above sea level.

They are rather more restricted in their choice of habitat. The ferns, especially those of the cool temperate world, are essentially woodland plants. The great majority of species revel in cool, shaded conditions in which not only is there a reasonably constant amount of moisture in the soil, but in which the atmosphere is also relatively humid. While this goes for the majority, there are of course ferns that will grow in extreme conditions. Many of the dwarf ferns that inhabit walls and rocky cliff faces grow with their fronds fully exposed to the sun: it will usually be found, however, that their wiry roots have penetrated a deep crevice and are cool and damp at all times. At the other extreme there are the ferns that grow with their roots in perpetually saturated soil, at pondsides.

Ferns vary greatly in their shape of fronds, the bi-pinnate (doubly divided) leaf form of bracken being usually thought of as a typical fern frond. Other ferns, such as the maidenhair spleenwort *Asplenium trichomanes*, have pinnate fronds, while the true maidenhair fern *Adiantum capillus-veneris*, has uniquely-shaped cordate pinnules. Other ferns, such as the hart's-tongue *Asplenium scolopendrium*, have entire fronds—fronds, that is, which are not divided in any way.

The majority of ferns present their sporangia (spore cases) on the backs of their fronds and these sporangia vary very greatly in their colour and in their arrangement on the backs of the leaves. Indeed, it is these variations in the presentation of the sporangia that are used by botanists to classify ferns. Some ferns produce sporangia on the backs of all their leaves, as is the case with the hart's-tongue: others, such as the hard fern *Blechnum spicant*, produce both fertile and infertile fronds, only the fertile fronds carrying the sporangia. In the case of the hard fern the difference between the fertile and the infertile fronds is not strongly marked, the fertile fronds being erect and narrow, the infertile ones more flaccid and spreading. In other ferns, such as the lady fern *Athyrium filix-femina*, there is no differentiation at all. In others, as is the case with the adder's-tongue *Ophioglossum vulgatum* and with the moonwort *Botrychium lunaria*, the fertile frond appears to bear no resemblance to the infertile frond, the fertile fronds of both species looking, at a quick glance, very much like the seed head of a plantain—although a closer examination shows that the fertile frond is, in fact, only a modified infertile frond. Indeed, by comparing the fertile and infertile fronds of the hard fern and the moonwort it can be seen that the differences are of degree rather than of type.

At the present time there appears to be a growing interest in ferns, in the wild, in the open garden and in hermetic gardens. The last occasion on which there was a similar interest was in Victorian times when there was a veritable fern fad. It is interesting to note that just as the permissive society is giving way to a society of greater moral integrity, so the Victorian Age, an age characterised by a high sense of moral purpose, was also preceded by an age of permissiveness, the Georgian era. It seems that a permissive society is a society without purpose: in a more puritanical society what has been lost in open-mindedness is compensated for by a positive gain in driving force. These things are reflected in the aesthetic tastes of the times. It is almost as though the Victorians found the flamboyance of flowers, not so much vulgar nor even sensual, as frivolous, and found in ferns a sense of functional purpose that matched their own thoughts and outlook. Be that as it may, it seems that with a change in moral outlook society is again returning to an interest in ferns as part of a general change in aesthetic taste.

In Victorian times the fad for ferns was ubiquitous. Every household had its fernery or its terrarium or Wardian case in which ferns were grown. Indeed, the Wardian fern case was as essential a piece of decorative furniture as were the waxed fruits under glass domes, the stuffed birds in glass cases, the bouquets of dried grasses and peacock feathers, the velvet-hung mantleshelf and the occasional tables bearing a bounty of bijouteries. Many of these items are also making a return to fashion, along with the bottle gardens and fern cases. The cabinet makers and factories of Victorian times specialised in producing fern cases to suit all homes, rich or poor, and they produced these cases in a vast variety of designs, varying from quite small pieces suitable for keeping on a table to huge pieces the size of small glass-houses. Some were of simple design, while others were extremely ornate. People filled these cases with ferns, and itinerant plant sellers, called 'Botany Bens', scoured the countryside for ferns and went from door to door, a basket of ferns over their arm, hawking the ferns. Breeders and selectors spent a great deal of time and money collecting and breeding plumose, cristate, tasselled and foliose forms of common ferns.

Over 1,800 different varieties of British native ferns has been recorded, and one species, the lady fern *Athyrium felix-femina*, is recorded as having almost three hundred different cultivars.

Ferns were of course the ideal plant for the terraria* of Victorian parlours: under conditions of hermetic cultivation they are as indifferent to neglect as it is possible for a plant to be, and they were as tolerant of gloom as troglodytes. Yet there was one undesirable side-effect of the fern fad. The Botany Bens appear to have collected British native ferns with such enthusiasm that they seem to have brought about a depletion of stocks, from which it is doubtful whether the ferns have yet recovered. There is reason to believe that such ferns as the rusty-back *Asplenium ceterach*, and the true maidenhair, *Adiantum capillus-veneris*, were much more common before Victorian times than they are now. It would indeed be a sad thing if a new craze for ferns were to bring about a similar depletion of natural stocks.

*Closed cases like miniature greenhouses, and very popular in fashionable Victorian parlours.

CHAPTER TWO

The Life-Cycle of the Fern

Ferns are non-flowering plants. Since they do not flower, they cannot produce seed. Yet this fact is not always apparent to the uninitiated observer. Many ferns, such as the royal fern *Osmunda regalis*, produce fertile fronds that certainly look very like primitive flowers and which may indeed have been one of the experiments that led, ultimately, to the evolution of flowering plants.

Ferns reproduce by means of spores. Since there are no flowering stalks these spores are carried on the undersides of the fronds. This is true even where fertile and infertile fronds are differentiated as they are in the case of the royal fern, *Osmunda regalis*, the parsley fern, *Cryptogramma crispa*, and the adder's-tongue, *Ophioglossum vulgatum*, to name but a few. In all these cases close examination will show that the fertile frond is but a modified leaf: so of course, are the petals of a flower, although there the modifications have been far greater.

The life cycle of ferns is highly complex and extraordinarily fascinating. Ferns, like all plants lower than themselves in the evolutionary ladder, go through what is known as the alternation of generations. That is, there is a sexual phase and there is a non-sexual phase. Whereas in the true mosses and the liverworts it is the sexual phase that is the one normally called moss or liverwort and the non-sexual generation normally passes unnoticed, with the ferns it is the other way about: it is the non-sexual generation that is usually noticed, and the sexual generation that passes unnoticed. It is a curious but often overlooked fact that this peculiar mode of reproduction takes place in all plants including the flowering plants, although in these higher forms of plant life the alternation of generations takes place internally within the seeds, and not externally as in the lower forms of plant life.

The spores of ferns are situated on the undersides of the leaves. Sometimes they occur in symmetrical patterns each side of the central rib, and sometimes round the edges of the underside of the fronds. In each fern the arrangement of the spore cases is different, and it is this that is used by botanists when classifying or identifying ferns. While with mosses and the lower forms of non-flowering plant life spores are produced virtually throughout the year, ferns, together with clubmosses and horsetails, produce spores only at particular seasons. This is important, because ferns have a definite and seasonal cycle of growth: mosses and lower forms of plant life can be found in all stages of their life cycle at all times of year.

The spore cases form conspicuous brown or black clusters on the undersides of the fronds. A microscope is needed to see the details of these organs and how they work, but there is a simple experiment that can be tried, and it is rather interesting. Take a frond of any fern with its brown or black spore cases showing clearly and lay it down on a piece of white paper, with the underside of the leaf touching the paper. Leave it in a dry place for a couple of days, making sure that it is not disturbed. Then carefully lift the frond off the paper, and you will find a delicate tracery of brown or black dust that follows exactly the pattern of the spore cases on the underside of the frond. This dust is made up of millions of spores. These spores really are tiny. Even with a powerful hand magnifying glass they are still minute.

a Mature non-sexual generation fern
b Fertile pinnule with sori
c Spores being released from mature sporangium
d Spores (× about 120)
e Spore germinating and beginning to lengthen into a prothallus
f Prothallus
g Sperms on the left and archegonium on the right. The archegonium contains the egg cells which when fertilised will produce a new non-sexual generation fern.
h Young fern beginning to grow from the prothallus. The young fern lives as a parasite on the prothallus until strong enough to adopt an independent existence.

THE LIFE-CYCLE OF A FERN (not to scale)

The spores are produced in enormous quantities because, for reasons that become apparent later, only a relatively small proportion survive to become mature plants. The spores are collected together in clusters on the undersides of the leaves. It is these clusters that are so conspicuous late in the year as the spores are ripening. Each spore cluster is usually protected by a tiny umbrella-like object called an *indusium*.

Because of the minuteness of the spores a microscope is needed to see the intricate structure of the spore cases, and the infinite cunning with which the spore cases operate. The spore containers of most ferns are like minute spheres carried on short and incredibly thin stalks. Around the middle of each sphere is a belt of cells with toughened walls. When these cells reach a certain degree of dryness they straighten out tearing the sphere apart as they do so. This operation is very much like that of certain seeds that explode by dehydration. The bursting of the seeds of broom or of the common garden lupin (which can fling its seeds up to twenty yards away) can often be heard on a still day. The spore containers of ferns are much too small to explode noisily, but the mechanism is much the same. When the spore container is torn asunder it flings the spores into the air. It does not fling them a great distance: it does not need to. The spores are extraordinarily light, and they can be carried truly incredible distances on the wind.

Only if the spore falls on wet ground will it start into growth. The fact that it can only grow on wet ground is one of the many reasons for the ferns' prodigal production of spores: those that fall on dry ground will never begin to grow. The spore will need uniformly wet conditions if it is to continue growing and to produce another non-sexual generation plant—another reason for the enormous quantity of spores produced.

The first thing a spore does when it falls on wet ground is to absorb water, which it does by osmosis. With the absorption of water the inner contents of the spore begin to swell. This swelling causes the tough, outer wall of the spore to burst, allowing the growing tissue to break through. As soon as this has happened the spore-cell divides in two. One part becomes a rhizoid, growing into a long, slender thread, while the other part grows more vigorously and contains green cell bodies called chloroplasts. These colour bodies enable the growing spore to photosynthesise.

The upper part of the growth (the part containing the chloroplasts) continues to extend itself, becoming a long green thread. This thread is made up on a continuous line of single cells joined end to end like the carriages of a train. After about a week of growth the growing tip begins to multiply sideways. The cell at the growing tip of the thread is then divided into three parts by two slanting cell walls. The organism then continues to grow both forwards and sideways. Instead of being just a green thread it becomes a green ribbon.

This green ribbon is extremely fragile. It is only one cell thick. It has no internal structure that would give it either strength or rigidity. It is simply a ribbon of single cells that lies on the ground. By the time that the organism has reached this stage the original rhizoid has become inadequate: it can no longer supply sufficient moisture to maintain the whole plant. The ribbon then develops independent rhizoids. These grow out of the lower surfaces of some of the cells. Usually they are produced only by the cells nearest the middle of the ribbon.

Aided by these additional rhizoids, the tiny plant continues to grow. At full growth it will be a small, fan-shaped object with a slight notch at the end. This notch occurs where the end-cell of the original thread terminates. In many ferns this stage is reached after about twelve weeks of growth. At this stage the cells in the centre of the ribbon will be two cells thick, although the rest of the plant will remain only one cell thick.

This tiny plant, now at its full growth, is called a *prothallus* (plural *prothalli*). It is the sexual generation of the fern (the noticeable generation with the decorative fronds being the non-sexual generation). The prothalli are usually small, sometimes very small, and they are easily overlooked. Often their nature is not realised, and many people who have tried growing ferns, especially if they have tried growing them indoors either in pots or in hermetic gardens, have mistaken these prothalli for baby liverworts, which they very much resemble. The liverworts are indeed built on very similar lines, but they are usually larger than prothalli.

The *antheridia* or male organs of the prothallus (the organs that will produce the spermatozoa) are produced on the underside of the prothallus, either in amongst the rhizoids or else on the edge of the prothallus. They are small round bodies, and when they are ready to discharge their spermatozoa they burst open, and spermatozoa are released in millions. However, the antheridia can only burst open if they are in contact with water: of the millions of prothalli that grow, thousands will be growing in conditions that are too dry for this to happen. Each spermatozoon consists of a long, thin nucleus coiled in a spiral with a small bladder filled with food substances attached to one end. This bladder falls away when it is no longer needed. The spermatozoa can swim actively in water, and they do this by means of swimming-hairs which are attached to the spiral nucleus. These hairs thrash the water incessantly, spinning the spermatozoa along. This animal-like movement of the spermatozoa may seem something totally unexpected in a plant, but in fact it is found in the spermatozoa of all lower plants.

The *archegonia*, the female reproductive organs, are situated on the top of the prothallus. Each archegonium consists of a tiny flask containing a single egg-cell. When the eggs are ripe, and ready for fertilisation, the neck of the flask opens and a quantity of mucilage oozes out. This contains a chemical 'scent' which attracts the spermatozoa. In ferns this activating agent is malic acid: in the mosses it is a sweet mucilage. This 'scent' attracts the spermatozoa, which swim in the manner already described from the underside of the prothallus all the way round the edge and onto the top of the prothallus, across the top and into the open neck of the flask, where they fertilise the egg-cell.

Once fertilised, the egg-cell is not liberated from the flask. It stays inside the flask and develops there. This being the case, the growing embryo fern draws nourishment from the prothallus, and it continues to draw it from the prothallus until it is large enough to support itself, at which time the prothallus withers and dies. In a great many of the lower plants this sort of parasitism of the young plant upon the parent body is common.

As it grows in size the young fern puts down rhizoids of its own. Once this has happened the prothallus gradually degenerates, so that the change-over from feeding off the prothallus to becoming self-supporting is a gradual one.

The young fern plant that grows on the prothallus is a true fern, and its fronds, although very much smaller, are definitely fern-like. Growth continues, both above ground and below ground, until the winter comes and the plant begins its period of dormancy.

In many ferns, however, growth underground continues during the winter. The rhizoids continue pushing their way down into the soil, forming what is really a subterranean stem known as a rhizome. The surface of the rhizome is covered with a mass of minute feeding hairs. These extract nutrients from the soil and store them up in fleshy tissue for use by the plant when growth begins again.

In the spring top-growth begins again. Swellings appear on the upper surface of the rhizome. These are the leaf-buds. They grow longer and longer and gradually push their way up through the soil. When they emerge they are seen to be tightly coiled: it is this coiling, which is unique to ferns, that protects the tender young fronds from damage incurred as they thrust up through the soil.

In most ferns the fronds are rolled as they emerge from the soil. They are curled up rather in the manner of a bishop's crook. As they elongate they gradually unfurl. If the fronds are bi-pinnate, each of the side-branches of the frond is also curled.

As spring changes to summer the young fronds uncurl, opening themselves like fans to expose the maximum area to the sunlight. As summer progresses the spores begin to form on the backs of the fronds, which often turn a deeper green as the summer goes by. As summer changes to autumn the spores ripen and are released. Then with the deciduous species the fronds turn to shades of yellow, white or bronze, before falling to the ground to rot away during the winter. As the fronds rot away they form a usually acid mould which is highly moisture-retentive—an ideal place for the spores to grow into prothalli. And so the whole cycle begins again.

CHAPTER THREE

The Geographical Distribution of Ferns

Both the evolutionary history and the natural history of ferns have an intimate bearing on their geographical distribution. Both, in fact, exert a limiting factor on their distribution. Because ferns evolved in a world that was considerably wetter than the present-day world and because they can only reproduce in relatively wet surroundings, the ferns are denizens only of the damper places in the world of today. Moreover, the world was not only wetter, but also warmer, and this too has a bearing on the geographical distribution of ferns: they require a high degree of atmospheric humidity, and this in turn means that they are confined to those areas of the world that are moderately warm. A further evolutionary factor affecting their geographical distribution is that, as far as climatopalaeologists can tell, the world in which the ferns evolved was one of almost incessant rain. Although there were in those distant days no broad-leaved trees to shade them, there was no need for such trees, since the sun would probably never have shone directly on the fronds of the ferns, being obscured from them either by the rain and the clouds that brought it, or else by a very thick blanket of mist. As a result of this modern ferns normally grow in situations where their fronds are shielded from the direct rays of the sun, while the few that grow in exposed situations almost invariably do so on the tops of mountains where they are more or less perpetually dampened either by rain or mist.

As might be expected of plants that evolved in a world where a virtually tropical climate obtained, the great majority of the ferns of the modern world are denizens of the tropics, and in particular of the warm, wet regions of the tropics. While the great majority of fern genera have a number of species that are tropical, and a few species that are not tropical, there are relatively few genera which have no tropical species at all. Indeed, of the 243 fern genera known to science, only fifteen do not occur in the tropics. Similarly, of the ninety-four genera known in the northern hemisphere, only eight do not occur in the tropics. As might be expected of plants that are so dependent on moisture for their individual and group survival, it is only in the tropics that the larger, lusher ferns are found (including the tree ferns) while the ferns of the cooler, relatively drier temperate regions are, in the main, dimunitive species, adapted to surviving in conditions of greater exposure to sunlight, dry air and even frost.

The one factor above all others which controls the distribution of ferns is moisture, whether in the soil or the atmosphere. It is worth looking at some specific distribution situations to see what effect rainfall has on fern populations. The British Isles serve as a useful example for an analysis of this type, being very small (only one thirty-eighth the size of the United States) and the annual mean temperature varying by only trivial amounts from one part of the country to another. The variation in rainfall on the other hand is substantial, the rainfall in the west of the country is substantially higher than that in the east of the country. Thus whereas in parts of Cornwall and Wales the rainfall may exceed 70 inches a year (going up to over 100 inches a year in the West Highlands of Scotland), in East Anglia the rainfall seldom exceeds 20 inches a year, and in places is as little as 15 inches a year. This variation in rainfall is directly reflected in the fern populations of the east and the west of the country. Thus in Caernarvonshire in Wales where, in the region of Mount Snowdon, the rainfall is in the region of 100 inches a year, about forty species of fern are found, while fewer are found in East Anglia, with less than 20 inches a year.

It is not only the composition of the fern populations that is richer in the wetter regions and poorer in the drier regions, but also the density of the populations. Thus in East Anglia the hart's-tongue fern, *Asplenium scolopendrium*, is found only as a rare inhabitant of wells and damp ditch walls, while in the wetter Wales the same fern is found in abundance, in places forming a dominant feature of the flora, as for example, in some of the limestone woods where it completely clothes the floor. It is not only fern populations, however, that are affected by rainfall: it is also notable that those parts of Britain with the highest rainfall are also among the most heavily forested parts of the country, and there is a relationship between this and the fern populations, for the great majority of temperate ferns are woodland plants.

The higher rainfall in the west of the country plainly encourages both the ferns and the woodland trees to thrive, but there is a still more intimate relationship between forest and ferns than this. Forest exerts a moderating influence on climate. It moderates the violence of wind, sunlight, frost and the force of rain and fluctuations in temperature, while increasing atmospheric humidity (a point of particular relevance to natural populations of ferns). Nor are these influences minimal: they are substantial. So far as fluctuations in temperature go, the floor of a forest is normally at least 4° C warmer on the surface than the ground outside, while it may be as much as 7° C warmer six inches under the soil: in summer the air temperature inside the forest may be between 7° and 10° C cooler than that outside the forest. And, while some seven per cent of the rain falling on the forest will never reach the forest floor (being absorbed by the leaves of trees or evaporated on their surface), the actual amount of rain reaching the forest floor is normally higher than that falling on ground outside the forest, since the forest itself will become a focal point for precipitation.

The total rainfall in the forest area will, therefore, be higher than that outside it: more important than that, so far as ferns are concerned, is the fact that, having fallen, a higher proportion of the rainfall will be retained by the forest floor, shielded as it is from direct sunlight, than is the case in non-forest areas. Another factor of great significance to ferns is the higher humidity inside the forest, the air usually being up to fourteen per cent more humid than the air outside it.

The figures given above refer to cool temperate forests, the differences in the tropics being far more pronounced. In those regions the differences are exaggerated to the point of absurdity with, on the one hand the tropical rain forests where the air is so saturated with moisture that even if it did stop raining no one would ever notice it because the moisture already in the air is continually condensing on the leaves of trees and climbers and causing a perpetual drip, while at the other extreme there are the deserts which are defined as areas in which the annual rainfall is less than five inches, but which also differ from the tropical rain forests in that, instead of having perpetual rain, the rain, when it does fall, comes in storms of great and destructive violence: fifteen or even twenty years may elapse between one rain storm and the next but, when it does come it will disgorge a whole twenty years' worth of rain in a couple of weeks.

It is worth considering in this context the cultivation of the tree fern, *Dicksonia antarctica*, in Great Britain. On account of its peculiar mode of growth (a mode of growth which it has in common, incidentally, with many other tree ferns), it affords an excellent index of atmospheric humidity. This beautiful tree fern with its finely divided bi-pinnate fronds will in time form a substantial trunk as much as 15 feet high: it is in the nature of this trunk that its main peculiarity lies. The trunk is not a trunk at all—at least it is not like the trunk of a tree: it contains no hard wood, no xylem, no cambium, no outer layer of new cells. Nor does it serve the basic function of a trunk, which is to conduct the products of photosynthesis carried out by the roots to other parts of the tree. It conducts nothing in either direction. It is not, in that sense, a trunk at all. It is what is known in fern terminology as a caudex, a neatly packaged collection of humus formed by the decaying leaf stalks and roots of the fern. Each year the fern puts on another thirty fronds or so, the previous year's fronds gradually dying. However, the base of the old fronds is very tough and fribrous, and decays much more slowly than the outer part of the fronds. What happens is that the fern sits on top of a pile of humus formed by previous seasons' growth, this humus being held in place by the tough fibre of the old fronds: each year the pile of humus gets a little higher, but the fern continues growing on the top of it. This in turn means that each year the fern has to push its roots further and further down through this pile of humus to reach the soil. These roots run only just under the outer layer of the trunk, and in their turn help to hold the trunk together. In effect a tree fern is an epiphytic fern growing on a stem that it has formed itself.

When this fern is grown in a conservatory its trunk has to be damped down every day. This is because the roots need moisture along their whole length if they are to go on functioning. Out of doors it will grow only in those parts of the British Isles where the atmospheric humidity is sufficient to keep the trunk damp at all times. It succeeds out of doors in those areas of very high rainfall which have already been noted as being most conducive to natural fern populations. It will not succeed out of doors at all in the drier parts of the country.

The same trunk-forming process can be observed in other ferns that are natives of the cool temperate regions, in particular in the case of *Polystichum* or *Dryopteris* species, which can form caudices of up to six or eight inches in height, though this feature is only to be observed on very old plants.

A fern's moisture requirements, together with its ability to withstand cold in varying degrees, determine within pretty precise limits the geographic distribution of that fern. Dr H. Christ of Basle, who is generally regarded as the world expert on the distribution of ferns, has divided the world into twelve regions, each with its distinctive fern flora. Any fern may therefore be referred to as belonging to a particular regional grouping: for example, *Athyrium filix-femina* may be said to belong to the Cosmopolitan group of ferns, a group with a singularly wide geographic distribution, whereas *Adiantum capillus-veneris* belongs to the Mediterranean group, being typical of that part of the world. The grouping is useful since it provides a ready terminology for defining the distribution of any particular fern. The regions applicable to the ferns described in this book may be summarised as follows:

(1) *Cosmopolitan ferns*   These are species which may be found in the new as well as the old world, in both the northern and the southern hemisphere, as well as throughout much of the tropics.

(2) *Pantropical ferns*   These are species which occur almost exclusively in the tropics and throughout the tropics. One or two of these species do however have outlying stations in the temperate regions.

(3) *Circumpolar ferns*   These species occur, as their name implies, in a ring round the north pole: their distribution is confined, however, to the northern temperate zone only.

(4) *Arctic-alpine ferns*   These species again are confined to the northern temperate regions, but they are found further north than the Circumpolar

ferns: many also occur as high mountain ferns in the Circumpolar region.

(5) *Bi-polar ferns*   These, unlike the circumpolar ferns, are found in the temperate regions surrounding both the North and South Poles: they are not, however, found in the tropics.

(6) *Atlantic ferns*   These are species confined to the Atlantic seaboard of both the old and the new worlds.

(7) *Mediterranean ferns*   These are confined mainly to the Mediterranean region.

(8) *Australasian ferns*   Embraces ferns endemic to Australia, New Zealand and related to Pacific islands.

(9) *Antarctic Alpine ferns*   High mountain ferns of Australasia.

Each of the ferns referred to in the descriptive sections of the text will be related to these pteridological regions.

CHAPTER FOUR

The Identification of Ferns

Everyone with an interest in ferns is bound sooner or later to want to learn how to identify those species with which he is not already familiar and, as has already been mentioned, almost anyone with any sort of interest in plants, or simply in the world around them, knows a few of the commoner fern species—the hart's-tongue, the polypody and bracken for example.

The ferns as a group are not difficult to recognise: they have characteristic modes of growth and a characteristic type of leaf—known properly as a frond—that are both quite distinct from anything encountered in the angiosperms. Indeed, so easily recognisable is a fern frond and so different from the normal sort of leaf encountered in flowering plants that when a flowering plant has a finely dissected leaf it is often simply described as 'fern-like'—and most people know what to expect when a leaf is so described.

The identification of fern species is, however, a much more difficult matter than recognition of the group as a whole. The features used to identify flowering plants are, in the main, rather obvious ones, shape of leaf, type of flower, colour of flower, season of flowering, shape of seed and seed capsule, season of ripening and so on. With ferns there are no such obvious features. In the first place there are no flowers, and those parts of ferns which take the place of seeds can really only be studied with a hand lens.

For botanists, however, the problems are not so great. They do not make their identifications by what we might here call the macrofeatures, but by the microfeatures, chiefly the arrangement of the reproductive organs of the plants, and this goes as much for ferns as for flowering plants. For botanists one of the keys by which ferns are classified is the arrangement of the spore cases on the fronds and the details of those spore cases, these being slightly different in every species. A hand lens or linen-tester with a magnification of × 10 is adequate for this purpose and is an essential part of the equipment of anyone interested in ferns.

For the non-botanist, those microfeatures are the last details to be looked for. There are bolder features to be looked for first. Identifying a fern is largely a matter of eliminating all the unlikely suspects quickly and efficiently, and then concentrating on the microfeatures of the few remaining suspects. Thus, for example, if you find a fern growing in Scotland you can eliminate from the list of suspects those ferns that are endemic only to three offshore islands of Tierra del Fuego: you can eliminate all those ferns too that are not found in the cool temperate regions of the world. If the fern is growing in woodland you can eliminate all those ferns that normally grow in bogs, in walls, in cliffs, on mountaintops or in scree. You then need to decide whether the fertile and barren fronds are of the same general form or are different. If they are different you can eliminate all those ferns in which the two are the same. You then need to determine the shape of the frond, its branching and so on. By determining these macrofeatures, a huge number of ferns can quickly be eliminated from the possibilities.

It is then that one has to start looking for the microfeatures. There is no one feature of any fern by which it can positively be identified at first glance. It is more a matter of finding the number which opens the combination lock: identification must rest wholly on the coincidence of a number of features.

Thus far all you need is a deerstalker, calabash pipe, a large magnifying glass and an address in Baker Street, London, W.1. But now the real problems begin. You have to learn, if only to a limited extent, the jargon of the trade. Without it, you will have enormous difficulty in relating botanical descriptions to the plant you wish to identify.

Botanists have not invented their jargon with the sole object of confusing the uninitiated—although it sometimes seems as though they have—nor have they invented it so that they can keep their discoveries to themselves. As with other types of jargon—the jargon of astronautics, for example—it is simply a kind of shorthand. By using the jargon one can explain in one word what it would otherwise take a whole sentence to explain. One might describe a frond segment as 'truncate', which is rather shorter than saying that it terminates abruptly as though it had been cut off. Almost every jargon word used is used simply because it offers this sort of shorthand alternative to a long-winded explanation. In this book every attempt has been made to keep the jargon to a minimum. Nonetheless the reader will need to acquire a little skill in this language. A glossary is provided at the back of the book for ready-reference. Most of the terms used will be discussed in the part of this chapter devoted to the procedures to be adopted when identifying ferns.

FERN IDENTIFICATION SCHEDULE

When the reader comes to the section of this book dealing with the descriptions of the ferns he will find that in each instance the same features have been mentioned in the same order. This is done not only so that the reader will get used to looking for particular identification points in the same part of each description, but also so that he will get used to looking for the same features on each fern in the same order each time. In time it should become a habit. The point is that one must always work methodically.

Since the aforementioned jargon is used (though as little as possible) in the descriptions, the relevant terms will be explained in the run-down on the procedure to adopt when setting about identifying a fern.

The first thing to notice about a fern is where it is growing—i.e., its habitat. This is usually a simple enough matter. Either the fern is growing in woodland, on a wall, on a mountain or in one of the other habitats under which the ferns in this book have been grouped. Usually ferns stick to their recognised habitats, but ferns, like people, do occasionally fail to conform, and one does find woodland ferns obstinately growing in walls or on mountains. With experience one will quickly learn under which alternative habitats to look.

The next thing to notice is the general form of the fern, particularly its size. It may be large, medium, small, or even dwarf. The next thing to observe is whether it presents its fronds in a basket-like tuft, whether it presents them in a group of tufts (i.e., in several basket-like tufts growing from a single crown) or whether it is a creeping species, throwing up fronds at intervals and branching so as to form an irregular mat of fronds.

One has then to see whether the plant is *monomorphic* (i.e., has both barren and fertile fronds of the same type) or *dimorphic* (has fertile fronds different in form from the barren fronds).

The final stage of the preliminary investigation is to decide whether the plant is deciduous or wintergreen (ferns are usually referred to as wintergreen rather than evergreen—though it is perhaps a distinction without a difference). It is not necessary in most cases to wait until winter to find out whether a fern is wintergreen or not. Those species which are wintergreen have more *coriaceous* (leathery) fronds than most deciduous species. Furthermore, the fronds of wintergreen species take longer to decay once their period of active growth is over than do those of deciduous species, and even in midsummer the previous season's fronds will be found on the ground round the base of wintergreen species, dried, brown, brittle, occasionally retaining some green, but still there, which is rarely the case with deciduous ferns.

These, the macrofeatures, are all mentioned in the introductory paragraph to each fern description. These are followed by the microfeatures, each under its own heading. These are invariably explained in the same order, and that order is followed in this explanation of the microfeatures.

Stock All the ferns described in this book, with the one exception of *Anogramma leptophylla*, an annual which is endemic to Jersey and Guernsey, are perennials. There is therefore, throughout the whole of their lives, whether wintergreen or deciduous, a part of each fern permanently in the ground from which the new fronds will arise. This part is known as the stock. It can vary to some extent in its characteristics. A typical stock is fairly stout

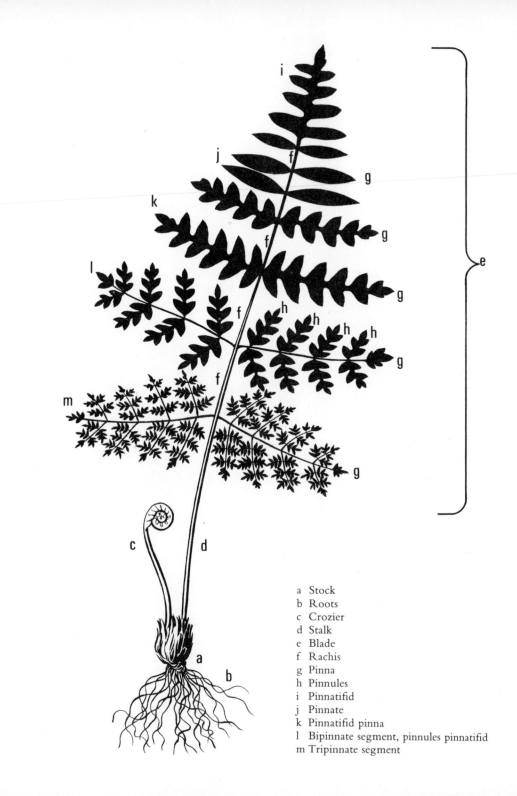

a Stock
b Roots
c Crozier
d Stalk
e Blade
f Rachis
g Pinna
h Pinnules
i Pinnatifid
j Pinnate
k Pinnatifid pinna
l Bipinnate segment, pinnules pinnatifid
m Tripinnate segment

and covered with the old frond bases: the younger parts are usually more or less densely covered with hairs and/or scales. It may grow erect or horizontally. If it grows erect it may form a single crown or be *caespitose* (tufted), that is, with several crowns forming on the same stock. If erect, the stock may form a short trunk known as a *caudex*. All ferns with the types of stock described so far present their fronds in more or less basket-like arrangements.

Some ferns, however, rather than having a stock in the manner just described, have what is often called a rhizome. For the sake of simplicity this terminological difference has been ignored in this book. Such a stock is simply described as narrow and creeping. Ferns with stocks of this type usually present their fronds in more or less dense mats, since such stocks invariably branch frequently. Such stocks, incidentally, usually creep just over the surface of the soil, but are occasionally subterranean.

The roots which arise from the stock are not normally described unless there is something of special interest about them.

Fronds These are the most obvious part of the fern. Indeed, to most people they *are* the fern. They are, however, composed of several elements—stalk, rachis and blade—each of which is described separately. Under this heading will be found only a very general description of the fronds, giving details about height, presentation (whether in tufts or otherwise) colour and leatheriness.

Stalk The stalk of any fern frond forms an important element in its identification. It can vary in a number of ways, the most obvious being its length. This may vary from almost negligible to equal in length with the blade. Since the same fern growing under different conditions will attain greater or lesser size, the length of the stalk is given as a proportion of the length of the blade, rather than as an absolute measurement. It may thus be described as being from a third to a quarter as long as the blade, or equal in length to the blade. The stalks of different species vary in section. Most are more or less round in section, but many are flattened on the face and rounded behind: some are also grooved on the face. The colour of the stalk also varies between species, but is usually darker and often swollen towards the base. In many genera the stalk is covered with hairs or scales, and again, these are described where present, or their absence is noted.

Rachis The rachis is the continuation of the stalk into the blade itself. It is usually similar in form, colour and hairiness or scaliness to the stalk, but this is not invariably the case.

Blade This is the leafy part of the frond and, for all its basically simple structure, probably the most difficult part to describe. It has, therefore, been broken down into a number of further headings: branching, pinnae, pinnules. Under the heading 'blade' the only information given concerns its shape in outline. It is important to be quite clear what is meant by outline. If one takes a frond of the common hart's-tongue fern and lays it on a piece of paper and puts a series of dots at the outermost tips of each of the sections of which the blade is composed: one then removes the blade and joins up the dots, thus arriving at its outline. With practice these shapes can be recognised without pencil and paper.

A number of special terms are used to describe the outline of a frond. They are the same terms that are used for describing the shape of a leaf, so anyone familiar with the terminology of other branches of natural history or horticulture should have no difficulty recognising them. Anyone not familiar with the terminology is referred to Figs. 2 and 3, which show the shapes delineated by their various terms.

Unfortunately the terminology was invented after the fronds had evolved, and the fronds do not therefore always conform precisely to the shapes subsequently laid down for them by botanists—a failing of most systems designed to classify natural phenomena. Thus, for example, a fern that is narrower than the proportions laid down for lanceolate but too broad for the term linear (and is therefore intermediate between the two) is described as linear-lanceolate, which denotes the relationship of form with an acceptable degree of accuracy. In other cases the term needs qualification. Thus a blade that is triangular will almost invariably need to be qualified as being either broadly or narrowly triangular. By constant reference to fig. 3 one will soon become familiar with the terminology of blade outlines.

Branching The blade of a fern may be either simple or compound. Very few are simple, the hart's-tongue, *Asplenium scolopendrium*, and the adder's-tongue, *Ophioglossum vulgatum*, being examples. The great majority are compound, and one has to master the terminology used to describe the differing degrees of complexity in compound blades. The simplest form of branching is that known as pinnate. In this a number of leaflets (known as *pinnae—singular pinna*) are arranged on either side of the rachis or main stem. The pinnae themselves may be opposite or alternate, but in a great many cases they are not arranged precisely opposite or precisely alternate, in which case they are described as being sub-opposite, meaning that they are more nearly opposite than alternate. The next degree of branching is that in which the pinnae themselves are pinnate: in which case the branching of the blade itself is known as a bipinnate. And if those pinnae themselves are still further branched the frond is known as tripinnate, and thus may branch again to become quadripinnate.

Pinnae The term pinna is given to the first degree of branching in a fern

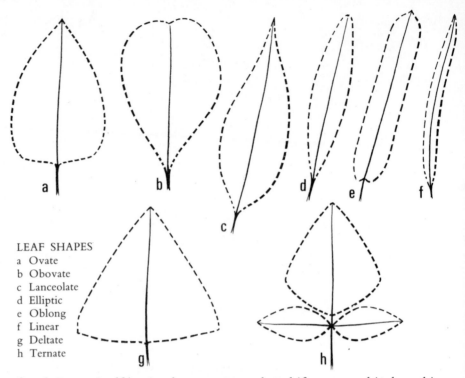

LEAF SHAPES
a Ovate
b Obovate
c Lanceolate
d Elliptic
e Oblong
f Linear
g Deltate
h Ternate

frond. It may itself be simple or compound, and if compound its branching will conform to the terminology used for the blade as a whole. Under this heading the degree of branching of the pinnae and their outline is usually given.

Pinnules This heading only occurs where the segmentation of a blade is bipinnate or still more finely divided. The pinnules themselves may be pinnate or even bipinnate. Again, the degree of branching and the general outline of the pinnules is described under this heading.

Having grasped the essentials of whether a frond is pinnate, bi-pinnate or tri-pinnate, the next distinguishing feature to look for is the degree to which the frond is incised (i.e. cut) although this is not given a separate heading of its own. A frond may be pinnate and yet not incised right up to the midrib or rachis. Each of the varying degrees to which the frond is incised has its particular name. Each of the sections divided is called a *segment*. If the segments are divided only by shallow incisions, the segments are called *lobes*, and a shallowly incised pinnate frond is known as *pinnately lobed*. If the incisions are deeper, reaching to about halfway from an imaginary line drawn round the outside of the frond joining the tips of the segments and the midrib or rachis, then the frond is said to be *pinnatifid*. If the incisions are very deep, reaching almost to the midrib or rachis, then the frond is said to be *pinnatisect*.

In ferns, unlike angiosperms, the pinnate character of the frond may not be distinct over its entire length (using the word entire in its normal sense). It is more usual, as is the case with the common polypody, *Polypodium vulgare*, for the pinnate quality to be more pronounced towards the base of the frond than at the tip. Where this occurs the change in character is usually described by the use of the verb 'to become', the action of becoming progressing from the base of the frond towards the tip. The frond of the common polypody might thus be described as pinnatifid becoming pinnately lobed.

A further distinguishing feature in compound leaves is whether the pinnae have stalks attaching them to the mid-rib or do not have stalks. If they are stalkless they may be referred to as *sessile*.

Two further words used in the descriptive sections with which most readers are highly unlikely to be familiar are acroscopic and basiscopic. *Acroscopic* refers to that side of a pinna or pinnule which faces towards the apex of the frond, or that side of the pinnule or pinnulet which faces towards the apex of the pinna. *Basiscopic* refers to that side of a pinna or pinnule which faces towards the base of the frond, or that side of the pinnule or pinnulet which faces towards the base of the pinna. The point is that in quite a large number of cases one of the features by which one species can be distinguished from the others in its genus is that the acroscopic side of the pinna may be markedly different from the basiscopic side.

It is worth remarking, and this is not done merely to confuse the reader, that the shape of individual pinnae may vary considerably according to their position on the frond, those nearest the base often being substantially different in shape from those nearer the tip. On careful analysis these differences will be found to be largely of degree, rather than of basic character, there being a general tendency for those pinnae nearest the tip of the frond to become simpler in shape than those at the base. It is thus not uncommon to find ferns in which the frond is tripinnate at the base, becoming bipinnate at about three-quarters of its length and simple but pinnately loved at the tip.

The margins of fronds also vary in a number of ways important to identification, and again there is a precise vocabulary to describe these variations. The margin of a frond may be *crenate* (scalloped, with rounded teeth or nothces), *serrate* (with pointed teeth), *crisped* (curled), *entire* (without teeth or notches of any sort), *incised* (deeply cut), *inflexed* (curled inwards and upwards), *reflexed* (curled downwards and outwards) or *sinuate* (wavy).

There is a similarly precise vocabulary to describe the possible variations on the tip or *apex* of a frond. The apex may be described as *acuminate* (drawn to a point), *acute* (which is sharply pointed but not drawn out into a point), *incurved* (applying to the pinnae of a compound frond rather than to the apex of the frond itself, and meaning curved so that it points towards the apex of the frond), *mucronate* (ending in a short, straight point), *obtuse* (rounded or blunt), *recurved* (again applying to the pinnae rather than to the apex of the frond, and meaning curved downwards towards the base of the frond), and *spinulose* (ending in a small spine). Each of these terms may be applied to the pinnae as well as to the frond.

The variations in the shape of the *base* of the frond or pinnae are described as being *cuneate* meaning tapering, *decurrent*, meaning running down the mid-rib or rachis, *truncate*, meaning cut off abruptly, usually at right angles to the mid-rib or rachis, or truncated, or *unequal*, meaning that the base of the frond terminates unequally. Indeed, the segments at the base of a frond can show a marked degree of inequality, the segment on one side of the rachis being truncate, that on the other side being decurrent.

Venation   In any full botanical description of a fern species the venation is always given. It is not included in every instance in this book, though it is given in a number of the commoner species. Venation in ferns may be thought of rather in the manner of finger-prints—to which indeed venation imprints bear some resemblance.

While it would be misleading to go so far as to say that each species of fern has its own distinctive type of venation, the venation within any given species, and often within a whole genus, is usually fairly constant. Because of this it has become one of the cornerstones of identification, and a number of standard types of venation have been described and are generally accepted. Not all the types of venation recognised are, however, found in the temperate fern flora: in fact as few as eight types of venation are encountered. Before detailing these types it is necessary to explain briefly the terminology used to describe the branching of the veins themselves. The veins can, incidentally, usually be seen more clearly on the underside of the frond than from above, and are even more apparent if the frond is held up to the light.

The main rib of a frond is called the *primary vein:* the term is also, indeed more usually in this context, used to refer to the mid-rib of one of the segments. Veins branching from the primary vein are called *secondary veins*, and veins branching from them are, perhaps not unexpectedly, called *tertiary veins*. Any further veins are usually dismissed under the name of *venules*. The terms *acroscopic* and *basiscopic*, already encountered in the terminology relating to the divisions of the frond, are also used to describe venation, usually to describe the tertiary veins. Thus tertiary veins occurring on the side of the segment nearest the apex of the frond are called *acrpscopic* tertiaries, while those occurring on the side of the segment nearest the base are called *basiscopic* tertiaries.

The eight types of venation encountered in temperate ferns are as follows: (the names of the different types of venation are derived from various fern genera, those of types 1, 2 and 5 being named after living fern genera, the remainder after fossil fern and pteridosperm genera).

(1) *Coenopteridian:* in which there is a single unbranched mid-rib in each undivided frond or segment of a divided frond.

(2) *Ctenopteridian:* in which a series of pinnately arranged secondary veins arise from the primary vein or midrib.
 The following three types of venation are all forms of the ctenopteridian form, but are distinguished from that form and from each other by the angle at which the secondary veins leave the midrib.

(3) *Taeniopteridian:* in which the secondary veins leave the mid-rib at approximately right angles: the secondaries then continue straight out towards the margin of the frond: any tertiary veins run parallel with the secondaries.

(4) *Sphenopteridian:* in which the secondary veins leave the mid-rib at an acute angle: the secondaries, together with the tertiaries which leave the secondaries at an acute angle, then run straight to the frond margin.

(5) *Eupteridian:* in which the secondaries leave the mid-rib at an angle that is intermediate between those described above.

(6) *Neuropteridian:* in which the secondaries leave the mid-rib at an acute angle as in the sphenopteridian type, but from which they differ in that the secondaries, instead of running straight to margin of the frond, turn sharply towards it, curving convexly in relation to the mid-rib. The tertiary veins leave the secondaries at an acute angle, and run parallel with them towards the frond margin.

(7) *Pecopteridian:* in which the tertiary veins leave the secondary veins in a pinnate arrangement.

(8) *Cyclopteridian:* this differs from any of the other types in that the mid-rib disappears completely at the base of the frond blade or segment (as the case may be), the subordinate veins branching repeatedly in a fan-like formation.

 It is an interesting point that in nearly all temperate ferns the vein endings are free. In other parts of the world closed venation is found, in which the venules at the outer edges of the fronds fuse together, containing the whole network of veins within an outer vein rim. There is a very small number of temperate ferns in which the venation is closed, examples being the rusty-back fern, *Asplenium ceterach*, and the adder's-tongue *Ophioglossum vulgatum*.

Sori The final, and probably most conclusive element in fern identification relates to the reproductive organs of the ferns. As has already been explained in the chapter devoted to the life-cycle of a typical fern, ferns do not flower: they reproduce by means of spores. In the great majority of ferns there is nothing as distinctive as a flower by which they can be identified. On most ferns the spores are carried on the backs of perfectly normal fronds. There are, however, a number of ferns on which the spores are borne on special fronds: examples are the hard fern *Blechnum spicant.* the two ferns belonging to the genus Ophioglossum, and *Botrychium lunaria.* These are, however, the exceptions. On a typical fern the spores are borne on the backs of undersides of the fronds (and thus in the position least exposed to sunlight and the drying influences of wind). The precise placing of the spores and the spore-cases on the fronds is one of the most definitive keys to fern identification.

The spores, which are minute, dust-like particles, are normally clustered together in cases known as spore-cases or *sporangia.* The sporangia themselves are usually, though not always—an exception being the moonwort *Botrychium lunaria*—grouped together in clusters known as *sori* (singular *sorus*). The sporangia invariably arise on a vein, although occasionally they occur between two veins, their outer edges reaching to the veins. They are normally borne on the top of a small swelling called the *receptacle.* In most ferns the sporangia are set on stalks. In most cases the stalks are long in relation to the size of the sporangia, but in some cases the stalk is very short, while in others there is no stalk at all: in some cases the sporangia are actually sunk into the receptacle.

Indusium The groups of spore-cases or sporangia known as sori are frequently protected by a thin, membraneous covering known as an *indusium.* Where the sorus is not protected by an indusium it is known as *naked.* The purpose of the indusium is undoubtedly to protect the spores and the sporangia. Ferns normally shed their indusia: in some cases however the indusium merely curls back. Indusia which are shed are said to be *deciduous:* those that are shed early in the season are called *fugacious* (i.e., fleeting): those which are retained are said to be *persistent.*

The indusium having been either shed or curled back, a further process is necessary before the spores can be released. This is the opening of the sporangia. This process is normally achieved by means of a process known as *dehiscence.* This in effect amounts to the drying out of the sporangium and its consequent splitting, or opening. In the case of aquatic ferns, however, no dehiscence occurs, and the spores are released when the sporangia decay.

Habitat The ferns have already been grouped together into chapters according to their habitats, but under this heading will be found more detailed information regarding their habitat.

Geographical type Under this heading the fern under discussion is simply referred to the group of geographical types already discussed.

Distribution This is simply a list of the continents or countries from which the fern under discussion has been recorded. It is sometimes helpful in clinching an identification where one finds that there are two almost identical species, but that each of them grows on one side of the Atlantic only: since the species you thought you had identified grows only on the other side, it is plainly the other species you have found.

Cultivation This just gives some brief hints on the general cultivation requirements of each fern. The cultivation of ferns is discussed in more detail in the following chapter.

Varieties These follow the sub-heading cultivation, as in general gardeners are rather more interested in them than are botanists and natural historians. Botanists on the whole tend to dismiss them as mere monstrosities. It is worth pointing out, however, that the majority of varieties cultivated by gardeners and fern enthusiasts were originally found in the wild. Many of them are very beautiful—at least to unprejudiced eyes. Furthermore, they are often more difficult to assign correctly to their species than are the species themselves. Anyone with an interest in ferns should at least be aware of the existence of varieties and of the frequency with which they occur in the wild. There are only a standard number of ways in which ferns can vary from the typical, and these are discussed in the next chapter.

Finally, it should be stressed that, even to the quite experienced, accurate identification can only be made from mature fronds. They need not necessarily be the largest fronds on the plant, but they should be typical of the plant as a whole. In the case of dimorphic ferns both fertile and barren fronds should be collected. What is wanted for identification is a whole frond, including the stalk, and this is easily detached from the stock by taking hold of the stalk just above its point of junction with the stock and exerting a sharp downward pressure. The frond will usually come away cleanly.

It is *never* necessary to uproot the whole plant in order to identify it.

IDENTIFICATION OF VARIETIES
During the Victorian era of pteridomania almost every fern that was found that differed even in the slightest degree from the norm was given a name. The result was a vast proliferation of named forms, many of them virtually worthless. Thus, for example, one frequently comes across forms of the hart's-tongue fern *Asplenium scolopendrium* in which the fronds are slightly digitate or slightly crested, or occasionally both. In most cases the deviation from the norm is relatively slight. Probably thousands of such varieties are

encountered every year by fern enthusiasts, yet they are simply not worth giving individual names. To earn an individual name a plant must be really outstanding. However, man has an irrepressable urge to name and classify almost everything with which he comes into contact, and it is therefore worth knowing the broad divisions into which fern varieties are divided.

The classification of ferns into groups is relatively simple, since there are only a limited number of ways in which ferns can vary. Either the variation is in the shape of the frond, or it is in the shape of the pinnule. Frequently the two conditions appear together. The analysis of variations given here follows the modified systematisation of fern varieties by Reginald Kaye, one of Britain's leading pteridophiles, and a fern nurseryman, and J. W. Dyce, Secretary of the British Pteridological Society.

CHANGES IN FROND SHAPE

Cristate, is a term which describes the commonest of all forms of variation found in ferns. In it the frond apex and pinnae, or apex, pinnae and pinnules are divided to a greater or lesser degree into tassels or crests. But there are so many variations on this theme that the following sub-categories have been devised:

Capitate, in which the frond apex alone is crested.

Cristate, in which the frond apex is crested in one plane like a fan, and the pinnae are similarly created. The apical crest is not as wide as the frond.

Percristate, in which the frond apex, the pinnae and the pinnules are all crested.

Corymbose, in which the frond apex is divided into a number of tassel-like crests in different planes, the crest not being wider than the frond itself, the pinnae similarly crested.

Grandicipital, in which the most noticeable feature is the apical crest, this being wider than the frond itself. The pinnae may be crested, reduced or absent.

OTHER CHANGES IN THE FROND SHAPE

Cruciate, in which the pinnae have much reduced pinnules, the pinnae arranged in pairs set at right-angles and forming a series of crosses up each side of the rachis.

Ramose, in which the lower part of the frond divides once or several times.

Congested, in which the rachis is much shortened so that the pinnae are very close, usually so close as to overlap. The pinnules are also close and overlapping.

Angustate, in which the fronds are very narrow with very short pinnae, which can also be twisted, reflexed or ball-like.

Deltate, in which the frond is very broadly triangular in outline.

CHANGES IN PINNULE SHAPE

Plumose, in which the pinnules are pinnate or bipinnate and the sori scanty or absent.

Foliose, in which the pinnules are wider than normal, giving a more leafy appearance than in the type plant.

Dissect, in which the pinnules are finely divided into minute teeth.

Depauperate, in which the pinnules are much reduced, irregular, or altogether absent.

Divisum, a classification used only for certain varieties of *Polystichum setiferum* and embracing those forms more specifically referred to as acutilobe, divisilobe or decomposite.

Heteromorphic, which embraces any other possible variations in pinnule shape, these being usually the rounded, the linear or the jagged.

The point of this classification is that if one finds a fern in the wild, or even if one finds a specimen growing in a deserted garden that is sufficiently interesting to bring into cultivation, but perhaps not worth naming, then one can at least classify it as *Asplenium scolopendrium capitatum* if it fits the capitate conditions. Frequently ferns will be found in which more than one condition is combined. For example, the ramose condition is often found in association with the cristate condition, in which case one's fern would be *ramo-cristatum*.

CHAPTER FIVE

The Cultivation of Ferns

Ferns are among the easiest of plants to cultivate. In the first place, they will thrive on neglect—as may be observed when visiting the gardens of old houses, where it will often be found that the ferns may still be flourishing from plantings made during the heyday of the Victorian fern craze, although all the flowering plants have long since disappeared (such gardens often not having been cultivated at all for twenty or thirty years); even so, that is not to recommend neglect as an ideal mode of cultivation. In the second place, ferns are ideally adapted to growing in those shaded corners for which it is so difficult to find effective flowering plants.

The great era of the fern garden as such has passed, probably for ever. No one today would attempt to emulate those gardens of the Victorians that were wholly devoted to the cultivation of ferns, those woodland walks whose path sides were lined with ferns, both native and exotic, those grottoes constructed quite often for no other purpose than the cultivation of some very special fern species and varieties or those rockeries full of ferns and hostas. Such gardens, while they may have suited the austerity of the Victorian age, seem dull masses of greenery today. There are one or two such gardens still in existence, not newly created but maintained since Victorian times, but it is unlikely that such gardens will ever be created again.

There are two reasons for this. In the first place the Victorian gentleman had a garden large enough to devote considerable areas of it to the cultivation of ferns and nothing else, while keeping his colourful bedding schemes in other parts of the garden. Gardens today are, by and large, too small for such clearcut distinctions between the various elements that go to make them up. Secondly, the great era of the fern garden occurred before the introduction of all those hardy herbaceous perennials that are the mainstay of most modern gardens.

The simple fact is that today more and more people live in urban and suburban environments, the houses crowded together on relatively small plots of land. In Great Britain three-quarters of all gardens are a quarter of an acre or less. In continental Europe, particularly in Belgium and The Netherlands, the gardens are even smaller. In such gardens, if they are to be effective as gardens, it is simply not possible to give over large areas wholly to the cultivation of ferns and nothing else. Even the true pteridomaniac will

1 *Adiantum venustum* (page 82).

2 (Right) *Asplenium
adiantum-nigrum* (page 113).

3 *Asplenium septemtrionale*
(page 119).

find his ferns all the more satisfying if there is the contrast with gaudy patches of colour in other parts of the garden.

The successful gardener is the one who studies the natural history of his garden, its climatic position, its microclimate—even the microclimates within his garden—his soil, aspect and the other factors that affect the cultivation of plants, and who then grows those plants in those situations which suit them best. To do this he also needs to study the situations in which the plants he wishes to cultivate grow in the wild. He needs to know their hardiness, whether they grow in sun or shade, and whether they grow in acid or alkaline soils.

WHERE TO GROW FERNS

The first thing to decide when considering the cultivation of ferns is where to grow them. As has already been stressed several times, the great majority of the ferns of the cool temperate world—that is the majority of those ferns mentioned in this book—are woodland ferns. This means that in the wild they grow in conditions of more or less dappled shade, in a light, leafy and usually well-drained soil. These are therefore the ideal conditions under which to cultivate ferns. The reality, however, is that very few people have woodland gardens in the middle of New York or London, or even in the suburbs. However, even in a quarter-acre garden many shrubs will do service for trees in providing the necessary shade. As buildings get closer and closer what shade is lost by the felling of trees is more than made up for by the shade cast by the buildings themselves, and the foot of a north wall provides an excellent spot in which to grow many fern species. The foot of a north-facing fence also provides a good spot for many ferns. Indeed, there can scarcely be a garden anywhere in which there is not some shaded wall or corner providing conditions under which ferns would thrive. The majority of hardy species do not even seem to mind atmospheric pollution, and will thrive in the centres of industrial cities.

The soil conditions suitable for growing ferns require somewhat more consideration, though as a group they are not particularly fussy plants—with a few very notable exceptions. Although most ferns, in particular the woodland ferns, grow in moist conditions, it is important to appreciate that the expression 'moist conditions' does not embrace heavy, cold, ill-drained soils. The soil on the floor of a wood is moist, but is also springy and well-drained. It is moist not because the water cannot drain away, but because it is retained in the sponge-like humus that has been built up by many years, possibly centuries of leaf-fall, and also because the canopy of branches above the woodland floor prevents that sort of drying out that results from the sunlight scorching the soil. Furthermore, the atmospheric humidity inside a wood or forest is invariably higher than it is outside. On the rare occasions when one does find ferns growing in cold, heavy, ill-drained soils they will

c

invariably be found growing at the top of a slope from which excess water can drain away very rapidly.

PREPARATION

Although ferns are little trouble to grow, and will put up a passably effective show even when neglected, and even though they may initially only be planted because it has been found that flowering plants will not thrive in the position selected, it is well worth going to what little trouble is required in preparing the soil for them. The preparation of the soil amounts to very little. Basically all that need be done is to dig the soil to a depth of one spit, breaking it up well in the process, and mixing in liberal quantities of peat, leaf-mould and grit. The peat should be of the fibrous sphagnum type. The finely powdered black sedge peat is virtually useless for ferns. It has little body or substance, and tends to crack when it dries out. The grit should be coarse. The addition of the grit is extremely important, and it is an element in the growing medium that is often overlooked. It may be objected that ferns, especially the woodland ones, do not grow in gritty soils. In fact they do, but the grittiness of the soil is cancelled by the accumulation of years of leaf-mould over the top of the soil. Furthermore, in woodlands there are the roots of the larger trees pushing through the soil and providing a similar drainage action.

The best types of leaf-mould to use are oak and beech. These should be well-rotted. Precisely how well rotted is difficult to define, but as a rule the leaves should be half-rotted, and should be of a crumbly consistency. If one has room to keep a leaf-mould frame and gather one's own leaf-mould, then the leaves gathered in the autumn, topped with a few spade-fulls of earth and allowed to settle over winter are ideal. If the leaf-mould is gathered from woods, then the light leaves that sit on the top and do not rot in the course of the winter should be scraped away to reveal the half-rotted leaf-mould. The leaves of other broad-leaved trees are of less value, though they are better than nothing. Conifer leaves should never be used, except in situations where the soil is being prepared for ferns that are specially mentioned as normally growing in coniferous woodlands—of which there are just one or two.

The proportions of grit to humus (which is what the peat and leaf-mould provide) should be varied according to the nature of the soil. On lighter soils, more humus should be added: on heavy soils more drainage material. On the heaviest of clay soils more than merely coarse grit may be needed, and the majority of ferns find broken roofing tiles (of the old-fashioned clay type—not the modern coloured concrete ones), broken bricks and even old clinkers congenial.

Compost is an acceptable source of humus—though more acceptable in the preparation of the soil than as a mulch. If an activator is used in the preparation of the compost, care should be taken to make sure that it is a lime-free activator if the ferns to be grown in the bed are calcifuge subjects: calcareous matter such as egg shells should also be excluded from the compost, since, although they provide grittiness, they too are a source of free lime. These considerations do not matter if the ferns are calciphile subjects.

Animal manure should on no account be used, either in the preparation of the fern bed or as a top dressing. The natural mulch for ferns is leaves. Manure is too rich for them: it will produce (if it does not kill the ferns outright) lush, soft growth that is ready prey for pests and diseases, from which ferns are generally remarkably free.

Artificial fertilisers should on no account be used. In many cases they will prove poisonous to the ferns.

Having prepared the fern bed by digging and incorporating liberal quantities of drainage and humus materials, it only remains to give the bed a light dressing of bone meal. This should be applied at the rate of four ounces to each square yard, and should be lightly forked into the top six inches or so of the bed. Bonemeal is a slow-acting fertiliser and will get the young plants off to a good start.

Once the fern bed has been prepared it should be allowed to settle for two or three months before any ferns are planted in it. Unless this settling period is allowed it will be found that the air spaces in the soil will cause the roots of the newly planted ferns to dry out rapidly.

PLANTING

In contrast with the angiosperms, which are normally planted during the dormant period, from October to March in the northern hemisphere, ferns should be planted while they are in active growth, between March and October. The dormant period should be avoided, and ferns should never be planted in mid-winter, no matter how mild the weather may seem. A dull, grey day is the best day to choose for actually planting the ferns, and if you can hit a patch where a week or two of dull, grey days, preferably with some light rain as well, will follow the planting, so much the better. Ferns should never be planted during heat-waves or during periods of extremely high wind. The planting period in effect dictates that the fern bed should be prepared during the winter months.

The ferns with which the bed is to be planted may be acquired in one of four ways: they may be bought from a nurseryman, they may be grown from spores, received as a gift from a friend or collected from the wild.

Where ferns are bought from a nurseryman, unless the nurseryman in question happens to be a specialist grower, of whom there are lamentably few, the chances are that he will send the ferns out at the same time as he sends out the rest of his plants—during the dormant period when ferns should not be planted. Most nurserymen will, however, if you ask them nicely enough, send the ferns either very early in the autumn or very late in spring, so that they can be planted either at the very end or the very beginning of the proper season for planting ferns. If ferns do arrive at the wrong season, then one must put a brave face on the situation, plant them, protect them from drying winds and dessicating frosts, and talk to them encouragingly. If they arrive during a period of heavy frost they should be heeled in deep boxes full of peat that is only just damp, and kept in a frost-free place until the weather turns more mild.

Ferns received from nurserymen should be unpacked immediately on arrival. They should be examined at once to find out firstly whether the species sent is true to name and is, in fact, the species that was ordered. If it is not, you should complain by return of post but you need to be very certain that it is the wrong species that has been sent. The roots of the plant should then be examined to see if they are dry: if they are they should be soaked in cold (but not frosted) water for a few minutes—not more than about half an hour—and then they should either be planted or heeled in. If they are in a condition to be planted right away, then they should be planted right away, weather permitting.

Ferns received as gifts from friends will, especially if the friend is also a fern lover, be given during the correct season for planting, and should be planted at once. If they are going to have to travel some distance then they should be wrapped up in a plastic bag or placed in a large plastic sweet jar for their journey. If the friend does not know much about ferns and offers them at the wrong season, then it is always worth asking whether you could collect your gift during the proper planting season: it will, after all, stand a better chance of survival if planted at the right time, for which both giver and receiver should be grateful.

The business of raising ferns from spores is dealt with later in this chapter, but a great many species will need to be grown on in a nursery bed or cold frame until large enough to fend for themselves in the fern bed.

Collecting plants from the wild is something that calls more for discretion and self-discipline than for any particular skill. In many parts of the world, particularly in Great Britain, but also to a lesser extent in the U.S.A., some species have been collected from the wild almost to extinction. Indeed, in the United States, certain species are now protected by law. In Britain two species, *Adiantum capillus-veneris* and *Asplenium ceterach* were both collected to virtual extinction in Victorian times, and are only very gradually re-establishing themselves, and even now in only a few of those haunts in which they were once plentiful.

Even some of the commonest species were heavily over-collected in the past. The Botany Bens of the Victorian era were indeed proud of the fact that in some localities they cleared every single fern that could be seen from haunts where the whole woodland floor was covered in nothing but ferns. In some such places the ferns have never returned. It does not take a craze on the scale of the Victorian fern craze to deplete natural stocks: the common primrose, once a familiar sight in almost every hedgerow and woodland edge in southern and western Britain, less common in the eastern parts, is now a rare plant in the wild, and its depletion has not been brought about by a craze for primroses, but simply by occasional passers-by digging up a few and taking them back to their gardens.

Naturally, it is not the commonest of ferns that people wish to grow in their gardens. It is the rarer species, and it is the variations that they want. Yet these are precisely the very ferns that should never be dug up from the wild. In the case of rare ferns it is much better to collect a mature frond and grow the plant from spores—a slow but generally reliable means of building up a good stock—and a means that is not at all difficult.

With the forms the first important thing is to make sure that it is a form that is really worth collecting. Only then should it be dug up—never pulled up—carefully wrapped and rushed back to a suitably prepared bed. Particular care should be taken to ensure that it is being transplanted at a season when its success is likely to be ensured. And never try to take home a fern variety—no matter how desirable it may seem, unless you are certain that you can provide a congenial home for it. If, for example, you have a calcareous soil, do not even attempt to take home a fern variety that you know will only thrive on an acid soil: far better to leave it where it is, and tell some friend about it who does have the right soil or conditions in which to grow it. If you lose the satisfaction of growing it in your own garden, you may be compensated to some extent   if the variety turns out to be a really worth-while one—by having it named after you.

The general rule to be followed when planting is that the plants should be well firmed in the soil. They should, in general, be planted to the same depth as they were growing originally, whether in the wild or in the nursery. The exceptions, however, are those species which are caulescent (i.e., which form a caudex or pseudo-trunk). In these the oldest parts of the caudex will usually be found to consist entirely of matter that is completely dead—a mass of old leaf stalks and dead roots. The dead part of the caudex should be trimmed away with a sharp knife until firm, living tissue is found. The fern should then be planted with the crown level with the soil. It will grow away much better if this procedure is followed than it would if it were not followed: indeed, if left untrimmed, the fern may not survive at all.

It is not always easy for the beginner to know how far apart to space his plants. As a general rule about a square yard should be allowed for each of the stronger growing species. For the really large species, including, for example, the osmundas, considerably more space will be needed. The dwarfer ferns need only about a square foot each. With the spreading species one needs to determine to what extent one is going to allow them to spread, and then control them. Young plants can, of course, be planted closer together. They will not suffer from having to be moved later, provided that they are moved at the right season.

CULTIVATION

Having planted the ferns, they should be well watered in and then just left alone and enjoyed. During their first season or two a certain number of weeds will be inclined to appear, but they diminish the longer the ferns are left alone. Weed seeds normally only germinate in the top couple of inches or so of soil. If they are buried deeper than that they will lie dormant—for amazingly long periods. Thus the more frequently the soil is turned over, the more weed seeds will germinate, and the more weeds there will be to pull out. The rule with fern beds is to remove the weeds by hand: no large fork should ever come near a fern bed, and even a small hand fork should be avoided as far as possible. Persistent weeds, such as dandelions and bindweed, which are not easily pulled out by hand, should be destroyed by dabbing with a hormone weedkiller: but tremendous care should be taken that no such highly toxic substance comes into contact with the ferns.

Beyond that, the only regular routine maintenance required is an annual or biennial mulch with fallen leaves. The mulches, which should be made in spring before new growth starts and additionally in the autumn if sufficient leaves are available, will provide all the foodstuffs the ferns need to keep them in good condition, and will, furthermore, help to keep down the weeds. Those few weeds which inevitably appear will be far more easily pulled out if the soil is kept well mulched than if it is not.

The mulching is particularly important if the ferns are being grown in beds under trees or within the reach of tree roots. There they will have to compete with the roots of the tree for nourishment and the tree, being the larger of the two, is likely to get the lion's share of the available nourishment. On the other hand, it should be remembered that, with a great many ferns, the only place where they normally grow in the wild is under trees. There is, however, a difference. In the wild the ferns do not grow under the one or two large trees in a garden; they grow under trees in woodland. And they don't grow under every tree, or only exceptionally so. They grow under those trees around which the blown leaves of the other trees of the wood accumulate in autumn, and thus in situations where the amount of humus accumulating year by year exceeds the amount needed by the individual tree to sustain itself.

It is not always easy to provide similar conditions in the garden. What can be done, however, is to make sure that the fern is planted where it is not in direct competition with the roots of the trees. A little digging around will soon reveal places where the ground is relatively free from tree roots, and it is in these places that the ferns should be planted. They should be planted in a small pocket of soil prepared as one would prepare an ordinary fern bed. Of course the tree roots will make straight for this, but it will take them a year or two to get there, during which time the fern will have had a chance to become established.

Where ferns are grown under trees the annual or preferably biennial mulching is particularly important: indeed it is essential. Since one is likely only to be growing the more robust species under such conditions, a mulch a good four or five inches thick, both spring and autumn, is what is really needed. If, in addition, the ferns can be grown in association with other shade-loving plants, preferably dwarf shrubby evergreens, and these can be so planted as to catch both the leaves that fall from the tree and those blown about the garden by the equinoctial winds, then the tree itself can be left to do much of its own mulching.

Although a situation under a tree may seem the natural and obvious place to grow ferns, there are two severe disadvantages to growing them in this position. In the first place, the ground under trees becomes very dry during summer (a silver birth tree only 15 feet high or so will have some 5,000,000 leaves and will evaporate some 15 gallons of water a day during grey weather in summer, and considerably more when the sun comes out). Adequate provision should, therefore, be made for watering, preferably by means of spraylines. Secondly, if the trees develop greenfly the ferns growing under them will quickly become covered in an unsightly—but not harmful—sticky honey which the greenfly exudes. The presence of greenfly is easy enough to detect on a small plant, but it often goes unnoticed on a large tree. Indeed, you may not discover that that particular tree is regularly infested with greenfly every year until you try growing some ferns under it.

There is no practicable remedy: it is out of the question to spray the whole tree if it is a large one—apart from which the spray would almost certainly be harmful to the ferns. You either fell the tree or move the ferns—the latter generally proving the easier and more sensible course of action. Indeed, if it is at all possible to plant the ferns in such a situation, the ferns will generally be happier slightly away from the tree but still in its dappled shade, than they would be directly underneath it.

MOISTURE-LOVING FERNS

It is, of course, only those ferns that are at heart woodland ferns that will grow in the positions so far described, although several of the ambiguous ferns that also grow on walls—such as the common polypody, *Polypodium vulgare*, along with *Polypodium australe* and *Polypodium interjectum*, and their forms, will also grow under these conditions, doing very well at the foot of a north wall. Such conditions are not, however, suitable for the real moisture-loving ferns like the osmundas, which really need bog conditions and will only put up a mediocre performance in a normal fern bed, and the mountain and wall species which, apart from looking ridiculously small in flat fern beds, by and large simply will not tolerate such conditions.

Of the two extremes, the bog garden probably requires less effort to create than does a suitable environment for the mountain and wall ferns. In a few gardens, especially in the larger, older gardens, one may have an area in which bog conditions exist already—though unless one is a certifiable pteridomaniac one will probably have had the area drained. Alternatively one may have a stream running through the garden, and all the bog ferns will thrive on the stream side.

If neither of these conditions exists then one will have to set about the task of constructing an artificial bog garden. The task is not a difficult one, provided one keeps the scale of the operation within one's capabilities. A bog garden is, essentially, an area of impeded drainage. Basically anything that will impede drainage can be used to construct a bog garden. It is important to realise that a bog garden is *not* an area with no drainage whatsoever. The traditional method of making a bog garden is to dig out a shallow depression and then line this with a six-inch layer of impervious clay which is 'puddled' —that is, hammered with one's fists until it forms a smooth coherent mass. The depression is then filled with a rich, peaty soil. The method is an ideal one on a fairly heavy soil, but it does pre-suppose that one has ready access to a reasonable quantity of impervious clay—which is not a substance one can buy readily from garden centres or sundries shops. A more practical method, and one which is certainly better suited to light, sandy soils, is to line the shallow depression with a really heavy-gauge plastic sheet, or even with two layers of plastic sheeting, in the lower parts of which a few small holes have been pierced. This should then be filled with a similarly rich, peaty soil. Such a bog garden is highly effective. One does, however, have to take care that in subsequent cultivations one does not put a fork through the plastic sheeting.

Such bog gardens, by their very nature, need to be reasonably wide in order to achieve sufficient depth. Small bog gardens built by these methods will not be large enough to grow the strong-growing bog ferns, but they will be ideal for the smaller moisture-loving ferns. On the other hand there are methods of building bog gardens which provide the necessary depth of growing even the most robust of bog ferns in a relatively small ground area. Curiously enough, they are in some ways harder work to construct than the larger, wider, bog gardens. These methods involve quite simply obtaining an old laundry copper or better still a modern circular plastic water cistern and sinking it in the ground. One or two small drainage holes should be made in the bottom of the copper or the plastic cistern. The hard labour comes about because one has to sink a hole in the ground two or even three feet deep, but quite narrow in relation to its depth. One is usually surprised when one measures the hole one has dug to find what a small distance one has gone down. Once the hole is excavated, the soil should be returned round the cistern or copper, and the container itself filled with a rich, peaty soil. Ideally the top of the container should be level with the soil, so that small ground cover plants can be grown round the fern which will spread and cover the edge of the container. This method is ideal if one wants to use a strong-growing osmunda, for example, as a specimen plant in the midst of a bed of lower-growing ferns. Provided one has sufficient room it will prove even more effective if one can use three or five such containers, each containing a strong-growing plant.

ROCK GARDENS

For those ferns which will not readily thrive in the ordinary fern border or in the bog garden, some sort of raised garden using rocks or stone slabs is necessary. All the mountain wall and cliff ferns will be happy only in situations where they can push their roots into crevices between rocks. But, before embarking on the construction of some form of rock garden it is worth considering the real purpose of constructing such an object.

The ferns which grow on walls, cliffs and mountains are all ferns which like to have their heads in the sun and their roots in the shade. In fact, they usually push their roots a considerable distance into crevices in the rocks or cliffs and, if one could part the rocks, one would find that the roots were in fact quite wet—not with stagnant water, but just damp to the right degree. Whatever it is that one constructs in one's garden to grow these ferns, it must emulate these conditions. All too often the rockery of the suburban garden is nothing more than a mound of soil with some rocks scattered on the top: nature organises things somewhat differently. Indeed, a mountain might be regarded as a large rock with a little soil scattered on the surface. Certainly to view the structure needed to grow mountain ferns in that light puts the matter in its proper perspective. There should be more rocks than soil: the soil should be little more than small pockets between the rocks.

Unless one has a sloping garden, it takes quite a lot of room to construct a rock garden which, to look ornamental as well as to fulfil its ecological function, must rise up from the level. This will require quite a large area. Furthermore, consideration must be given to the fact that there will be a shaded side as well as a sunny side to the rock garden. By and large the ferns that will do best on the sunny side are the smaller ones, and the ones that will do best on the shaded side are the larger ones.

In small gardens there are two practical alternatives to the construction of the normal type of rock garden. The first is the *doline*, the second is the raised bed in one of its many forms.

A *doline* is basically a keyhole-shaped hole in the ground. The term is a Yugoslavian one; dolines are frequent in the Karst country of Yugoslavia, where they occur in rocky landscapes. In the garden a doline (of which there is a fine example at the University Botanic Garden in Cambridge—the doline there being part of the earliest rock garden constructed in the British Isles) is dug so that the tail of the keyhole forms a reasonably steeply sloping path downwards into the round part of the keyhole, this being the deepest part of the doline and usually having a level floor. The soil removed in excavating the hole is banked up round the edges of the doline, thus increasing its relative depth without having to increase its actual depth unnecessarily. To be of much use, that is, to grow as wide a range of ferns as possible, the deepest part of the doline needs to be a good seven or eight feet deep, which will usually mean excavating the soil to a depth of about five feet. The walls of the doline should be almost vertical, but leaning back slightly to support the weight of the soil behind them, and can be constructed either from large rocks such as one might use for a rock garden, or from the type of split stone normally used in constructing dry walls. Both are effective from the cultural point of view: the choice is one mainly of taste and partly of expense.

Variations can be made on the doline theme. The path leading down to the rounded end can be wide, and the diameter of the hole quite large. In this case the sides of the path can be planted with ferns, as well as the walls, while at the foot of the walls of the round part there could be further fern beds. For the glutton for hard work there is also the possibility of sinking a short well-shaft at the deepest part of the doline: it will be found that ferns that are normally tender will often survive in such conditions. Alternatively a copper or plastic cistern could be sunk at the deepest part of the doline, particularly if it is oriented south, in which to grow a bog fern. Or the doline can be narrow, the path only just wide enough for one person to pass down it, curved, and not opening out into the round part of the keyhole until the path itself has already reached a depth of seven or eight feet. Again, in such a doline it will be found that ferns that would normally be tender can be grown well in such conditions.

The orientation of the doline can be designed with the particular ferns you want to grow in mind, but in general it is best, if possible, to have the path leading into the doline entering it from the west, so that one wall of the rounded part will be in sun much of the day, the other in shade. The banks sloping away from the doline can be planted with dwarf conifers, heathers and other such plants as associate well with ferns.

A raised bed is a far more easily constructed affair, and again it is a theme that can be varied. Essentially a raised bed is a rectangular affair constructed of split stones sloped slightly inwards, containing a gritty, well drained compost and topped with coarse grit. Its formality makes it in many ways better suited to modern small gardens than a properly constructed rock garden—which, if it is to resemble a natural outcrop of rock, should have smaller outlying outcrops occurring in the lawn just where it is most awkward to mow round them. The bed need not, of course, be rectangular. It could be circular, kidney shaped or indeed any shape that takes one's fancy. The larger ferns should be grown in the lower parts of the walls, and the smaller ferns higher up. Sun-loving ferns could be grown on the side exposed to the sun, shade-loving ferns on the other side, while the top can again be planted with dwarf conifers, heathers, daphnes and other trouble-free alpines.

The choice of rocks for the construction of rock-gardens, dolines or raised beds will to some extent both determine and limit the ferns that can be grown successfully in those structures. If limestone is used, it will not be possible to grow those ferns that are pathologically calcifuge. If acidic rocks are used then a limit will be set on the possibilities of growing calciphile ferns. The obvious answer is to choose a completely neutral rock: unfortunately the few rocks that are virtually neither acid nor limy are also virtually useless from the cultural point of view. Most such rocks are exceedingly hard, exceedingly non-porous (and therefore do not hold the moisture during the drying summer months) and also exceedingly prone to getting very hot during summer—something which is definitely not wanted.

In general the sandstones are probably the ideal stones to use where growing ferns: they are porous, hold the moisture well during summer and do not get too hot. They vary considerably in texture, some being quite hard, others soft enough to rub away in the hand. It is worth selecting the grade you want, even if it means a little travelling around. The harder types of sandstone are used for building dry walls. Limestone is only suitable if calciphile subjects are to be grown. Granite is generally considered too hard a rock for growing ferns: it has very little porosity, and gets very hot during summer.

CULTIVATION IN PANS AND POTS

A further possible way of growing ferns—and this is a mode of cultivation that is particularly suitable for town and small suburban rather formal gardens, or for gardens in which there is no shade—is pan culture in an adaptation of a bonsai garden. The only structure needed is of the type that can easily be built by the average-to-competent handyman. It consists of a wooden fence, 9 or 10 feet high (and this can often be achieved by putting standard-size fence panels one on top of another) with a roof of slats of wood, each 2 or $2\frac{1}{2}$ by 1 inch, spaced their own distance from each other, supported at the end away from the fence by stout uprights and a cross beam.

Alternatively, the fence need only be 5 feet high, and the upper 5 feet of the back wall constructed of vertical slats like the roof. Then add staging to suit your needs, and you have an excellent environment in which to grow ferns in pans. In such surroundings you could even grow a few bonsai trees to make a change from the ferns, while one or two of the stronger-growing ferns could be grown in borders within the shelter of the enclosure.

There is no 'secret' to success with growing ferns in pans. The principles and formulae are simple. It is watering that will make or mar the ferns, and the amount of water to apply and when to apply it is something you will really only learn by experience. The first essential with growing anything in pots or pans—and this applies to ferns as much as to any other plants, is that the pots or pans should be scrupulously cleaned before use. If the pots are brand new they should be soaked for an hour or two before using. If they have been used previously they should be scalded with boiling water, and then scrubbed inside and out until they look as good as new. In addition it is a wise precaution to soak them in a mild solution of disinfectant. The crocks should be cleaned as thoroughly as the pots themselves. Plastic pots should also be cleaned thoroughly, though most types will not stand being scalded in boiling water.

The pots or pans (and a pan is simply a shallow pot but is by and large more suitable for growing ferns than a pot, since most ferns are relatively shallow-rooting) should then be properly crocked. There is more to crocking a pot than simply throwing a few pieces of broken flower pot into the bottom. Firstly the drainage holes should be covered with a piece of perforated zinc. The purpose of this is to prevent the entry of slugs. Over this should be placed a relatively large crock, a piece large enough to cover the hole adequately. This should be laid with its convex side upwards. The point of crocks is to shed the water: if they are placed with the concave side up they will tend to collect the water, which in turn will tend to turn the compost sour. Above this large crock should be placed two or three smaller ones, and above them even smaller ones—still all convex side up. These should be topped off with a layer of coarse peat—the purpose of which is to prevent the compost being washed down into the crocks and so blocking the free drainage they have been placed there to provide.

The pans are then filled with a compost. A John Innes No. 1 potting compost, mixed in the ratio of two parts of John Innes to one of sphagnum peat, makes a good compost for ferns for those living in cities and unable to obtain the raw materials for making their own compost. If one has the oppurtunity to mix one's own compost then a good mixture is one part of coarse sand, one part of good turf loam and two parts of well-rotted leaf-mould (parts by volume). A pinch of granulated charcoal should be added to each potful of the mixture made up, and also a pinch of hydrated lime (except where the compost is to be used for growing calcifuge subjects, when the lime should be omitted). The compost should be damp but not wet when it is wanted for use.

The potting of ferns is a very simple matter: the pot chosen should be the smallest one that will take the roots of the fern. If a larger pot is used the roots will not spread into the outer reaches of the compost, and compost which is not being actively used by the roots of plants rapidly becomes sour.

The fern should be held with one hand while the compost is added with the other. The compost should be poured in loosely until it is level with the rim of the pot. The crown of the fern should then be pressed down, and the soil firmed round it. The soil should not be made too firm—only firm enough to hold the plant: ferns grow naturally in light, open soils. In compacted compost they will have great difficulty in making root growth. Once potted the ferns should be either watered or, in the case of very small plants, plunged up to the rim in rainwater at atmospheric temperature, and then allowed to drain. They should be kept in a shaded place out of the sun for several days, and will not need watering again for quite a while.

The true art of growing ferns in pans is the art of watering them. More plants die of over-watering than of under-watering, but to keep ferns in good heart one needs to steer a happy middle course, which is easier said than done. Some ferns need more watering than others, while some flower pots dry out faster than others, even though they may seem to have exactly the same amount of drainage material in them, the same compost and similar ferns. In the old days one used to be able to buy little wooden hammers with which to tap the pots to find out whether they needed watering or not. If a tap with the hammer produced a dull sound, then the pot was still wet enough. If the tap produced a more resonant sound, then watering was needed. If the pot positively rang, the plant was probably dead anyway. In the absence of a little wooden hammer—another of those devices which the handyman can easily make for himself—knuckles are a serviceable substitute. The trouble is that, although they do replace themselves, they wear out rather quickly! If one is growing a substantial number of ferns in pans one's knuckles can become exceedingly sore during dry hot periods in summer when some of the ferns will need attention every day.

Fortunately modern science has come up with a device that, though more expensive than either knuckles or a wooden hammer, is also more accurate. It consists of a needle which is inserted into the soil, on the top of which is a dial, with a moving needle which indicates whether the pot is wet, dry or just right. The point of the instrument is just plunged into the soil and gives an instant reading.

When it comes to repotting the rule again is that the fern should be moved into a pot only one size larger. It is bad practice to move it into a much larger pot in the hope that this will save having to repot again in the near future: in fact the soil that is not being actively used by the roots will become sour, and could do the fern permanent damage. If the plant has made a number of crowns and one wants to divide it, the time to do this is when repotting. The crowns should be separated with a sharp knife, and any moribund parts of the stock should be trimmed away at the same time. Early summer is generally the best time to repot ferns, just as growth is beginning.

One is often advised to allow moss to grow over the soil at the top of the pot, the theory being that the health of the moss will be a good guide to the health of the fern. This is one of those theories that sound convincing but in practice just don't work. It really is better to use other means for judging whether the fern needs watering or not.

FERN BORDERS

From all that has been said so far it may appear the ferns form a distinctive group of plants and should accordingly be grown separately from other plants; in other words one would have a fern border which is wholly devoted to ferns just as one might have a herbaceous border wholly devoted to herbaceous plants. Of course one can do this, and if ferns are the only plants one really likes growing then this is probably just what one will do, but in general ferns can be grown together with other plants and probably are most effective grown in this way. It may seem heresy to anyone wholly devoted to ferns, but the fact is that the common polypody, *Polypodium vulgare* and its varieties, and *Polypodium australe* and its varieties make excellent ground cover plants beneath flowering shrubs, as indeed does *Blechnum spicant* and its varieties. *Blechnum tabulare* makes ground cover very much in the idiom of the polypodies, but on a more robust scale.

To the real fern enthusiast a fern border should contain ferns and nothing else: to plant anything else in a fern border would be a sheer waste of space. And indeed a border planted with nothing other than ferns can have a calm and restful quality that cannot be created in any other way in the garden. Although all ferns are green, there are ferns that come in almost every shade of green, some are virtually light yellow while others are so dark as to be shading into brown. In general, however, the purely fern border is probably something that belongs rather to the botanic garden than to the ornamental garden.

Most people will find that the ferns in a fern border will gain by contrast with other plants. Plants such as the bergenias, with their big bold round leaves, or the hostas with their also usually large, often variegated leaves help to reveal just how finely dissected are the fronds of the ferns. There are other plants grown in the garden more for their foliage than their flowers which also contrast well with ferns, including the acanthus species, alchemilla and, very differently, *Phormium tenax* in its various colour forms, the purple-leaved form looking particularly effective among ferns.

If one wants to concentrate one's cultural attentions on the ferns themselves, then there are a number of plants that can be grown amongst the medium to strong-growing ferns which will virtually look after themselves (and help to keep the weeds down). The most obvious of these is the common lily-of-the-valley, *Convallaria majalis*, which is itself a woodland plant, and will run through the fern border happily, needing no attention. For those who dislike the common single white form there is a single pink-flowered variety, *Convallaria majalis* 'Rosea', though it is a rather dowdy pink and probably at its most effective when contrasted with the white form. The finest of all, though unfortunately hard to obtain, is the double white 'Flore pleno', in which the flowers are both larger and longer-lasting. There is also a form with very broad leaves which are variegated with white stripes. It is not a particularly striking variegation and the form seldom flowers, but it may well appeal to many fern enthusiasts.

Rather similar to the lily-of-the-valley is the twin-leaved mayflower, *Maianthemum bifolium*, which might well be described simply as a dwarf, unscented lily-of-the-valley. It grows no more than two inches high and forms a carpet of its small, oval leaves. Another charming white-flowered woodlander that will creep around happily in the leafy soil of a fern border and will again provide good ground-cover is *Chamaepericlymenum canadensis*, better known under its old name of *Cornus canadensis*. Though usually classified as a shrub it is really only a perennial with rather woody little stems that persist through the winter after flowering before decaying away. It sends up masses of shoots each only two or three inches high bearing a whorl of typical dogwood leaves on the top of which sits a tiny flower surrounded by conspicuous white bracts, like those of the shrub *Cornus kousa*. In addition to its flowers the plant is attractive on account of its autumn colour and its bright red fruits.

Another group of pseudo woody plants that love the shaded conditions of the fern border are the epimediums. These are attractive in spring, when their delicate heart-shaped leaves come through a pretty pink changing to copper before turning green. The epimediums have small flowers in white, yellow or pink. There are several species, and they are all good.

Other ground-covering plants—though they are rather slow to cover it— that are ideal for the fern border are the shortias and their relatives, the schizocodons. The shortias are very low-growing evergreens with round, leathery, polished leaves about two inches across, and they need a little nursing when first planted, it being essential to ensure that they are shaded and kept moist until established. Once established they can be left to spread slowly into a dense carpet. The finest of the shortias is *Shortia uniflora* 'Grandiflora' which produces its charming shell-pink cyclamen-like flowers in early spring on wiry stems about two inches above the leaves. The petals are delicately fimbriated, which adds to their charm. The schizocodons are closely related but have less leathery leaves. In *Schizocodon macrophyllus* the leaves are about two and a half inches across, but in *Schizocodon soldanelloides* they are no more than an inch across, with the flowers proportionately smaller. Both flower rather later than *Shortia uniflora* 'Grandiflora'.

Another group of plants that will often prove useful in the fern border are the violets. *Viola cornuta* is one of the strongest growing species, with large bright green leaves and huge white flowers, at least an inch across and very conspicuous in its season. It is completely deciduous, springing up again each year from a stout creeping rootstock. Very different and in some ways almost shocking, but very effective if you like being shocked, is *Viola labradorica*, which has purple leaves and pale violet flowers. It is an evergreen species, and will spread itself quite rapidly both by runners and by seed into large colonies, through which only the occasional weed seedling will appear.

Also low-growing, but rather more spectacular in flower than anything mentioned so far, are the gentians, some of which will grow quite happily in the fern border, though in general they prefer only light shade. The easiest two to grow under fern border conditions are *Gentiana septemfida*, which flowers in August and seeds itself freely in positions where it is happy, and *Gentiana sino-ornata*, which is even more spectacular and does not flower until October. It spreads reasonably rapidly both by seed and runners into fairly dense colonies. Much stronger growing, up to two feet, is *Gentiana asclepiadea*, which bears its rather heavy blue trumpets on willowy, arching stems in September. It lacks the gayness of the dwarfer species, but competes better with the stronger ferns.

More spectacular in flower are the woodland primulas, which will seed themselves happily in a woodsy soil in a shaded situation, provided that it does not become too dry during summer. Any of the woodland species are suitable, but among the best are *Primula sieboldii* with its large soft mauve flowers borne in staggering profusion, *P. saxtilis* and *P. polyneura*, together with some of the candelabra primulas such as *P. japonica*. *Primula rosea* will grow in any part of the fern border that is really wet, and is a very beautiful plant with its flowers of a singularly vibrant pink, while the drumstick *P. denticulata* will grow well in any shaded border that is not too acid. There are purple, mauve and white forms, and they will all interbreed freely.

Another group of plants which need no looking after and which will seed themselves freely once established are the hellebores. The best known of these is the Christmas rose *Helleborus niger*, which, in a mild season, will be in flower at Christmas. The finest form is known as 'Potter's Wheel', and is sufficiently superior to the average seedling to be worth some trouble in hunting down. Even earlier flowering is *Helleborus atrorubens*, which produces its large deep pink flowers as early as the beginning of December in most seasons. It is perhaps all the more effective for being fully deciduous, unlike most of the hellebores. The most useful of the group for the fern border are the Lenten roses *Helleborus orientalis*, which flower from March till May. These range in colour from whites through palest pinks to deeper pinks, and to a form that is virtually black. If one starts with a good dark form and a good white form, intermediates will soon appear among the self-sown seedlings. A border in which these plants have become established is a joy for months on end.

Another group that is easily satisfied with a leafy soil and a shaded border is the genus trillium, of which the best known is the Trinity flower *Trillium grandiflorum*. This produces clumps of foot-high stems with a whorl of green leaves topped by a large white three-petalled flower. *Trillium undulatum*, known as the painted wood lily, is similar but the petals are stained with pink. *Trillium erectum* has similarly shaped flowers of a rich claret colour, looking like highly polished patent leather. All three are effective plants, and when happy will seed themselves, though not with the freedom of the primulas or the hellebores.

There are a number of more spectacular plants which just happen to thrive in the conditions of the fern border: indeed, they are difficult to satisfy in other conditions. The lilies at once spring to mind, the majority of them being true woodlanders at heart. They like their roots in the shade and constant moisture at the root, and these are just the conditions the fern border provides. There are numerous species and even more numerous hybrids, and most of them will do well in the fern border. Two dwarf, stoloniferous species which are particularly suitable for small gardens and for growing among small ferns are *Lilium duchartereri* and *Lilium langkongolense*, both of which produce white densely spotted flowers of the turk's cap type, and both of which spread underground, forming dense but delicate clumps.

Even more exotic are the orchids, of which the lady's slipper orchids are particularly suitable for the fern border. *Cypripedium calceolus* is probably the easiest to obtain, and has charming yellow and brown flowers. *C. macranthum* is more striking, with deep rich purple flowers, while *C. arietinum* is usually considered the prize of the genus, with very large flowers, white with a deep pink pouch. There are several other species, and all are beautiful. They take a little time to settle down to flowering, but once established perform well year after year, gradually spreading into small clumps. Other orchids that grow well among ferns are *Orchis maderensis* with its huge densely packed spike and brilliant purple flowers, and the slightly smaller but otherwise similar *Orchis latifolia*.

Then there are those plants which are strange rather than beautiful, and these somehow seem to fit very well into the fern border. The arisaemas at once spring to mind as representative of this type of plant. The loveliest of these, and also the hardest to obtain, is *Arisaema candidissimum*, which produces quite large, soft green hastate leaves and a white or slightly pinkish spathe with darker vertical stripes running up to it. It grows from a swollen tuber which needs to be planted about six inches deep, and has the disconcerting habit of not appearing above ground until late June—just about the time one is starting to think of digging around to find out what killed it. A well established clump will produce many spathes and make a striking sight against the darker foliage of the ferns. *A. ringens* is similar, but a little smaller growing. *A. shikokianum* is rather smaller and has a purplish-brown spathe striped white, with a white inside. All produce red berries after flowering, and seedlings will appear when the plants are growing in conditions which suit them well.

In general any plant which grows in woodland in its native haunts will grow well in a fern border, and by and large the woodlanders make a harmonious group with the ferns, in general having rather subdued flowers. There are many more species that could be grown together with the ferns, and it is always worth keeping a sharp look-out for anything unusual.

Ferns are seldom troubled by either pest or disease, though the plants that may be grown together with them may. Care should be taken in the use of insecticides and fungicides, as some can be very damaging to the ferns. It is worth the small effort required to read the instructions on the packet or aerosol to see if ferns are included in the list of plants on which the pesticide should not be used. There are plenty of pesticides on the market which will not damage the ferns.

Thus the fern border can range from being a border wholly devoted to the cultivation of ferns to a border of ferns with a few flowering plants in it to a flower border with a few ferns in it. The mixture can only be one of personal choice.

GROWING FERNS UNDER GLASS
Since this is a book devoted to the ferns of the cool temperate world, most of the ferns mentioned in it can easily be grown out of doors in such conditions. However, some of the ferns mentioned are undoubtedly on the tender side and better grown in the sheltered environment of the greenhouse, especially where one is attempting to grow, in more northerly latitudes, ferns which basically come from the more southerly latitudes and enter the cool temperate world only at the outlying extremes of their range.

All that is needed for such ferns is a cold greenhouse (i.e., a greenhouse that is not heated at all). The main consideration is in siting such a greenhouse for ferns. All books on greenhouses assume that you want to grow sun-loving plants in them and instruct you accordingly on the orientation required to gain the maximum entry of sunlight, either opting for maximum sunlight during summer, or a less degree of light in summer but a higher level of light in winter. But such considerations are irrelevant to the growing of ferns. What is needed is a greenhouse that receives the maximum shade throughout the year. In a conventionally orientated greenhouse, the only place where ferns can be grown is in the borders under the staging. For many people, whose interests in gardening embrace other groups of plants than the ferns, this is probably all that is required. The ferns can either be planted directly into the border, or grown in pans placed on a gritty surface under the staging.

For the enthusiast, however, this is not enough. A greenhouse which is to be wholly devoted to the growing of ferns should be placed where it is in shade for most of the day during most of the year. An ideal greenhouse for ferns would be a lean-to type sited against a north wall. Here both the staging and the under-staging could be used, while at the foot of the wall a small rock-garden could be built in which further ferns could be grown. The wall above the rock garden could be adorned with epiphytic ferns grown on pieces of cork bark and wired to nails in the wall. They would need frequent watering with a fine mist spray.

Ideally the bench should be designed for capillary watering, which means that the ferns need to be grown in plastic pots. Rain-water from the guttering should be brought into a butt in the house, with an overflow leading outside again, and tap water should generally be avoided for watering the ferns themselves. The rain-water should be passed through a filter before being used in the capillary header tank. The ferns will need an occasional overhead spray, especially during the summer months, and the floor should be damped down daily during the same season. It is important not to indulge in too frequent overhead spraying, as many ferns will not tolerate this, though they like a humid atmosphere. The damping down of the greenhouse path, together with the presence of the water butt, should create sufficient humidity for their needs.

Where the greenhouse is not in an ideally shaded situation provision for shading must be created. Lath blinds are undoubtedly the best for this purpose, though expensive, and scrim blinds will serve as well, although they have a shorter life. The advantage of blinds is that they can be operated electronically, to provide shade only when it is needed, and not when it is not. An alternative is to create a lath structure similar to that used in the bonsai-type fern garden to create shade. The laths should lie north-south so that the shadows they cast will cross the ferns quite quickly with the passage of the sun. The structure should be detachable, so that it can be removed during the winter. In general, the types of washes applied to the outside surface of the glass to create shade are not satisfactory for ferns: they create just too much shade during dull weather.

A final and highly important point is the provision of adequate ventilation. Ferns do not like a still atmosphere. They grow best where there is a constant but subdued movement of air, and this applies in winter as much as in summer. Ideally the ventilators should never be closed completely, except perhaps during gales (when, if they are left open, the house is likely to be damaged).

BOTTLE GARDENS AND FERN CASES

The idea of growing ferns in hermetically sealed glass containers is, like the fern craze itself, a Victorian one. Fern cases, variously known as Wardian cases or terraria, were as essential a part of any Victorian parlour as were the potted aspidistras, the palms, the bouquets and the velvet mantle covers.

The discovery that plants could be grown in hermetically sealed containers was made by accident by the man who also discovered the aquarium and the vivarium. He, Dr Nathanial Bagshaw Ward, had a practice in the grimy East End of London, where he found that the soot and fumes made it impossible to grow his favourite plants, the ferns, out of doors. The principle of growing in a sealed container is simply that, if the case is properly constructed, and proper growing medium used and the right amount of water supplied, an indoor garden can be created which, once planted, will need no further attention for as much as perhaps twenty years.

The great advantage of growing ferns under these conditions, whether in Wardian cases or in bottle gardens, is that they are protected from the hazards to which most house plants are exposed—sudden changes of temperature, pollution of the air by tobacco smoke, coal fumes or gas fumes, dust on the fronds and dessication by central heating. For these reasons, hermetically sealed fern cases should be just as popular today as they were in Victorian times.

At its simplest level a Wardian case is nothing more than an ordinary glass aquarium with a sheet glass lid. Such a receptacle is still perfectly usable today, indeed perhaps the more so because of its simplicity, but the Victorians went in for very ornate Wardian cases, or terraria, as they called them. They were, in effect, miniature greenhouses designed to stand on the bureau or on a table top. The most elaborate were miniature versions of the Crystal Palace, or the Palm House at Kew, while others had miniature ponds in them, complete with miniature fountains. Most had fronts that could be opened like the front of a doll's-house, so that cultural operations could be carried out. Such pieces seem to have completely vanished with the passing of the Victorian era, thrown out, no doubt, in that enthusiasm which ushered in the new Edwardian age and decreed that everything Victorian should be banished. Certainly today, with its revived interest in all things Victorian, a genuine terraria is an almost unobtainable object: you can't even find them in museums.

Though people who have terraria and bottle gardens like to give the impression that the whole thing is complicated and that there is some 'secret' formula involved, the cultivation of ferns and other plants in hermetically sealed containers is really very simple. Firstly the container should be made of clear glass and should be sterilised before use. Basically the terraria or bottle should then be prepared just as though one were going to grow the fern in a pot. Firstly a layer of coarse drainage material is put in, and it is important that there should be an adequate layer of drainage material. In a terraria where one can get one's hands inside easily crocks are as good a drainage medium as any other, but in a bottle garden, where all cultivations have to be carried out through a small hole in the top, small pieces of broken brick or gravel are more suitable. Over this layer should be placed a layer of granulated charcoal. This is most important, for the charcoal has the power of absorbing noxious gases created by the growing plants, and prevents the compost from going sour. Above this should be added a layer of coarse sphagnum moss, whose purpose is to prevent the fine soil working its way into and impeding the effectiveness of the drainage material.

The compost for the bottle garden is the most important factor in its success. It needs to be a good open compost that will retain moisture and yet be well drained. An ideal mixture, provided that one has facilities for sterilising soil, is one part good loam, two parts coarse gritty sand and two parts leaf-mould or fibrous peat, to which should be added a thimbleful of John Innes base. If one does not have the facilities for sterilising compost then a good mixture would be one part of John Innes potting compost No. 2, one part fibrous peat and one part coarse gritty sand.

The next operation is planting the terraria or bottle garden. With a terraria this presents no problems, but with a bottle garden it is not quite so easy. The compost will have been added to the drainage material through a funnel in a fairly dry condition. It needs to be levelled, and any dusty particles that may have adhered to the side of the bottle or carboy need removing with a piece of cotton wool attached to the end of a kebab skewer. The compost should then be watered: this is most easily done by the controlled use of a pippet, a surgical syringe, or some such instrument—anything, in fact, which will allow the water to be added drop by drop. Water can be allowed to trickle through at a controlled rate by squeezing the tubing. The object is to get the compost damp but not positively wet. It is better at this stage to err on the side of under-watering rather than over-watering. Water can be added later more easily than it can be removed, which can only be done by allowing to evaporate—a slow process.

The plants for a bottle garden must be very small when planted, otherwise they will not pass through the neck of the bottle. The technique is to make two instruments out of a heavy gauge wire: each consists of a long straight piece which is the handle and which should be long enough to rest on the compost, while leaving sufficient of itself sticking out of the neck to manoeuvre it. At the end of each of these a small hook should be formed, and bent at right angles to the handle. The fern to be planted is then hooked between roots and fronds, and lowered carefully into the bottle. The other instrument is then used to create a hole in which to plant the fern: the fern is lowered into the hole and the compost returned to its roots with the free instrument. This is then used to hold the fern in position while the instrument with which it was originally held is disengaged and removed from the bottle. It is helpful to make one hook larger than the other, the larger of the two being used as the cultivating instrument.

Once the ferns are in position they should be sprayed lightly overhead with a fine spray (an old perfume spray is ideal for this purpose), and the bottle sealed. The garden must be watched carefully to see whether sufficient or too much moisture has been added. A well-balanced bottle garden is one in which just sufficient free moisture remains to form a dewy film on the upper part of the bottle. If this condensation assumes the proportions of droplets of water, then too much has been put into the receptacle and the top should be removed to allow the excess to evaporate. If insufficient water has been added to condense then a little more should be added with the sprayer.

Considerable care needs to be taken in the selection of plants for a bottle garden: they will invariably grow larger than they would out of doors. Filmy ferns, for example, which grow to perfection in bottle gardens and terraria, will just romp away and smother anything planted with them. The same is true of most of the selaginellas, which are often planted as ground cover in bottle gardens.

Once planted the bottle garden or terraria should be put in a light position, but not one where it will receive direct sunlight. It can then be left alone and enjoyed for years without any further attention. Only when the ferns in it become too large should it be broken up and a new garden created.

PROPAGATION AND HYBRIDISING

In any branch of gardening the propagation of one's favourite plants forms one of the most rewarding aspects of that hobby, and this is particularly true of the ferns, and even more of their varieties. One may have many reasons for wanting to increase one's stock of a fern: simply so that one has more plants of it to dot around the garden; to gain sufficient plants for ground cover; for swapping; or, in the case of the varieties, if one is raising them from spores, it may be in the hope of 'making a break'—of coming up with some new and startling form. Whatever the reason, the propagation of ferns is a fascinating subject.

The great majority of ferns are most easily increased quite simply by division. Many species have creeping rootstocks, and any portion of the rootstock may be used to produce another plant. In the case of plants that form crowns, all that needs to be done is to wait until a sufficient number of crowns have formed, and then to divide them, trimming off the moribund parts of the stock or caudex with a sharp knife and making sure that each crown has sufficient stock and roots to ensure its survival. With some of the varieties, many of which are sterile, the crowns may build up only very slowly, and it is not advisable to attempt to divide these plants until they have built up a good number of crowns.

Division is certainly the easiest method of increasing ferns, and it is a method that can be used for the great majority of cool temperate ferns. It is the only way of increasing some of the varieties. The reason for this is that many varieties are sterile, while others quite simply do not come true from spores: they may produce some good things among the sporelings, but they will not be identical with their parents.

There are other methods of vegetation propagation that can be used in one or two instances, but their application is strictly limited to a very small number of species. Again the reason for using the alternative methods is almost invariably because the plant itself is sterile. All these methods depend upon the production of bulbils upon one part or another of the fronds.

The hart's-tongue fern forms are a special case, especially when it is realised that most of this fern's most desirable forms are completely sterile. The method of producing the bulbils is very similar to that used for producing young plants from the large-leaved begonias. An old frond of the hart's-tongue is snapped off the stock, and the dead portions are trimmed away, leaving only the section of the stalk that is still green. (It will be found, on a close examination of any hart's-tongue, that the stalks remain green for as much as three years after the blade has turned brown.) The stalk portions are then rested lightly on top of a layer of sand over a fern compost in a shallow pan, and covered with a pane of glass. They are kept moist, close and well shaded for some weeks, after which it will be found that they have formed small white bulbils. These can be detached and potted on into tiny pots as soon as they are large enough to handle. Again, they need to be kept relatively close and shaded until true fronds can be seen emerging.

The soft shield fern *Polystichum setiferum*, also has the power of producing bulbils, and will do so fairly readily with good cultivation. The bulbils are produced along the lower parts of the living rachis, and they are evident on the plants only as buds swelling the rachis. All that is needed to encourage them to turn into bulbils and then into plants is to detach the frond and peg it down onto a really gritty fern compost, and keep it under close conditions—in a frame or greenhouse—until the young plants start growing away. They can then be detached and potted on into the smallest pots that will accommodate their roots.

There are, of course, one or two ferns notable for the production of bulbils, *Asplenium bulbiferum* being perhaps the most obvious example. In the case of this particular fern the bulbils will form small plants on the frond before dropping off, when they will start to grow quite readily, provided only that a suitable fern compost is provided for them to fall onto.

There are a number of ferns and fern varieties which reproduce themselves by non-sexual methods. Two different physiological processes are involved, though for practical purposes the differences between these may not seem very important. The first is known as apospory, in which the prothallus grows directly out of a deformed spore capsule or directly from the frond, pinnae or pinnule tips (when it is known as apical apospory). In the case of apical apospory it is possible to produce young plants simply by pegging the tips of the fronds down into a suitable growing medium. The other method is known as apogamy, where the young fern is produced directly from a bulb-like bud on the prothallus instead of by sexual fertilisation. What happens in this case is that the spores are so formed that the prothallus contains the full compliment of chromosomes and is therefore self-fertile, not seeding the doubling-up of sexual fusion to produce a young plant.

Spores are of course a fern's natural mode of reproducing itself, and they form a ready means of increase for most species. When it comes to the varieties their usefulness becomes a rather more dubious affair. Some varieties will come 95 per cent true from spores, while others will produce only 2 per cent or 3 per cent true from spores.

The propagation of ferns from spores is something that calls for strict regime of cleanliness. Basically there is nothing difficult in raising the sporelings, except in getting them to come through before mosses, algae and liverworts beat them and swamp them. It is worth remembering that in the wild only one or two out of the thousands and thousands of spores produced by each fern each year actually succeed in germinating and growing into mature plants. But one needs to achieve a rather higher success rate than this to make it worth growing ferns from spores.

There are a number of techniques that can be used, and any fern enthusiast will always tell you that his method is the right one and that all the others are useless. The choice is really a personal one, depending to some extent upon the amount of time one has available to tend the spores and the facilities at one's disposal.

The traditional method is to sow the spores straight into a shallow pan of ordinary sterilised fern compost, plunge the pot in water up to the soil level, cover with a piece of perfectly clean glass, and then stand to drain, subsequently keeping the pan in a shaded situation and watering from below whenever the compost appears in the slightest bit dry. After a few weeks in most cases, but occasionally it is a matter of months, the little green prothalli will appear and, if growing conditions are kept correct, these will in time grow on into small fern plants. In Victorian times it was usual to sow the sporelings onto sterilised brick-dust instead of the usual fern compost. The advantage of using brick-dust (which should, incidentally, contain a few good sized chippings for drainage) is that once the plants have appeared they are more easily lifted out of the pan for potting on than is the case when fern compost is used.

A very different method which works well is to sterilise a pan, fill it with moist sphagnum moss and then invert it, standing it in a shallow saucer of sterilised water. The spores are then sown on the bottom of the pan, and the whole structure is then covered with a bell jar. While this is a very successful method so far as rate of germination foes, the prothalli must be potted on when they are still very small, and this can result in losses unless one is

4 *Asplenium ceterach* (page 115).

5 *Matteucia struthiopteris* (page 148) in autumn.

particularly careful.

Yet another method which can be adopted is to sow the spores under similar conditions to those of a bottle garden. All one needs is a plastic sweet jar, which must be sterilised before use, although not with boiling water: once the spores have germinated the plastic jar can simply be cut open with a sharp knife when the time comes to pot on the young ferns. The lid should first be removed and the plants gradually hardened off before the jar is cut. With this method the critical factor would appear to be the amount of moisture in the jar, which should be rather higher than that needed for a bottle garden.

The sporelings will take about two to three years to show their paces. Those sporelings which have come true to type or which show some interesting new break should be kept, and the rest ruthlessly thrown away. Unless one does this one will quickly accumulate an enormous number of inferior forms.

It may be thought that having to wait two or three years for the young ferns to show their paces is a long time to wait, but in fact if one sows a batch or two of spores every year, one always has some at all stages of development, which makes the process seem a lot less slow.

The need for absolute hygiene when growing ferns from spores cannot be stressed too strongly.

Spores should be collected from mature and well-developed fronds in late summer. The fronds should be examined with a hand lens to make sure that they are ready to shed their spores. Once picked, the frond should be placed, folded if necessary, into a clean white envelope and clearly labelled. After two or three days a brownish dust will collect in the envelope—the spores. The spores of most ferns will remain viable for several years, but in general the sooner they are sown the higher the success rate. There are exceptions, however, the osmundas being the most notable. In their case the spores remain viable for a mere two or three days, and after that they are useless.

Though the existence of hybrid ferns in the wild has been known for some time, it is only recently that growers have shown an interest in trying to raise deliberate hybrids. As with flowering plants, the best chances of successful results come from closely related genera.

The simplest method of hybridising ferns is to mix thoroughly the spores of the two species to be crossed and sow them very thickly. Once they have germinated the pan should be flooded, the idea being to enable the male sperms to swim from one prothallus to one of the other species. The flooding should be repeated several times, since the sexual organs of different prothalli will mature on different days.

A more certain but much more difficult method is based upon the fact that the male and the female reproductive organs of the ferns are produced on different parts of the prothallus and are recognisably different. The male

D

organs, the antheridia, are situated on the basal part of the prothallus, while the archegonia, the female reproductive organs, are situated just behind the 'notch' in the heart of the heart-shaped prothallus. A little simple surgery with a very sharp instrument enables one to remove the antheridia and present them to the archegonia of the other species being crossed. The simplest method of putting the theory into practice is to sow the spores of the two plants to be crossed in different pans, and, at the right moment, remove the male organs from the prothalli in both pans and transfer them to the opposite pan.

The success of this method depends entirely upon choosing precisely the right moment at which to carry out the operation. If it is done too soon, the male organs will die before they have released their sperms: if it is done too late the sperms will have already been released to fertilise the archegonia of the prothallus on which they were growing. The right moment is the moment at which the neck of the archegonium opens, and this can be determined only by careful examination of a sample prothallus under a microscope: a hand lens is not strong enough to reveal this detail.

The labours involved in hybridising ferns are well worth the trouble. If successful, you may have created an entirely unique plant, something which even nature had never produced; something, moreover, which is entirely your own. It may even be a rather attractive plant.

CHAPTER SIX

Maritime Ferns

All the ferns in this section are plants which grow naturally fairly close to the sea. Two species, the maidenhair fern *Adiantum capillus-veneris* and the sea spleenwort *Asplenium marinum* are both most often found growing in cliffs actually overlooking the sea, while the other ferns in this section inhabit rock crevices and walls in mainly maritime localities—although there is increasing evidence that the maidenhair fern, *Adiantum capillus-veneris*, is spreading to more and more inland sites.

The sea-cliff species seem to grow by choice in those rock crevices that are most inaccessible to man: it is quite likely, in fact, that this is simply due to over-collecting in the past, having reduced the viable populations on the more accessible levels of the cliffs.

Close examination shows that the crevices in which those ferns grow usually contain a considerable amount of humus and that they are usually very wet: there is often a continual trickle of water across the roots of the ferns. This not only supplies the roots with the moisture they require, but also contributes to keeping the atmosphere in the immediate environment of the ferns highly saturated.

The maritime ferns are most frequently found growing in positions where they are sheltered from direct sunlight and the worst excesses of the weather an an overhang of rock. In such positions they are shaded from direct sunlight but, being on sea-cliffs which are open to the reflected brightness of the sea, they still receive a lot of light.

Adiantum capillus-veneris
The true maidenhair fern

This is one of the most delicate and charming of all the ferns native to the cool temperate regions of the world. Like the other adiantums that grow in the cool temperate regions, it is, in a sense, out of its element, the genus as a whole being an essentially tropical one. The genus is quickly recognised by the very characteristic shape of the pinnules

DESCRIPTION: diminutive monomorphic evergreen creeping fern. *Stock:* creeping, rather thick in relation to the general delicacy of the species, up to 5 mm in diameter, densely covered with narrow chaffy scales. *Fronds:* up to 30 cm tall when held upright but more often held more or less horizontally and rather shorter. *Stalks:* very slender, dark brown to shining purplish-black, the lower parts somewhat covered in light brown chaffy scales, about equal in length to the blade. *Blade:* up to 15 cm by 10 cm, more or less ovate in outline, of delicate appearance and texture. *Branching:* bi to tripinnate. *Pinnae:* widely spaced on blackish-purple hair-like stalks. *Pinnules:* wedge-shaped and quite unlike those of any other fern of the regions of which it is a native, up to 12 mm broad, the outer margin deeply cut. *Venation:* Cyclopteridian. The fertile pinnules differ from the barren pinnules in their more or less truncate apex, and in the way in which in segments of the margin are incurled acting in effect as indusia, each one some 3 mm long. *Sori:* small, produced in clusters of two to ten each pinnule. *Indusium:* absent.

HABITAT: sheltered maritime cliffs, usually on calcareous formations.

Adiantum capillus-veneris

GEOGRAPHICAL TYPE: cosmopolitan.

DISTRIBUTION: throughout the tropical and warm temperate regions of the world, rarely in the cool temperate regions, being more common in the northern hemisphere than in the southern hemisphere. Western and north-western Europe, through southern Europe into Africa: thence through China to Japan: in North America confined to the south and western states. Guatemala, in South America from Colombia southwards into the Amazon basin: in Australia confined to Queensland: Ceylon: Polynesia.

CULTIVATION: this beautiful plant can only be grown out of doors in mild areas in Britain and the U.S.A. Elsewhere it needs the shelter of a frost-free house.

VARIETIES: earlier authors have recorded several beautiful varieties but none of these is now known to be in cultivation. Some may crop up again in the wild and are well worth looking for.

Asplenium billotii★
Asplenium lanceolatum
Asplenium obovatum
The lanceolate
spleenwort

A charming dwarf tufted wintergreen fern, relatively uncommon throughout most of its range. It is easily confused with *Asplenium adiantum-nigrum*, from which it differs chiefly in its lanceolate blade, which is slightly narrowed towards the base (which is not the case with *A. adiantum-nigrum*). Other features by which it may be distinguished from that species are the less leathery and brighter green pinnae, which are somewhat, though not pronouncedly crisped, and further by the placement of the sori, these being nearer the margin than the midrib of this species, but nearer the midrib in *A. adiantum-nigrum*.

DESCRIPTION: dwarf tufted monomorphic wintergreen maritime fern.
Stock: short, tufted, erect or creeping, densely clothed with blackish-brown shining scales each of which terminates in a hair-like point.
Fronds: produced in basket-like tufts, several tufts pressed closely together on each mature plant, varying between 10 cm and 40 cm in length.
Stalks: $\frac{1}{3}-\frac{2}{3}$ as long as the blade, semi-circular in section, dark, reddish-brown to purplish-brown, with a few hair-like scales, particularly towards the base.
Rachis: of similar shape and colour, but with very few scales.
Blade: lanceolate in outline, slightly narrowed towards the base, rather stiff in texture, bright green.
Branching: bipinnate.
Pinnae: opposite to sub-opposite up to about 20 on either side of the rachis, lanceolate in outline, very shortly stalked, pinnate at the base, becoming deeply pinnatifid with the ultimate segment entire.

★The first name given is that now regarded as correct. The other Latin names are synonyms still in use.

Pinnules: oblong to obovate in outline, coarsely toothed the acroscopic basal pinnule usually larger than the others, and itself deeply lobed to almost pinnatifid.

Venation: Pecopteridian.

Sori: oblong, situated close to the pinnule margins.

Indusium: oblong, entire, opening inwards.

HABITAT: coastal cliffs, rarely found away from coastal districts.

GEOGRAPHICAL TYPES: Atlantic.

DISTRIBUTION: the Atlantic coasts of western Europe including the British Isles; the north coast of the Mediterranean; Algeria; the Azores; the Canary Islands; Madeira.

CULTIVATION: can only be successfully cultivated out of doors in coastal districts, where it needs a vertical crevice in a rock garden. Elsewhere it makes an interesting specimen for a pan in the cold house.

VARIETIES: none recorded.

Asplenium marinum
The sea spleenwort

This spleenwort is distinguished from the other spleenworts mainly by its peculiarly leathery fronds and also by its purplish-brown stems.

DESCRIPTION: dwarf monomorphic wintergreen tufted maritime fern.

Stock: tufted, erect or creeping, densely clothed with purplish lanceolate scales.

Fronds: produced in tufts but very variable in size according to the richness of the particular habitat, varying from as little as 5 cm to as much as 50 cm.

Stalks: varying from $\frac{1}{2}$–$\frac{1}{3}$ as long as the blade, reddish-brown to purplish with a few scattered lanceolate scales towards the base: smooth: somewhat shiny.

Blade: again very variable but always variable in proportion to the whole plant, from 4–40 cm long, narrowly to broadly lanceolate, rather coriaceous.

Branching: pinnate.

Pinnae: sub-opposite to alternate again becoming sub-opposite towards the apex, bright green, oblong in outline, somewhat lobed on the acroscopic side close to the rachis, the margin broadly toothed.

Venation: Eupteridian.

Sori: linear, occurring on the acroscopic sides of the forks of the secondary pinna veins.

Indusium: linear, opening inwards.

HABITAT: maritime cliffs, usually on acid formations.

GEOGRAPHICAL TYPE: Atlantic.

DISTRIBUTION: the Atlantic coasts of Europe from the Orkneys to Gibraltar and the more westerly islands of the Mediterranean: the

Azores, the Canary Islands, Madeira.

CULTIVATION: this species can really only be cultivated in the open in coastal areas, where it needs a vertical crevice in a rock garden, and where it needs to be grown in an acid soil. Away from the coast it needs cool house treatment.

VARIETIES: several interesting varieties have been recorded in the past but none is now known to be still in cultivation.

Asplenium marinum

CHAPTER SEVEN

Mountain Ferns

The ferns of mountains are, as might be expected of plants that grow in a harsh environment, on the whole rather diminutive. The majority are extremely hardy, being used to exposure to dessicating winds, strong sunlight and very low winter temperatures. Many are also beautiful plants, especially for the rock or peat garden. A large number are, unfortunately, exceptionally difficult to cultivate successfully in lowland gardens.

The reasons for this are several. Mountains to tourists may just be a charming part of the scenery, but to anyone who actually goes looking for ferns on the sides of mountains it very quickly becomes apparent that mountain sides are not just a single habitat but a complexity of micro-habitats. Many mountain ferns grow in a similar fashion to most wall ferns, with their heads in the sun and their roots penetrating deeply into fissures in the rock (from which, incidentally, it is virtually impossible to dislodge them without severing their roots unless one is prepared cautiously to chip away the mountain immediately around them with a geologist's hammer): others grow in similar crevices but on the shaded side of the mountain. Those that grow in sun can usually be cultivated relatively easily on the sunny side of a rock garden or dry stone wall: those that grow on the shaded side would prefer the shaded side of a rock garden or dry stone wall, though they often do equally well in a peat bed, especially if grown in the vertical interstices between the peat blocks.

The really difficult mountain ferns to cultivate are those that grow in the screes. The problem here is that these ferns have their heads in the sun and their roots reaching right through the scree, under which it will very often be found that there is a stream. The result is that they grow in full sun, in perfect drainage, and yet have a constant supply of water at their roots. Such conditions are quite remarkably difficult to reproduce in the garden. Most success is usually achieved with these ferns by growing them on a peat bed to which at least equal parts of granite or limestone chippings have been added, the surface also covered in chippings, and the whole watered frequently during dry spells. Limestone chippings should only be used where the fern comes from a limestone habitat. An alternative is to grow these difficult ferns near the base of the wall in a doline.

Many mountain ferns prove difficult plants to cultivate in pans, though one or two make excellent subjects for this treatment. The reason for failure of these ferns when grown in pans is an obvious one when it is pointed out but it is also one that is very easily overlooked. It is quite simply that one of the factors affecting the growth of ferns on mountains is that they are used to constant wind movement: when grown in pans they are usually kept in greenhouses, and the one thing people in general fail to realise about greenhouses is that, while they may heat them admirably in winter, and shade them admirably in summer, they very seldom ventilate them properly at any time of the year. If you want to succeed with ferns in a greenhouse, especially with mountain ferns, good ventilation, preferably by means of both intake and outlet fans, is imperative.

Adiantum hispidulum
The rough
maidenhair fern

Like all the maidenhair ferns, the rough maidenhair fern is of delicate appearance—in this case belied by the rather leathery texture of the fronds. The young fronds are a beautiful bright pink when unfurling.

DESCRIPTION: creeping monomorphic wintergreen mountain fern.
Stock: short, stout, creeping, branching sporadically and usually alternately, rooting beneath, producing fronds above at irregular but usually alternate intervals, hairy.
Fronds: up to as much as 25 cm but usually about ½ that height, held erect.
Stalks: black, erect, bristly, the bristles being in fact fine rather hard scales.
Blade: broadly and unsymmetrically triangular, pedately branched.
Pinnae: lanceolate, pinnate.
Pinnules: dark green when mature, alternate becoming sub-opposite, the acroscopic edge straight and at right angles to the rachis, the basiscopic edge ovate.
Venation: Cyclopteridian.
Sori: numerous occurring on the acroscopic and outer pinnule margins.
Indusium: absent.

HABITAT: originally from mountain ranges, but naturalised on waste ground, clay banks and crumbling masonry, old walls, etc.

GEOGRAPHICAL TYPE: Bi-polar.

DISTRIBUTION: native of Asia and southern Australia including Tasmania and New Zealand. Naturalised in the U.S.A. from Louisiana eastwards to Georgia and Florida.

CULTIVATION: grows well in southern gardens in the U.S.A. but in areas that are not free from frost it needs cold house treatment. Makes a beautiful plant for pan culture.

VARIETIES: none recorded.

Adiantum venustum
The hardy
maidenhair fern

This delightful diminutive mountain fern is generally similar to the so-called true maidenhair fern *Adiantum capillus-veneris* except that it is somewhat more frost-tolerant than that species. It differs from it mainly in its carpet-forming habit, in the bluer cast to the fronds and in the narrower shape of the segments.

DESCRIPTION: dwarf creeping deciduous monomorphic mountain fern.
Stock: creeping, branching frequently and usually alternately rooting beneath, producing fronds above, supraterrestial, up to 3 mm thick, densely clothed, particularly on the younger parts, with chaffy light brown scales.
Fronds: deciduous, up to 30 cm long, usually $\frac{1}{2}$ that length.
Stalks: about as long as the blade or slightly less, furry at the base but otherwise smooth and shiny, very dark brown to almost black.
Blade: triangular-ovate in outline, flimsy texture.
Branching: tri- to quadripinnate.
Pinnae: alternate, bi-pinnate.
Pinnules: longer and narrower than those of *A. capillus-veneris*, cuneate at the base, rounded at the apex, slightly cleft.
Venation: Cyclopteridian.
Sori: produced one to three in slight hollows at the pinnule apices, protected by the curled edge of the pinnule apex.
Indusium: absent.

HABITAT: moist peaty soil on mountains, alpine meadows.

GEOGRAPHICAL TYPE: Arctic alpine.

DISTRIBUTION: Canada, where it is locally abundant. Also reported from Kashmir.

CULTIVATION: a worthwhile plant, really requiring a sheltered peatbed. Given conditions that suit it, it will quickly form a delightful carpet of light green. The fronds turn sere at the first touch of frost, and remain on the plants until the new fronds appear in spring. The stock should be planted on the surface of the soil and allowed to find its own depth.

VARIETIES: none recorded.

Asplenium bradleyi
Bradley's spleenwort

A rather rare wintergreen mountain fern confined to rock crevices in rather dry positions on extremely acid formations. It seems to inhabit only those haunts which are almost inaccessible to man.

DESCRIPTION: tufted, monomorphic, wintergreen mountain fern.
Stock: short, creeping, erect, branching frequently, the younger parts clothed in dark brown hairs, the older parts in the almost black dead frond stalks.
Fronds: up to 26 cm in length, wintergreen.

Stalks: about ½ the length of the blade, sometimes less never more, very dark, shining brown.

Rachis: similarly of a dark, shining brown, quite smooth like the stalk, very wiry.

Blade: oblong-lanceolate in outline, less coriaceous than in some other species.

Branching: pinnate.

Pinnae: oblong-obovate in outline, deeply pinnatifid, appearing lobed, particularly on the lower pinnae, the lower ones distinctly shortly stalked, the others apparently sessile, up to 10 pinnae on either side of the rachis.

Venation: Pecopteridian.

Sori: small, numerous, dark brown, occurring on the tertiary veins midway between the midrib and the margin of the pinna lobes.

Indusium: somewhat inflated, membraneous, delicate.

HABITAT: rock crevices often on high mountains and frequently in rather dry situation, invariably on extremely acid formations.

GEOGRAPHICAL TYPE: Arctic-alpine.

DISTRIBUTION: North America, including New York State, thence to Georgia and Alabama and westwards to Arkansas.

CULTIVATION: difficult. Not only does this fern prefer rather drier conditions than those enjoyed by most ferns but it also enjoys an extremely acid soil. It will succeed in a shaded crevice high up on a large rock garden where the drainage is perfect, especially if protected from excessive winter wet by a sheet of glass. It makes an attractive plant for a pan in an alpine house. It is difficult in a bottle garden: it apparently dislikes the lack of air movement.

VARIETIES: none recorded.

Asplenium fontanum
The smooth rock spleenwort

A delightful small, tufted evergreen fern that is probably best briefly described as a small version of *Asplenium billotii*. It would seem that young specimens of *Athyrium filix-femina* are sometimes mistaken for this species, and this double possibility of mis-identification makes it difficult to be certain that all the reports upon which knowledge of its geographical distribution are based are in fact accurate.

DESCRIPTION: dwarf, tufted, monomorphic wintergreen mountain fern.

Stock: short, usually creeping, tufted, densely clothed with dark, blackish-brown scales terminating in long, hair-like points.

Fronds: 7–10 cm long, rarely more, lance-shaped in outline. Descriptions of this fern in earlier books occasionally refer to fronds up to 24–28 cm in length, but this almost certainly occurs only where the author is describing *Athyrium filix-femina* under this name in error.

Stalks: very short in relation to the blade, seldom more than 1 cm long, frequently less, bearing pale brown hairs at the base.

Rachis: green. It is this green rachis that is one of the main distinguishing features between this species and *A. billotii*, in which the rachis is purplish-reddish.

Blade: pinnately branched.

Branching: pinnate.

Pinnae: obovate in outline, much smaller at the base of the blade than higher up, teeth mucronate.

Venation: Pecopteridian.

Sori: oblong, running obliquely from the mid-veins of the pinnae and scattered pretty evenly over the underside of the fronds.

Indusium: absent.

HABITAT: essentially a mountain species from southern France and central Europe, it is not truly native to the British Isles, having been recorded from only a few locations, where it is presumed to have been a garden escape.

GEOGRAPHICAL TYPE: Mediterranean.

DISTRIBUTION: Belgium, Britain, France, Italy, Greece, Hungary, Spain, Switzerland and Siberia.

CULTIVATION: grows best in a good stony compost, preferably with some builders' rubble added and plenty of leaf mould; drainage must be perfect. Makes an ideal plant for a vertical crevice in a limestone rock garden.

VARIETIES: none recorded.

Asplenium montanum
The mountain spleenwort

A charming diminutive mountain fern closely related to *Asplenium ruta-muraria* and perhaps best briefly described as intermediate between that species and *Asplenium viride*. It does, however, have its own quite distinctive characteristics, among the most noticeable of which are the bluish-green colour of the fronds, its drooping habit and the way in which the sporangia are presented in linear groups on the secondary veins of the pinnules.

DESCRIPTION: dwarf wintergreen tufted monomorphic mountain fern.

Stock: short, creeping, the younger parts densely clothed with light brown hairs and scales, the older parts with darker brown chaffy scales; roots appearing through the chaff, black, wiry, matted.

Fronds: wintergreen, up to about 10 cm, rarely more.

Stalks: approximately $\frac{1}{3}$ the length of the frond, very slender and easily broken, brown at the base becoming green, smooth, hairs and scales absent.

Rachis: green, flattened on the face.

Blade: oblong-lanceolate in outline, somewhat coriaceous.

Branching: pinnate, the lowest pair of pinnae larger than the others, all decreasing in size towards the apex, opposite or nearly so, obovate in outline.

Pinnae: opposite, the lowest pair largest, the others decreasing in size towards the apex.

Pinnules: somewhat irregular in shape, roughly ovate-oblong in outline, sessile becoming decurrent.

Venation: Sphenopteridian.

Sori: few, confluent, forming short, almost straight lines on the acroscopic side of the secondary veins of the pinnules.

Indusium: absent.

HABITAT: rock crevices on mountains and cliffs, walls, usually on acidic formations.

GEOGRAPHICAL TYPE: Arctic alpine.

DISTRIBUTION: limited. Confined to the acid formations of southern New England in North America; Europe; and Asia.

CULTIVATION: easy in any well-drained, gritty soil. An ideal rock garden or pan plant.

VARIETIES: none recorded.

---

*Asplenium
pinnatifidum
The pinnatifid
spleenwort*

One of the most charming of the spleenworts, the pinnatifid spleenwort is like rather a large number of its relatives and seems only to grow in places which are almost inaccessible to man. It is a high mountain fern, growing in crevices, on acid formations, and in usually rather dry´ situations. It resembles the so-called walking fern, *Camptosorus rhizophyllus*, so closely that it was for a long time thought of as merely a form or variety of that species. It is chiefly distinguished from that species in that it most usually grows in isolation, not in colonies, in that the frond apex is less acutely or lengthily tapered, and in that the frond does not root. There are, however, one or two records of the tip having enlarged as though in an attempt to form a proliferous bud. The species may well have evolved from the walk-

ing spleenwort, and lost the power of regenerating itself in that way.

DESCRIPTION: wintergreen, tufted, monomorphic, high mountain fern.

Stock: short, erect, usually single, seldom branched, the younger parts clothed densely with minute very dark brown hairs, the older parts with the almost black bases of the old frond stalks: roots small, wiry, black, far-reaching, pressing into narrow fissures in rock.

Fronds: wintergreen, presented in a rather irregular tuft, up to 10 cm long, often shorter.

Stalks: $\frac{1}{3}$ the length of the blade, green, smooth, hairs and scales absent.

Rachis: similar.

Blade: broadly lance-shaped tapering to a long, tail-like apex, somewhat leathery in texture, dark green.

Branching: simple, deeply lobed, becoming almost pinnatifid towards the base, the lobes being sub-opposite, becoming decurrent.

Venation: Sphenopteridian.

Sori: very variable in shape, being straight or curved, occurring in groups on all lobes of the fronds.

Indusium: cusped, persistent.

HABITAT: crevices on high mountains on acidic formations, usually in rather dry positions.

GEOGRAPHICAL TYPE: Arctic alpine.

DISTRIBUTION: in North America from New Jersey and Pennsylvania to Illinois, thence southwards to Alabama and Arkansas. Absent from Britain.

CULTIVATION: difficult, requiring very dry conditions in a crevice high up on a rock garden composed of acid rocks, perfect drainage and protection from excessive winter rain by means of a pane of glass.

VARIETIES: none recorded.

Asplenium richardii
Richard's asplenium

A very dwarf tufted wintergreen fern of great character, native of high mountains in New Zealand. The frond in general rather resembles that of *Davallia mariesii*, but the habit is different, this plant being tufted, the Davallia creeping.

DESCRIPTION: dwarf, tufted monomorphic mountain wintergreen fern.

Stock: short, erect, branching, spreading by means of stolons to form small tufted clumps, the younger parts of the stock densely clothed with light brown scales, the older parts with the black bases of the fallen fronds.

Fronds: very variable in length, from as little as 5 cm to as much as 15 cm.

Stalks: green, the lower parts covered in light brown hairs, about $\frac{1}{3}$ the length of the frond.

Blade: triangular, bright green, coriaceous.

Branching: tri- to quadripinnate.

Pinnae: up to 8 pairs, opposite or sub-opposite, well spaced.

Pinnules: very finely divided into very thin segments, less than 1 mm across.

Venation: not established.

Sori: minute occurring on the upper half of the blade.

Indusium: absent.

HABITAT: crevices in rocks in high mountains.

GEOGRAPHICAL TYPE: Antarctic.

DISTRIBUTION: confined to New Zealand.

CULTIVATION: a pretty fern well worth attempting in crevices in the rock garden. Needs constant moisture at the root, but will not tolerate stagnant water nor dry conditions. Also an excellent pan plant.

VARIETIES: none recorded.

Athyrium distentifolium
Athyrium alpestre
The alpine lady fern

This might well be described simply as a high mountain form of the lady fern *Athyrium filix-femina*, which it closely resembles except in that it is smaller in all its parts.

DESCRIPTION: dwarf deciduous monomorphic mountain fern.
Stock: erect or ascending, usually simple but sometimes, though seldom, branched. The living stock is found embedded in the decayed stocks of former crowns, and each living stock carries on its lower parts the semi-decayed stubs of the old fronds. The younger parts of the stock are clothed with light brown or sometimes dark brown lanceolate scales.
Fronds: 20–30 cm, erect or gracefully spreading as with *A. filix-femina*.
Stalks: approximately $\frac{1}{4}$ or sometimes as much as $\frac{1}{3}$ the length of the blade, swollen and flattened towards the base, blackish in colour and covered with reddish-brown lanceolate scales.
Rachis: green covered with minute hairs.
Blade: 15–20 by 10–15 cm, lanceolate in outline, rather flimsy and light green.
Branching: tripinnate becoming bipinnate.
Pinnae: many, alternate, sessile or occasionally short-stalked, linear-oblong in outline.

Pinnules: alternate, oblong, usually overlapping the pinnules of adjacent pinnae: pinnately toothed.
Venation: Pecopteridian.
Sori: found only on the acroscopic sides of the lower pinnules of the lower pinnae. Its main distinguishing feature, apart from its smaller size, is the purely botanical point that the indusium is rudimentary or vestigial and disappears long before the sori ripen. The sori themselves are smaller than in *A. filix-femina* and are situated nearer to the margins of the pinnules.
Indusium: vestigial—absent.

HABITAT: confined to high mountains: essentially an alpine and sub-alpine species.

GEOGRAPHICAL TYPE: Circumpolar.

DISTRIBUTION: recorded in Great Britain only from the highlands of Scotland, but known otherwise fairly commonly throughout the alpine and sub-alpine regions of the northern hemisphere.

CULTIVATION: a hardy little fern growing well in a crevice in a rock garden or dry stone wall in a somewhat acid soil.

VARIETIES: *A.d. flexile*, a very dwarf fern differing from the type in its even smaller parts, the stalk being no more than 1–3 cm long, the frond no more than 7–10 cm long, and in its smaller, fewer sori.

It is a fern of doubtful status, the botanists having done little work on it.

Blechnum capense
The palm leaf fern

This could generally be regarded as a typical blechnum in that it is dimorphic, in that the barren fronds are very much like those of any others in the genus, but differing from the other species in its variability: it can grow from anything from 10 or 15 cm high to 3 m or more, being one of the most striking of temperate ferns when growing luxuriantly. The variation in size would appear to be due to environmental factors, not to genetic inheritance.

DESCRIPTION: creeping dimorphic wintergreen mountain fern of dwarf to robust habit.
Stock: creeping, very stout, up to 3 cm thick, densely clothed in rather coarse reddish-brown hairs, branching sparsely and usually alternately.
Barren fronds: lanceolate in outline, coriaceous.
Fronds: wintergreen, very coriaceous, very variable in length, from as little as 10 cm to as much as 3 m, the size of the fronds depending upon the conditions under which the plant is growing.
Stalks: thick, up to 4 cm diameter, the whole of the unfurling crozier covered densely in coarse reddish-brown scales, these being retained by the stalk, which is blackish towards the base, but

falling from the rachis, up to equal in length to the blade.
Branching: pinnate.
Pinnae: oblong to oblong-linear, acuminate, with a glossy upper surface, paler below and matt, the edges of the pinnae finely serrate.
Venations: not established.
Fertile fronds: linear, taller than the barren fronds and more upright; pinnae narrow-linear.
Sori: occurring on almost every pinna of the fertile fronds, and virtually covering the whole undersurface of every pinna.
Indusium: linear.

HABITAT: on mountains up to a considerable height, but very widely distributed on the mountains, growing in both shaded places and in ones exposed to full sunlight, on both acid and alkaline soils, in conditions varying from the relatively dry to the very wet.

GEOGRAPHICAL TYPE: Antarctic alpine.

DISTRIBUTION: endemic to New Zealand.

CULTIVATION: not very frost-tolerant though well worth trying out of doors in areas where severe frost is not experienced. It does not really show its paces well when confined to a pot. Not fussy as to soil, and producing most luxuriant growth when planted in a soil rich in humus in a shaded, sheltered part of the garden.

VARIETIES: none recorded.

Blechnum
penna-marina
The dwarf hard fern

A charming and useful dimunitive creeping wintergreen mountain fern of great character in spite of its minuteness.

DESCRIPTION: dwarf creeping dimorphic wintergreen fern.
Stock: creeping, slender, up to 1.5 mm thick, branching normally alternately, sometimes erratically, surpraterrestial, rooting below, producing fronds above, fronds produced alternately along the back of the stock, the younger parts covered in minute reddish brown hairs and scales, these becoming darker in colour on the older parts of the stock.
Barren fronds: wintergreen, coriaceous, up to 8 cm long, usually rather less: stalk about $\frac{1}{4}$ the length of the blade.
Stalks: leathery, green covered in minute reddish scales and hairs.
Rachis: green, having a reddish appearance produced by quantities of minute reddish hairs and scales.
Branching: pinnate.
Pinnae: up to 20 on either side of the rachis, close-set like the teeth of a comb, linear oblong with a slight curve towards the apex of the frond.
Venation: Eupteridian.
Fertile fronds: up to 10 cm long, erect as opposed to the barren fronds which tend to be spreading, pinnae narrowly linear.
Sori: produced on almost every pinna of the fertile fronds and entirely covering the whole undersurface of those fronds upon which they are produced.
Indusium: linear.

HABITAT: high mountains, usually creeping over mossy rocks.
GEOGRAPHICAL TYPE: Antarctic alpine.

DISTRIBUTION: endemic to New Zealand.

CULTIVATION: easy in any soil well enriched with leaf-mould. It does not require or particularly enjoy a deep, rich soil, and will also grow well in gritty soil, in crevices on the rock garden or on walls. Hardy except in areas of very severe frost.

VARIETIES: only one variety has been recorded: *B. p-m. cristatum*, a form in which the frond apex is neatly crested. It really has no greater garden merit than the type plant.

Camptosorus rhizophyllus
The walking fern

The walking fern is undoubtedly one of the curiosities of the fern world, though the phenomenon of leaf-tips rooting is not unknown in the angiosperms. This fern, which is a close relative of the hart's-tongue, *Asplenium scolopendrium*, fascinates even those who normally profess to be little interested in ferns, and it is not unknown for people who normally decry ferns as mere green things that never flower to raise themselves to considerable exertions to see the walking fern, especially when growing in its native habitat. In the parts of North America where it is at home it is almost as common there as the hart's-tongue is in Britain—while of course the hart's-tongue is quite a rarity in the U.S.A.

The fern derives its common name from its uncommon practice of sending out arching fronds with tapering tips, the tips forming young plantlets where they touch the ground. Usually once the young plant is established the parental frond withers, but occasionally it is possible to see two or three generations all walking together, the original fern having rooted at its tip, and the young plantlet having sent out a frond at the tip of which yet a further plant has formed. The plant reproduces not only by means of these apogamous fronds but also by the normal means of spores.

DESCRIPTION: small evergreen monomorphic mountain fern.
Stock: short, slender, erect, seldom branched, the younger parts slightly covered with rusty brown scales, the older parts with darker scales and the almost black bases of the decayed stalks.
Fronds: up to 10 cm long, wintergreen presented in a star-shaped tuft.
Stalks: about $\frac{1}{4}$ as long as the

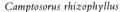

Camptosorus rhizophyllus

blade, often less, flattened and grooved on the face, dark brown and scaly at the base, becoming green and free of scales higher up.

Blade: simple, lanceolate extenuated into a long, tail-like apex, lathery, dark green, shining above, paler and less shiny below, smooth, arching, the tip rooting where it touches the ground.

Venation: Taeniopteridian.

Sori: scattered rather irregularly on the undersurface of the fronds, occurring normally on tertiary veins, but offering no particular pattern, some being parallel with the midrib, others oblique to it, others at right angles to it.

Indusium: inconspicuous.

HABITAT: limestone cliffs, less often on fallen tree trunks, boulders and rock outcrops, usually in situations facing north, and normally only in situations where there is a substantial growth of moss.

GEOGRAPHICAL TYPE: Arctic alpine.

DISTRIBUTION: in North America from sub-arctic Canada southwards to North Carolina and thence westwards: generally rare.

CULTIVATION: a decided calciphile, this fern must have adequate lime in its growing medium. Within its native range it is easily enough established in mossy situations on limestone rock-gardens, but elsewhere it is probably better grown in a pan.

VARIETIES: *C.r. auriculatus*, a form in which the basal lobes have become extenuated into long, saggitate appendages, sometimes as much as a third the length of the blade itself. Curiously, plantlets will form at the tips of these lobes in just the same manner as they do at the tip of the blade itself, though not with such regularity.

C.r. boycei, a form with a somewhat lobed blade, that looks as though it might be a cross between the species itself and *Asplenium pinnatifidum*, though there is as yet no evidence to suggest that it is in fact a hybrid.

Cheilanthes distans
Notholaena distans
The woolly rock-fern

An extremely pretty small tufted mountain fern, normally found growing in rocky, exposed situations on mountains.

DESCRIPTION: small tufted dimorphic wintergreen fern.

Stock: erect, tufted, the younger parts clothed with rather dark brown woolly hairs, the older parts with the almost black decayed stalk bases.

Barren fronds: up to 25 cm long, presented in closely pressed clumps.

Stalks: up to $\frac{2}{3}$ as long as the blade, dark brown almost black, covered with brown scales.

Rachis: similarly covered with light brown hairs, very dark brown, wiry.

Blade: triangular-ovate in outline.
Branching: pinnate.
Pinnae: up to as many as 15 pairs on each rachis, opposite widely spaced, broadly triangular, deeply cleft to almost pinnatifid, dark green and slightly hairy above, paler green and densely covered with thick, cotton-wool-like hairs below.
Venation: not established.
Fertile fronds: about ⅔ the length of the barren fronds, the pinnae much reduced and completely covered in sori, these forming a continuous line round the margins.
Sori: black.
Indusium: lip-like.

HABITAT: dry sunny situations in rock crevices.

GEOGRAPHICAL TYPE: Antarctic alpine.

DISTRIBUTION: New Zealand, Australia, Norfolk Island, New Caledonia.

CULTIVATION: reasonably frost-tolerant, and most satisfactorily grown in a sunny part of the rock garden. Not difficult, and not fussy as to soil. Slugs are its one great enemy, often attacking the young fronds. Precautions should be taken, since the depredations of these slimy invertebrates can quickly weaken a plant to a state of sickliness from which it is unlikely to recover.

VARIETIES: none recorded.

Cheilanthes sieberi
The smooth
rock-fern

This rather stiff little mountain fern is closely related to the woolly rock-fern from which it differs chiefly in the relative lack of woolliness.

DESCRIPTION: dwarf tufted dimorphic wintergreen mountain fern.
Stock: erect, branching, tufted, the younger parts densely clothed in chestnut-brown woolly hairs and scales, the older parts with the decaying stalk bases.
Barren fronds: up to 18 cm, presented in dense tufts.
Stalks: wiry, very dark reddish brown.
Rachises: of both barren and fertile fronds—rigid, reddish-brown,

becoming paler towards the apex, covered in woolly reddish scales.
Blade: linear-lanceolate in outline, dark green above, paler below, almost hairless on both surfaces.
Branching: bipinnate.
Pinnae: well spaced along the blade, opposite, triangular in outline.
Pinnules: triangular in outline, individually ovate.
Venation: not established.
Fertile fronds: shorter than the barren fronds, the entire surface of the reduced pinnae segments appearing to be covered in sori.
Sori: round, black.
Indusium: running round the edge of the fertile pinnae segments.

HABITAT: dry rocky mountain situations in full sun; will even grow on raw volcanic ash.

GEOGRAPHICAL TYPE: Antarctic alpine.

DISTRIBUTION: Australia, New Zealand, New Caledonia.

CULTIVATION: needs a situation in full sun and perfect drainage. Relatively frost-hardy, but probably better grown as an alpine house plant where severe frosts are experienced.

VARIETIES: none recorded.

Cryptogramma crispa
The parsley fern

A small tufted fern whose fronds, particularly when both the fertile and the infertile fronds are showing, so much resembles parsley that the derivation of its common name is obvious to anyone seeing it.

DESCRIPTION: dwarf dimorphic deciduous mountain fern.
Stock: normally creeping, tufted, about 3 mm thick, scaly and covered with the decaying stalks of the deciduous fronds.
Barren fronds: 5–15 cm long produced in a dense, spirally arranged tuft.
Stalks: long, usually twice as long as the blade.
Rachis: bright green, smooth, rounded.
Blade: triangular in outline.
Branching: tripinnate becoming bipinnate towards the apex.
Pinnae: alternately arranged along the rachis, though not evenly alternate, some pairs of pinnae appearing almost opposite.
Pinnules: tripinnate or bipinnate, always obviously alternate.
Venation: Ceonopteridian.
Fertile fronds: longer than the

Cryptogramma crispa

outer, barren fronds, sometimes as much as 30 cm long, the difference in length being accounted for mainly by the much longer stalk. The fertile fronds are basically similar in shape to the infertile fronds, but differ from them in that the venation is Eupteridian, and in that the margins of the pinnules are rolled back to cover the sori, the extent of the rolling being such that the outer margins meet at the mid-rib on the underside of the frond.

Sori: elliptical in outline. When the fertile fronds first appear the individual sori can be distinguished, but as the fronds mature the sori appear to run together forming a continuous band running parallel with the margin of the pinnule.

Indusium: absent, the rolled leaf-margins doing duty for them.

HABITAT: is found only in mountainous districts and is essentially a pioneer plant on acidic rocky screes.

GEOGRAPHICAL TYPE: Arctic-alpine.

DISTRIBUTION: found throughout northern and central Europe, including mountainous regions of the British Isles, extending its range northwards to Lapland, eastwards to Siberia, southwards to the Greek Islands and westwards to Spain. It also has stations in the mountains of Afghanistan and other parts of Asia Minor.

CULTIVATION: a difficult plant to cultivate, partly because it has a rapidly fatal intolerance of lime in any form, but more particularly because in its natural haunts it is normally found growing in loose screes under which there is a continuous trickle of water. It thus likes growing in conditions in which its roots are continually wet, but its fronds are permanently in the sun. Such conditions are plainly exceedingly difficult to reproduce in a garden without going to tremendous trouble and expense, unless of course you just happen to have such a scree in your back garden. It appears to grow well in a very heavy clay in a semi-shaded position. Alternatively it can be grown in a mixture of oak leaf-mould and fine granite chips, though it is important that it is never allowed to dry out.

VARIETIES: none recorded.

Cystopteris dickieana

A diminutive deciduous fern, so rare in the wild that it does not appear to have a common name. In the past some doubt has been cast on its specific rank, but since it comes perfectly true from spores, and is easily raised from them, there can be little doubt but that it is a true species. It differs from *C. fragilis* in its rough spores, those of *C. fragilis* being smooth. See also *C. fragilis*.

DESCRIPTION: dwarf deciduous monomorphic mountain fern.

Stock: very small, usually branched, creeping, the older parts covered with the decaying stalks of the deciduous leaves, the younger parts with minute yellowish-brown scales.

Fronds: oblong-lanceolate in outline.

Stalks: half as long as the blade, very brittle, breaking easily.

Rachis: green.

Blade: up to 7 cm long, often shorter.

Branching: pinnate.

Pinnae: deeply pinnatifid.

Venation: Pecopteridian.

Sori: presented in two rows, one on each side of the midrib of the pinnae.

Indusium: absent.

HABITAT: extremely rare, (information withheld in the interests of conservation).

GEOGRAPHICAL TYPE: Arctic-alpine.

DISTRIBUTION: northern and central Europe, extending northwards into Lapland. Generally rather rare.

CULTIVATION: an ideal rock-garden or alpine house fern, growing well in a pan. Though slow growing, it does in time form an attractive tight little mass of crowns. Owing to its rarity living plants should never be removed from the wild. Plants should be grown from spores, a process which presents no difficulty.

VARIETIES: none recorded.

Dryopteris abbreviata
The dwarf male fern

This, as its common name implies, is in effect a dwarf version of the true male fern *Dryopteris filix-mas*. In general appearance it could easily be mistaken for a stunted, high-mountain form of the male fern, but its specific status is in no doubt since it invariably comes true from spores and maintains its dwarf character.

DESCRIPTION: dwarf, deciduous monomorphic mountain fern.

Stock: stout in relation to the size of the plant, erect and usually branched and tufted, retaining the decaying stalks of the deciduous fronds on its older portions.

Fronds: 25–40 cm long, rather stiff.

Stalks: about $\frac{1}{4}$ as long as the blade, covered with blunt, pale brown scales.

Blade: broadly triangular in outline.

Branching: alternate, pinnate.

Pinnae: branching alternately from the rachis, the intervals between the pinnae increasing towards the base of the frond, the tips and edges of the pinnae upcurled, this being one of the distinguishing features of the species. The pinnae are deeply pinnatifid, the indentations reaching almost to the midrib and giving, at a superficial glance, the appearance of being bipinnate. The pinnae are crenately lobed, the teeth being broad and blunt.

Venation: Pecopteridian.

Sori: occurring only on the largest of the pinnae, and arranged on each side of the midrib.

Indusium: reniform, less than 1 mm across, with minute glands on the margins.

HABITAT: high mountains in rock crevices and screes, less commonly in stone walls.

GEOGRAPHICAL TYPE: Circumpolar.

DISTRIBUTION: recorded from mountainous regions of northwestern Europe including Britain, but not accurately known.

CULTIVATION: easily grown on the rock-garden, though tends to be larger in cultivation than in its natural habitat. The fronds die at the first touch of frost.

VARIETIES: none recorded.

Dryopteris fragrans
The fragrant
cliff brake

A relatively small wintergreen fern in general resembling the other Dryopteris species, but distinct from them both in its size and by reason of its fragrance. This fragrance comes from minute glands on the frond blades. It might be better described as a cliff fern than a mountain fern, for it is most often found growing on cliffs, rather than on the flatter slopes of mountains. It is usually found as an isolated specimen.

DESCRIPTION: low-growing, wintergreen monomorphic mountain fern.

Stock: short, stout, erect, the younger parts densely clothed in pale brown hairs, the older parts in the almost black stumps of the withered frond stalks: roots, black, rather coarse, rather sparse.

Fronds: wintergreen, up to 30 cm long.

Stalks: usually about ¼ the length of the frond, green, densely clothed with reddish brown scales towards the base, less so towards the base of the blade.

Rachis: green, lightly clothed with chaffy reddish-brown scales.

Blade: obovate in outline, narrowing towards both tip and base.

Branching: pinnate.

Pinnae: up to as many as 40 pairs, obovate-lanceolate in outline, alternate becoming sub-opposite to opposite towards the base, deeply pinnatifid.

Venation: Pecopteridian.

Sori: large, becoming confluent.

Indusium: kidney-shaped.

HABITAT: primarily cliffs, steep rocky banks, occasionally screes,

6 *Onoclea sensibilis* (page 150).

7 (Top) *Osmunda regalis* (page 153).   8 (Bottom) *Osmunda regalis* in autumn.

usually only on calcareous formations.

GEOGRAPHICAL TYPE: Arctic-alpine.

DISTRIBUTION: north-eastern United States, Canada from Newfoundland to Alaska, the Aleutian Islands, Kamchatka.

CULTIVATION: difficult, growing best where its roots can deeply penetrate a rock fissure—conditions difficult to imitate in the garden. Best in tight crevices in the rock garden. If grown in a pan it needs a very gritty medium to ensure perfect drainage.

VARIETIES: none recorded.

Gleichenia dicarpa var. *alpina*
The umbrella fern

This is one of those awkward little ferns that could equally well be placed in the chapter devoted to the ferns of wet places, since its natural habitat is sphagnum bogs: since however it only grows wild in sphagnum bogs occurring 4,000 feet up or so, in the mountains, it is probably most suitable for inclusion here. Like many ferns that will grow with their roots in really wet situations, this one grows in full sun in the wild.

DESCRIPTION: dwarf tufted monomorphic wintergreen mountain fern.
Stock: short, erect, branching, up to 3 cm thick, the younger parts clothed with light brown hairs, the older parts with the almost black decayed stalk bases.
Fronds: wintergreen up to 30 cm long, quite different in their manner of growth from any other fern, appearing to branch and rebranch dichotomously but in reality not in this fashion: the branching takes place on the horizontal plane.
Stalks: rather rigid, light green: slight whitish bloom when young.

Rachis: also rather rigid, light green.
Blade: of irregular outline, light green, whitish below.
Branching: irregular, branches bipinnate, oblong-linear in outline.
Pinnae: triangular in outline, alternate becoming sub-opposite, then alternate again towards apex.
Pinnules: linear.
Venation: not established.
Sori: small, produced in small groups of 2 or 3.
Indusium: absent.

HABITAT: sphagnum bogs on high mountains up to the snow line.

GEOGRAPHICAL TYPE: Antarctic alpine.

DISTRIBUTION: endemic to New Zealand.

CULTIVATION: easy enough when grown in established sphagnum moss in the bog garden in full sun or in a pan. Will not tolerate severe frost.

VARIETIES: none recorded.

Grammitis pumila

Very dwarf wintergreen creeping fern of unusual aspect.

DESCRIPTION: dwarf monomorphic creeping wintergreen mountain fern.
Stock: creeping, branching normally alternately occasionally erratically, rooting beneath, producing fronds above, the younger parts clothed in greyish scales.
Fronds: wintergreen, up to 2.5 cm, rarely more, linear in outline, erect, very thick and coriaceous in texture, entire, smooth.
Stalks: very short or almost absent.
Blade: simple, linear in outline, coriaceous.
Venation: not established.
Sori: large, obliquely places on the fronds.
Indusium: absent.

HABITAT: rock faces on high mountains, in crevices and on mossy boulders.

GEOGRAPHICAL TYPE: Antarctic alpine.

DISTRIBUTION: endemic to New Zealand.

CULTIVATION: this species is rather less hardy than the majority of New Zealand Antarctic alpine ferns, but will withstand slight frost. It makes a fascinating plant out of doors where the climate is mild enough, and is easy enough to grow given perfect drainage in soil that never dries out. Makes a good specimen plant for a pan in a cold house.

VARIETIES: none recorded.

Gymnocarpium dryopteris
Phegopteris dryopteris
Thelypteris dryopteris
Carpogymnia dryopteris
Polypodium dryopteris
The oak fern

This is one of those ferns that could almost equally well be included in the chapter on woodland ferns, but earns its place here since it is usually found only in woodland on the foothills of mountains. It is one of the most dainty and beautiful of the smaller, deciduous, northern temperate ferns.

Its nomenclature has suffered unduly at the hands of the taxonomists over the years. It was originally assigned to the genus Gymnocarpium: then, for a long while, it was known as *Polypodium dryopteris* (an enormous number of ferns have been assigned to the genus Polypodium at one time or

another): it has subsequently been known as *Phegopteris dryopteris*, *Lastrea dryopteris*, *Polystichum dryopteris*, *Dryopteris linnaeana* and finally —or almost finally—*Gymnocarpium dryopteris*. However, even then the taxonomists had still not quite finished with it. About a decade ago they suddenly decided that it should be called *Thelypteris dryopteris*. It has since been reinstated as *Gymnocarpium dryopteris*, and one hopes that it may stay with that name for a while.

DESCRIPTION: diminutive deciduous monomorphic fern.
Stock: very slender, seldom thicker

than 1 or 2 mm, black, glossy, the younger parts clothed in tiny, pale brown scales. The stock creeps just under the surface of the soil, branching sparingly. The stock never appears above the surface of the soil, sending up fronds at intervals. The stock is well adapted to running around in gritty soil and scree.

Fronds: varying from 10 to 35 cm, appearing singly from the ground. The new fronds, as they emerge and begin to unfurl, resemble three little green balls carried on slender, wiry green stems.

Stalks: very long, 2–3 times the length of the blade.

Rachis: bright green, flaccid when young, becoming firmer with age.

Blade: up to 15 cm long, broadly deltoid in outline, bent back at an angle from the stalk.

Branching: tripinnate.

Pinnae: opposite, usually presented in 6 distinct pairs, the lower pair being by far the largest, usually almost as large as the rest of the blade together.

Pinnules: those of the lower pair of pinnae ovate to oblong, sometimes entire, sometimes crenate and sometimes toothed: those of the upper pinnae resembling the lowest pinnulets of the first pair of pinnae.

Venation: Pecopteridian.

Sori: normally circular, the lowest ones sometimes elongated towards the oval, occurring on the secondary veins close to the margins of the pinnules, sometimes running together so that they appear to form a continuous band.

Indusium: absent.

HABITAT: mountainous districts, rocky woodlands, screes, rocky stream banks, locally abundant.

Gymnocarpium dryopteris

GEOGRAPHICAL TYPE: Circumpolar.

DISTRIBUTION: common throughout northern and central Europe, occurring less frequently towards the Mediterranean, thence eastwards through Asia Minor, through the western Himalayas and northwards through northern Asia into China and Japan. Its northern range takes it through Greenland and the Arctic into Canada and thence southwards through temperate North America as far south as Arizona, Kansas and Virginia.

CULTIVATION: an ideal fern for the front of a shaded fern border. It is also happy in the rock garden or in a peat wall, and thrives in openings among low-growing shrubs. It needs plenty of leaf-mould in the soil, and will not tolerate a soil that dries out.

VARIETIES: none recorded.

Gymnocarpium
robertianum
Carpogymnia
robertiana
Phegopteris robertiana
Thelypteris robertiana
Limestone polypody

A charming diminutive deciduous fern often confused with the closely allied *Gymnocarpium dryopteris* and, less often, with *Phegopteris connectilis*. It is, however, easily distinguished from these species, not only by its botanical differences but also and more importantly by its habitat. It is confined in the wild to limestone pavements, where it is found growing with its stock firmly established in deep fissures, and on limestone screes: the other species are not lime-lovers and generally prefer to grow in damper places.

DESCRIPTION: diminutive, delicate, monomorphic deciduous woodland fern.
Stock: black, creeping, 20 cm by 3.5 mm, covered in light brown hairs and scales.
Fronds: arising at irregular alternate intervals along the stock, varying from 15 to 45 cm in length.
Stalks: very long in relation to the blade, usually 1½, sometimes 2 times as long as the blade, exceptionally soft and flimsy when young, green, becoming darker and firmer with age.
Rachis: pale green, soft and flaccid when young, becoming firmer and almost wiry with maturity.
Blade: triangular in outline, of a dull mid green.
Branching: tripinnate at the base, becoming bipinnate and finally pinnatifid towards the apex.
Pinnae: always opposite, the lower pair of pinnae being substantially larger than the others and placed so far down on the stalk as to give the frond the general appearance of being composed of three large sub-fronds.
Pinnules: deeply pinnatifid, the segments normally oblong but occasionally truncate.
Venation: Pecopteridian.
Sori: small, round, forming rows on either side of and fairly close to the margins.

Indusium: absent.

HABITAT: locally common on limestone pavements and limestone screes, less often found in limestone woods and dry limestone walls.

GEOGRAPHICAL TYPE: Circumpolar.

DISTRIBUTION: found in Europe from Iceland southwards to the Pyrenees, Corsica and Italy and eastwards to the Balkan Peninsular and Afghanistan. In North America its range extends from Brook's Range to the Laurentian Plateau in the north, southwards to the Bay of Fundy and thence westwards to Iowa.

CULTIVATION: essentially a fern for a crevice in a limestone rockery where it can bury its roots and reach deep moisture while having its fronds in the sun.

VARIETIES: none recorded.

Gymnocarpium robertianum

Hypolepis millefolium
The thousand-leaved fern

This delightful mountain fern has probably the most finely divided fronds of any fern—at first glance somewhat resembling those of *Davallia mariesii*, but in fact even more finely divided.

DESCRIPTION: creeping winter-green monomorphic mountain fern.
Stock: long, slender, creeping just below the soil surface, branching frequently and irregularly, rooting beneath, producing fronds at frequent intervals along its upper side, the younger parts densely clothed in rusty-red scales.
Fronds: up to 30 cm long.
Stalks: pale yellow-brown clothed lightly with short, scattered hairs.
Rachis: pale yellowish green lightly clothed in short, scattered hairs becoming fewer towards the apex.
Blade: very finely divided, of a soft, velvety texture, light green, triangular to deltate in outline.
Branching: tripinnate.

Pinnae: lanceolate in outline, frond-like, with pronounced central rib.
Pinnules: deeply denate giving a delightfully lacy effect.
Venation: not established.
Sori: occurring in the sinuses of the lobes, numerous.
Indusium: formed by the pinnules margins.

HABITAT: woodlands on high mountains.

GEOGRAPHICAL TYPE: Antarctic alpine.

DISTRIBUTION: endemic to New Zealand.

CULTIVATION: relatively easy, reasonably frost tolerant though best grown in a cold house in all but the mildest districts. Though not fanatically calcifuge, it prefers to grow in conditions where little time is present.

VARIETIES: none recorded.

Hypolepis rugosula

A delightful creeping mountain fern, distinguished from *H. millifolium* by the very much more widely spaced pinnae, by the brownish-green of the fronds and the dark red, rather rough, sticky leaf stalks and pinnalmidribs.

DESCRIPTION: creeping winter-green monomorphic mountain fern.
Stock: long, creeping, very slender, up to 1 mm thick, densely covered in rather coarse reddish hairs, rooting below, producing fronds alternately on the upper surface.
Fronds: up to 1 m long, usually about half that length, soft and velvety in texture, of a curious brownish-green colour.
Stalks: up to $\frac{1}{4}$ as long as the blade, densely covered with sticky, rather coarse dark red hairs.

Rachis: and pinna midribs also similarly clothed.

Blade: broadly to narrowly triangular.

Branching: bipinnate.

Pinnae: frond-like, occurring in opposite pairs.

Pinnules: obovate in outline, opposite, somewhat irregular.

Venation: not established.

Sori: numerous on the upper part of the frond.

Indusium: formed by the pinnule margins.

HABITAT: light woodland on lower mountain slopes.

GEOGRAPHICAL TYPE: Antarctic alpine.

DISTRIBUTION: Australia, Japan, New Zealand.

CULTIVATION: prefers a lime-free soil, though will tolerate a little lime. Not very frost-hardy, and best grown in the alpine house except in relatively frost-free areas.

VARIETIES: none recorded.

Lastreopsis hispida

A charming wintergreen mountain woodland fern, in general appearance closely resembling plants of the genus dryopteris but differing in its creeping stock and in the way in which the prominent ridges of the main rachis are continuous with the blade edge.

DESCRIPTION: creeping woodland monomorphic mountain fern.

Stock: creeping, thick, up to 1 cm diameter, branching frequently and irregularly, covered with russet scales, fronds produced alternately.

Fronds: wintergreen up to 45 cm long, very coriaceous, rather rough to the touch, triangular in outline.

Stalks: light green, flaccid when young, becoming firmer with age.

Rachis: light green.

Blade: 23–46 cm. long, triangular, lancedate in outline.

Branching: tri- to quadripinnate.

Pinnae: triangular in outline.

Pinnules: and pinnulets deeply serrate.

Venation: not established.

Sori: large, numerous.

Indusium: orbicular.

HABITAT: thick woodland on high mountains.

GEOGRAPHICAL TYPE: Antarctic alpine.

DISTRIBUTION: endemic to New Zealand.

CULTIVATION: not particularly easy, needing a very moist growing medium and yet perfect drainage, and conditions of very heavy shade. Rather frost-tender and only worth trying out of doors in areas where frost is slight or rare, otherwise better confined to a fern house where its cultural requirements can most easily be met.

VARIETIES: none recorded.

Polystichum cystostegia
The mountain shield fern

A charming mountain fern producing tufts of thin, shiny fronds. In effect a dwarf version of *P. vestitum*.

DESCRIPTION: tufted wintergreen dimorphic mountain fern.
Stock: erect, sub-caulescent, rarely branched, densely covered in rusty-brown scales, the older parts thickly beset with the dead stalk bases.
Fronds: up to 20 cm long, usually about half that length, rather soft in texture, produced in a basket-like tuft.
Stalks: up to equal in length with the blade, covered with relatively large pale brown scales.
Rachis: green, also covered, though to a lesser extent, with rather large pale brown scales.
Blade: linear-lanceolate in outline.
Branching: bipinnate.

Pinnae: triangular-ovate in outline, alternate.
Pinnules: deeply toothed, acute.
Venation: not established.
Sori: large, produced on the upper half of the fertile fronds which otherwise differ little from the barren fronds.
Indusium: large, dome-shaped, pale brown.

HABITAT: alpine scrubland.

GEOGRAPHICAL TYPE: Antarctic alpine.

DISTRIBUTION: endemic to New Zealand and its offshore islands.

CULTIVATION: a surprisingly frost-tolerant species that succeeds well in any deep, rich, well-drained soil.

VARIETIES: none recorded.

Polystichum lonchitis
The holly fern

A charming low-growing tufted evergreen species of great individuality and character. It derives its common name from the stiff bristles at the tips of the larger segments of the pinnae. The whole frond, if one runs one's hand over it, has a threateningly bristly feel, though the bristles are not sharp enough to pierce the skin. It is occasionally confused with *Polystichum aculeatum* var. 'Cambricum': the confusion, however, normally only occurs when attempts are made to identify immature plants.

DESCRIPTION: low-growing, leathery monomorphic wintergreen mountain fern of distinctly bristly appearance and feel.
Stock: short, thick, erect, densely clothed in the decaying stalks of the old fronds, the younger part covered with light brown scales, some large, some small, evenly intermixed.
Fronds: lanceolate in outline, up to 60 cm long, usually less than half that length, presented very stiffly, of a decidedly leathery texture, deep green, glossy, above, paler green beneath.

Stalks: short, normally not more than $\frac{1}{5}$ the length of the blade, densely clothed with light brown scales, both large and small evenly intermixed.

Rachis: rather rigid, brownish green, paler towards the apex, covered in both large and small light brown scales evenly inter-mixed.

Blade: up to 50 cm long and 6 cm wide.

Branching: pinnate.

Pinnae: up to as many as 40 on either side of the rachis normally alternate except at the base where they become first sub-opposite and then opposite, set very closely together along the rachis so much so that the upper edge of each pinna often overlaps the lower edge of the pinna above it. The pinnae are simple but coarsely toothed,

Polystichum lonchitis

particularly towards the base, the largest of the serrations being so large as to be almost lobes, each tooth ending in a long, pointed bristle-like hair.

Venation: Neuropteridian.

Sori: appearing only on the upper half of the blade and forming a line along the secondary vein only on the upper and outer quarter of each pinna.

Indusium: circular, irregularly toothed.

HABITAT: rock crevices on high mountains.

GEOGRAPHICAL TYPE: Circumpolar alpine.

DISTRIBUTION: very rare in Britain, somewhat commoner in the northern mountain regions of continental Europe and relatively common thence eastwards through Asia Minor and northern Asia to the Himalayas. Its range then extends westwards from Greenland into North America, from Nova Scotia to Colorado.

CULTIVATION: the holly fern is one of the most difficult of the mountain ferns to cultivate, especially in lowland gardens. Mature plants wrested from their mountain crevices seldom survive the move to lowland gardens, and in Britain, where the fern is very rare, and in those parts of Europe where it is relatively rare, this should never be attempted, on that account alone. Far more success will be achieved if sporelings are raised from fertile fronds and these are grown on and planted out as young stock into tight crevices in the rock garden. In their native haunts they are usually found growing on mountains on basic igneous rock, particularly granite, but this is not a satisfactory choice of rock for lowland gardens, a more porous rock generally proving more satisfactory. The soil should be extremely gritty.

VARIETIES: though a crested variety has been recorded in Britain, it is now no longer known to be in cultivation. There is obviously a remote chance that a crested form may be rediscovered in one of the areas in which this fern is common.

Polystichum munitum
The Pacific coast sword fern

A very similar fern to the North American Christmas fern, *Polystichum acrostichoides* (see page 155), from which it differs mainly in its longer, more linear acuminate pinnae.

DESCRIPTION: wintergreen tufted monomorphic mountain fern.

Stock: short, horizontal to erect, variable, densely covered with mid-brown lanceolate scales on the younger parts, the older parts densely beset with the remnants of the old frond bases, roots black, coarse, numerous, growing both from the growing tip of the stock and through the old frond bases.

Fronds: up to 90 cm long, rather leathery, somewhat rigid and somewhat rough to the touch.

Stalks: about ⅓ the length of the blade, densely set with scales towards the base, becoming less scaly.

Rachis: green, beset with light brown scales, flattened and grooved on the face.

Blade: linear in outline.

Branching: pinnate.

Pinnae: linear, acuminate, serrate to biserrate, up to 40 pairs on each rachis.

Venation: not established.

Sori: occurring in two rows one on either side of the pinna midrib.

Indusium: circular, entire, tooth-edged.

HABITAT: mountain woodlands.

GEOGRAPHICAL TYPE: restricted.

DISTRIBUTION: coastal western North American mountains.

CULTIVATION: easy in any good garden soil well enriched with leaf-mould. Prefers some shade to give of its best, but will grow in a reasonable amount of sun.

VARIETIES: none recorded.

Polystichum vestitum
The large shield fern

A strong-growing mountain species producing a short stem topped by a thick crown of shining dark green fronds, of bristly texture.

DESCRIPTION: strong-growing, wintergreen monomorphic mountain fern.

Stock: stout, erect, somewhat caulescent, branching underground, the younger parts densely clothed with fox-red scales, the older parts beset thickly with the old frond bases, often almost black in colour.

Fronds: up to 1 m long, leathery, bristly, dark shining green above, paler and less glossy below.

Stalks: up to a ⅓ the length of the blade densely clothed with large brown scales, darker in the centres than at their margins.

Rachis: also densely clothed in similar scales.

Blade: narrowly lanceolate.

Branching: bipinnate.

Pinnae: oblong, acute.

Pinnules: ovate, somewhat auriculate but not so much so as in *Polystichum setiferum* (see page 229), toothed, the teeth terminating in sharp, bristly tips.

Venation: not established.

Sori: circular.

Indusium: small.

HABITAT: mountain scrublands.

GEOGRAPHICAL TYPE: Antarctic alpine.

DISTRIBUTION: Australia, Tierra del Fuego, Tasmania, New Zealand.

CULTIVATION: to show of its best this plant really needs to be grown in the open, not only so that it can develop its fronds to the full, but also to allow it to spread, as it does in the wild, by its branching sub-terranean stock into large, luxuriant patches. Unfortunately it is not very frost-hardy, and certainly demands cold house treatment in all but the very mildest areas of the U.K.

VARIETIES: none recorded.

Woodsia alpina
The alpine woodsia

A diminutive deciduous tufted mountain fern, this species is sub-stantially different in appearance from the others, particularly in the ovate or even triangular outline of the pinnae. It is not particularly decorative in the garden, but of interest to the enthusiast.

DESCRIPTION: diminutive mono-morphic deciduous mountain fern.
Stock: erect or somewhat obli-quely erect, sparsely branched, densely clothed with the decaying stalks of the old fronds, from among which the numerous fine roots appear. There are some light brown scales just above the points from which the roots spring, but they are largely obscured by the decaying frond-stalks and the roots themselves.
Fronds: 5–15 cm long.
Stalks: very variable in length, occasionally as little as $\frac{1}{4}$ as long as the frond, sometimes as much as $\frac{2}{3}$ as long, jointed about $\frac{1}{3}$ of the way between the stock and the blade, reddish-brown in colour, with a few light brown scales near the base.
Rachis: reddish-brown, lightly covered with a few scales becom-ing fewer towards the apex.
Blade: narrowly lanceolate or even linear-lanceolate in outline, bright green.
Branching: pinnate.
Pinnae: ovate or even triangular in outline, composed of 3–7 broadly rounded lobes, mainly alternate, but becoming sub-opposite to-wards the base, seldom truly oppo-site, the pinna widely spaced along the rachis, particularly towards the base, tending to run together to-wards the apex.
Venation: Pecopteridian.
Sori: circular, small.
Indusium: membranous, deeply lobed, cup-shaped.

HABITAT: moist rock crevices on high mountains.

GEOGRAPHICAL TYPE: Arctic-alpine.

DISTRIBUTION: Arctic and high mountain regions of the northern temperate zone. In Europe from Scandinavia southwards through north-western Russia across the Alps and down to the Pyrenees, eastwards through northern Italy and into the Carpathians: in Asia from the Urals to the Altai. Green-land into North America, across Canada from Labrador to Alaska and southwards in the U.S.A. as far as New York State.

CULTIVATION: like the other woodsia species, the alpine woodsia is surprisingly easy to cultivate, requiring the same conditions as those needed by *Woodsia ilvensis*. Like that species, it should be grown from spores rather than collected from the wild in those areas

where it is rare, and it is especially rare in Britain, being confined to a couple of cliffs in north Wales and a very few stations in Perth and Angus.

VARIETIES: none recorded.

Woodsia glabella
The smooth woodsia

A tiny and very rare, mainly North-American, wintergreen fern. It is easily mistaken for several others of the smaller mountain ferns including the alpine woodsia, *Woodsia alpina*, the green spleenwort, *Asplenium viride*, and the rusty woodsia, *Woodsia ilvensis*. It differs from these chiefly in its smaller size, its fewer pinnae, their wider spacing along the rachis, the more delicate texture of the blade and in its paler green colour.

DESCRIPTION: tiny, monomorphic wintergreen high mountain fern.
Stock: tiny, very slender, less than 1 mm diameter, upright, covered in mid-brown scales, the older parts bearing the remains of the stalks of previous seasons, the blades appearing to have snapped off rather than simply to have decayed away.
Fronds: up to 5 cm long, no more, presented in small, tight little tufts, forming small clumps.
Stalks: very short, often as little as $\frac{1}{8}$ the length of the blade, fragile, straw-coloured, the face flattened and grooved, jointed just above the base, smooth above, scaly below.
Rachis: green, smooth.
Blade: linear or very narrowly

lanceolate in outline, of delicate texture, light green, smooth.
Branching: pinnate.
Pinnae: as many as about 10 pairs, oval in outline, obtuse, lobed, usually consisting of 3 pear-shaped lobes: the pinnae opposite, sessile, distant, becoming closer.
Venation: Pecopteridian.
Sori: tiny, situated on vein endings very close to the margins of the lobes.
Indusium: tiny, disc-like with a few scattered hairs.

HABITAT: moist, shaded crevices on limestone rocks on high mountains.

GEOGRAPHICAL TYPE: Artic-alpine.

DISTRIBUTION: Canada from Labrador to Alaska, southwards to New York State and Vermont. Distribution probably not fully recorded owing to confusion with other species.

CULTIVATION: difficult, not taking to low altitudes well. Will occasionally succeed in a crevice in a limestone rock garden provided that there is a constant seepage of water through the crevice. Generally easier to cultivate either in a pan, in a fern house, or in a bottle garden.

VARIETIES: none recorded.

Woodsia ilvensis
The oblong woodsia

A diminutive tufted deciduous mountain fern of little garden value, but interesting to the enthusiast or to anyone trying to build up a comprehensive collection of herbaria material.

Woodsia ilvensis

DESCRIPTION: dwarf tufted monomorphic mountain fern.
Stock: short, no more than 4 mm thick, erect, branching, thickly covered with the decaying stalks of the old fronds and sparsely covered in scales.
Fronds: dull green, up to 10 cm but usually about half that length.
Stalks: half as long as the blade, jointed near the middle, pale brown in colour, sometimes reddish brown and clothed with reddish brown hairs and scales.
Rachis: green clothed with reddish brown hairs and scales.
Blade: oblong-lanceolate in outline.
Branching: pinnate.
Pinnae: 7–15 on each side of the rachis, alternate becoming sub-opposite and then opposite towards the base, very widely spaced on the rachis towards the base but closer together towards the apex, each pinna oblong in outline, deeply pinnatifid, each lobe somewhat toothed especially on the acroscopic side.
Venation: Pecopteridian.
Sori: circular, on the back of the venules.
Indusium: membraneous, deeply

lobed, cup-shaped.

HABITAT: moist rock fissures on high mountains.

GEOGRAPHICAL TYPE: Arctic-alpine.

DISTRIBUTION: throughout the Arctic and in mountainous areas of Europe from Iceland southwards through Scandinavia and at scattered stations all the way across Germany into Switzerland, and thence into Italy, eastwards into the Carpathians, the Crimea and the Caucasus and Asia Minor. Very rare in Britain. Greenland into Canada, and southwards through Iowa, Illinois, Kentucky and into North Carolina.

CULTIVATION: the oblong woodsia is probably the easiest of all the arctic-alpine ferns to cultivate, seeming to grow in any suitably moist crevice in a rock garden or in gritty soil in a shallow depression between the rocks. It should never be collected from the wild in those areas where it is rare, coming easily from spores.

VARIETIES: none recorded.

CHAPTER EIGHT

Wall Ferns

The term 'wall ferns' is used here to describe those ferns which will more often than not be found growing in walls: they are all species, indeed, which will seldom be found growing in any other positions. There are, by contrast, a number of ferns, such as the hart's-tongue, *Asplenium scolopendrium*, and the common polypody, *Polypodium vulgare*, which are, it is true, found growing on walls frequently, but these are found growing more often under other conditions—normally in woodland.

Wall ferns do not grow so much on as in walls. The conditions in which they grow resemble in some ways those of the screes: the plants have their fronds in the sun but their roots deeply embedded in the fabric of the wall, where they are cool and shaded. They may be found growing either on dry stone walls or on walls in which mortar has been used. In either case they will thrust their roots surprisingly deeply into the wall. It may look at first glance as though they are merely perched in a crack or crevice of the wall, but any attempt to dislodge them will quickly reveal that they have in fact pushed their very tough, wiry hair-like roots through splits in the stone or mortar-bonding, and it is these roots that really anchor them.

Wall ferns are not epiphytic ferns, though they might easily be mistaken for them. Epiphytes are essentially plants that grow on other plants but do not derive any nourishment from them: their roots are merely anchors and absorb nutrients mainly from the atmosphere. Wall ferns, by contrast, grow in minute pockets of soil that have gathered either in the gaps between the stones of dry stone walls or in incredibly small pockets of humus that have formed between the mortar and the bricks of brick walls. They will also quite often be found growing actually in the mortar on old brick walls, where the mortar has become soft with age. Such mortar contains an abundance of nutrients.

As might be expected of ferns growing in such tiny pockets of soil, wall ferns are invariably diminutive species, and are among the daintiest of all ferns.

The precise origin of wall ferns is not altogether clear. Plainly there were no walls around 30 or 40 million years ago when ferns evolved. It would seem most likely that their natural habitat is rock crevices and cliff faces. The fact is that the great majority of these ferns are seldom found growing in these conditions now. It seems likely that they would now be rare plants but for man's interference, for while man has brought about the extinction of so many species, both animal and vegetable, the wall ferns are one of the relatively few instances where he has actually created a habitat in which a declining group of plants have been able to re-establish themselves.

Asplenium
adiantum-nigrum
The black spleenwort

Asplenium adiantum-nigrum

The black spleenwort is typical of the spleenworts as a group. It is a violently calciphile plant, found growing usually in colonies in the decaying mortar of old walls or in dry walls of crumbling limestones. The roots grow horizontally between the slabs of stone or the brickwork, while the fronds are presented in a tuft, the outer fronds pressed flat against the walls, both above and below the stock. Though a very fern-like fern, the black spleenwort and its subspecies are less distinctive than some of the other aspleniums.

DESCRIPTION: a tufted wintergreen monomorphic fern, variable in size, occasionally as little as 7 cm on walls, but up to 21 cm where growing in richer conditions such as hedgerows, where it is sometimes also found growing.
Stock: tufted, the younger parts clothed with blackish-brown scales with long, hair-like points.
Fronds: up to 21 cm in length, usually about $\frac{1}{3}$ of that length.
Stalks: very darkly coloured, purplish-brown, swollen and scaly towards the base, normally as long as the blade but sometimes, especially on specimens growing in shaded conditions in hedgerows, as

much as two or even three times as long as the blade.

Blade: confusingly variable in outline, usually ovate but sometimes ovate-lanceolate or even narrowly triangular but invariably widest at the base (as opposed to being widest about $\frac{1}{3}$ of the way up the blade, as is the case with many other ferns). Texture firm, almost leathery, rather rough, dark green and shining above, paler below.

Branching: tri- or even quadripinnate at the base, tripinnate, bipinnate, pinnate and finally entire, but pinnatifid at the apex.

Pinnae: from few to as many as 15 but no more on either side of the rachis, alternate becoming subopposite towards the base, almost tripinnate at the base, becoming bipinnate then pinnate and finally pinnatifid.

Pinnules: alternate, the basal ones of the lower pinnae, pinnate or pinnatifid.

Venation: Sphenopteridian.

Sori: linear occurring on lateral veins closer to the midrib then to the margin.

Indusium: linear, entire, opening inwards.

HABITAT: rock crevices, walls; more rarely, hedgebanks.

GEOGRAPHICAL TYPE: Cosmopolitan.

DISTRIBUTION: throughout Europe, embracing the Faeroes in the north and the Atlantic Islands in the west, eastwards into western Asia and northwards across the Himalayas: North Africa, high mountain regions of East and West Africa, South Africa: Hawaii: North America.

SUBSPECIES: *adiantum-nigrum* is the type plant. It has blade and pinnae triangular in outline, and the stalk is never longer than the blade: furthermore the segments of the pinnules have acute teeth.

Subspecies: *onopteris* differs from the type plant in that the blade is always tripinnate with a tapering apex, and in that the pinnae are curved and also have tapering apices. The stalk is frequently longer than the blade, and the segments of the pinnules are narrowly lanceolate and have long, acuminate teeth. Less widely distributed than the type, being confined mainly to the Mediterranean region and parts of Great Britain.

CULTIVATION: like all wall ferns, the black spleenwort needs perfect drainage, and welcomes liberal amounts of old mortar in its growing medium. Wall ferns as a whole are not among the easiest of ferns to cultivate, preferring to be planted vertically in a dry stone wall, and proving extremely difficult when grown on level ground. They resent too much moisture on the fronds and are intolerant of close conditions.

VARIETIES: none recorded.

Asplenium ceterach
Ceterach officinarum
The rusty-back fern
The scaly spleenwort

One of the dwarfest of the wall ferns, and quite distinct from all the others on account of its sage-green fronds, which are almost completely covered on the underside with silvery scales which turn brown as the season advances—these scales covering the sori and giving the plant its common name.

DESCRIPTION: dwarf, tufted monomorphic wintergreen fern.
Stock: short, upright, tufted, clothed with almost black scales.
Fronds: up to 15 cm, usually about half that length, persistent.
Stalks: very short in relation to the blade, about ¼ as long as the blade, often less, clothed with

Asplenium ceterach

almost black scales very similar to those found on the stock.

Rachis: similar to the stalk, green above, white beneath, when young covered in silvery hairs which become black when the blade matures.

Blade: linear-lanceolate in outline, thick and exceedingly coriaecous, superficially appearing pinnate but in fact not so, merely very deeply pinnatifid, bearing on the upper surface a few scattered scales, these occurring mainly towards the mid-rib, the lower surface densely clothed in scales, silvery at first, becoming rust-coloured as the season advances: these scales are well worth examining under magnification; they are ovate-acuminate in shape and are attached to the fern in an overlapping fashion, rather in the way tiles are arranged on a roof: close examination reveals that they actually project beyond the outer margin of the segments.

Branching: blade does not branch but is deeply pinnatifid.

Venation: Neuropteridian.

Sori: linear, largely hidden by the scales.

Indusium: absent.

HABITAT: mortared walls, dry stone walls of calcareous rock and rock crevices in limestone. Far more frequent on walls than in more natural habitats. But for man and his walls it would now be a very rare fern indeed. It is rarely found growing as an isolated specimen, tending rather to occur in dense, though often very localised, colonies.

GEOGRAPHICAL TYPE: Mediterranean.

DISTRIBUTION: from the Mediterranean coast north-westwards into central Europe, along the Atlantic coast into Britain, eastwards to the Caucasus; north Africa; western Asia into the Himalayas.

CULTIVATION: one of the easiest wall ferns to cultivate, doing equally well in a crevice in a rock garden or in a pan. Must have lime present in the growing medium. Will grow in full sun provided that the roots are shaded, and indeed will probably grow in a sunnier situation than any other wall fern. Like one or two other primitive plants it has the ability—rare among ferns—of being able to recover when apparently dessicated beyond all hope.

VARIETIES: *A.c. crenatum*, a form in which the lobes of the deeply pinnatifid frond are themselves crenate. Quite distinct and interesting. This is the form that is normally found in Silverdale, in the English Lake District, so it appears to be a geographic variation. A foliose form has been found in Wales but has not yet been named and may possibly not be sufficiently distinct to warrant either naming or cultivation.

*Asplenium
ruta-muraria*
Wall rue

One of the commonest of all wall ferns, most frequently found inhabiting old mortared walls where it will often form huge colonies. Some really old walls are quite densely clothed by this fern. It is often found on old castle walls, on bridges and the walls surrounding churches.

DESCRIPTION: a diminutive, tufted, monomorphic wintergreen fern.
Stock: short, creeping, branching, the younger parts clothed with dark brown almost black scales with hair-like points.
Fronds: 3–15 cm long, usually shorter rather than longer.

Asplenium ruta-muraria

Stalks: as long as or twice as long as the blade, usually nearer the latter, dark purple-brown at the base, becoming green, clothed with minute hair-like scales when young.

Rachis: purple-brown to almost black with scale-like hairs.

Blade: triangular-ovate in outline, very leathery, usually dark green. There is however some variability in the species, and forms with the blade broader and darker green than normal may be found alongside forms with the blade longer narrower and lighter green than normal: it may well turn out that these are diploid and tetraploid subspecies, respectively.

Branching: pinnate to virtually tripinnate at the base.

Pinnae: no more than 4 or 5 on either side of the rachis, alternate, the basal ones usually sub-opposite, very widely spaced.

Pinnules: the lowest usually trifid, the degree of division decreasing towards the apex, the uppermost segment being entire or slightly lobed.

Venation: Sphenopteridian.

Sori: linear produced on the centre of the pinnules.

Indusium: linear, minutely crenate, opening inwards.

HABITAT: walls, especially mortared walls, less frequently rock crevices, particularly on limestone rocks.

GEOGRAPHICAL TYPE: Circumpolar.

DISTRIBUTION: throughout Europe, southwards into Algeria though not recorded from elsewhere in North Africa, westwards to northern Asia, southwards to Afghanistan and eastwards to the Himalayas; eastern North America and southwards as far as Alabama.

CULTIVATION: one of the more difficult of the wall ferns to establish in cultivation. In the wild it is usually found with its roots deeply buried in hair-line cracks between the mortar and the brick or stone work—conditions which it is almost impossible to imitate in cultivation. It can occasionally be established in old mortared walls by scraping a narrow gap in the mortar and inserting the roots into this gap, pressing them home with some loose mortar. Similarly, it can be established in dry stone walls if bedded into old mortar between the stones, but only the narrowest gap should be left for the roots. It is a fern that normally only grows in a vertical position, and it is this that makes it difficult to cultivate on the flat, though some success can be obtained growing it in pans if healthy, well-rooted specimens are obtained in the first place.

VARIETIES: none recorded.

Asplenium septentrionale The forked spleenwort

A most unusual fern of diminutive proportions with very finely divided fronds that give it, at a superficial glance, rather the appearance of a grass than a fern. Easily overlooked, but a real gem.

DESCRIPTION: tufted, wintergreen, monomorphic wall fern.

Stock: creeping, branched, tufted, the younger parts clothed with minute, almost black, scales with hair-like points.

Fronds: 5–14 cm long.

Stalks: up to 4 times as long as the blade, more commonly 2 or 3 times as long as the blade, never less than equal to the length of the blade, shiny black-brown at the base with a few scattered minute brown hairs.

Rachis: brown near the base becoming green towards the apex.

Blade: surprisingly tough and leathery considering its finely divided rather delicate appearance, difficult to fit into the normal classifications of pinnate or bipinnate, and best simply described as irregularly forked, of imprecise outline.

Pinnae: never more than 5 in all, linear, almost strap-shaped, appearing truncate at the apex at a superficial glance, but in fact acuminate or acute, the pinnae bearing few, very large teeth, so large they might almost be mistaken for segments.

Venation: Sphenopteridian.

Sori: linear, often covering practically the whole lower surface of the pinnae.

Indusium: linear, entire, opening inwards.

HABITAT: minute crevices on hard, usually basic rock (not limestone) and walls.

GEOGRAPHICAL TYPE: Circumpolar.

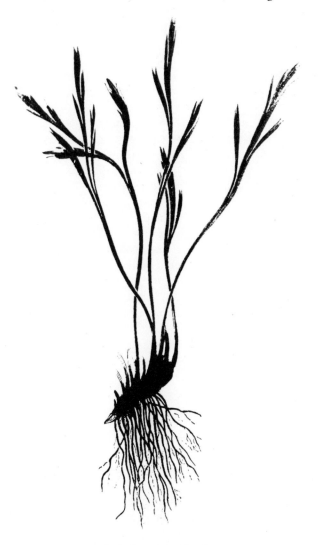

Asplenium septentrionale

DISTRIBUTION: throughout the mountainous regions of Europe from Norway in the north southwards to the Mediterranean, eastwards to the Caucasus, thence north-eastwards through northern Asia, across the Himalayas into the Altai mountains: in North America confined to mountain regions of the western U.S.A.

CULTIVATION: about as difficult to cultivate as most wall ferns, though somewhat easier to establish in a dry stone wall (provided the stone is not limestone) than some of the other aspleniums. It needs a north-facing position and seems to do best with some overhead shade from a small shrub. It is fairly easy in a pan, and when grown well makes one of the most delightful of all ferns for a pan.

VARIETIES: none recorded.

Asplenium trichomanes
The maidenhair spleenwort

One of the most delightful of all ferns, often charming even people who normally consider ferns dull. It is very distinct by reason of its entirely black rachis and neat, bright green segments.

DESCRIPTION: tufted, monomorphic, wintergreen fern.
Stock: creeping, densely branched, the younger parts clothed with dark brown scales.
Fronds: 5–30 cm.
Stalk: $\frac{1}{4}$ as long as the blade, often rather less, wiry, almost black, shiny, rounded behind and flat in front with a curious rather brittle, light brown winged border on the edges.
Rachis: shining blackish-purple, fading to green only towards the tip.
Blade: linear in outline.
Branching: pinnate.
Pinnae: up to as many as 40 on either side of the rachis, normally presented in opposite pairs, never alternate, but the pinnae about $\frac{1}{3}$ up from the base occasionally becoming sub-opposite, ovate in outline, slightly crenate at the apex, dark green, glabrous, becoming smaller towards the apex. The pinnae last just over a single year before falling from the rachis, which persists for several seasons: the pinnae leave a small tooth-like projection on the rachis when they fall away.
Venation: Eupteridian.
Sori: linear occurring on the acroscopic branches of the secondary veins.
Indusium: linear, entire on microscopically crenate, opening inwards.

HABITAT: rock crevices, walls especially in maritime areas.

GEOGRAPHICAL TYPE: Cosmopolitan.

DISTRIBUTION: throughout the temperate and sub-arctic regions of both hemispheres and, less frequently, the high mountain regions

9 (Right) *Azolla filiculoides* (page 167) showing how this fern reddens when grown in sunlight.

10 (Below) *Asplenium scolopendrium conglomeratum* (page 184) in the foreground with the type plant growing behind it.

11 *Asplenium scolopendrium muricatum* (page 189).

of the tropics. Throughout Europe and southwards into North Africa, eastwards to western Asia thence across the Himalayas into China and Japan: Australia (including Tasmania), New Zealand; North America, Central America and South America as far south as Peru; the Hawaiian Islands; Cape Province of South Africa; Madagascar. Both diploid and tretraploid forms occur throughout the range, though the diploid is relatively uncommon.

SUBSPECIES: two subspecies have been recognised, *trichomanes* and *quadrivalens*. Neither is easy to distinguish with the naked eye. It is rather groups of characteristics than any particular characteristics which distinguish the subspecies. Their distribution is probably generally the same as that for the type plant but, owing to the difficulty in recognising them, they have almost certainly been under-recorded.

Subspecies *trichomanes* differs from the type plant in that the scales on the stock are lanceolate rather than linear-lanceolate and bear a reddish-brown central stripe. The rachis is reddish-brown instead of blackish-purple. The pinnae are of a rather delicate, as opposed to leathery, texture, auriculate. Sori occurring only on the middle pinnae.

Subspecies *quadrivalens* differs from the type plant in that there is a dark brown central stripe on the stock scales, in that the rachis is dark brown, and in the differing shape and texture of the pinnae, these being very tough and usually oblong but with parallel sides.

CULTIVATION: one of the easier

Asplenium trichomanes

F

wall ferns to cultivate, growing readily in dry stone walls, clefts in rock gardens or in pans.

VARIETIES: *A.t. bipinnatum.* It would appear that two different plants have become confused under this name. The original Welsh find was in fact a bipinnate form, the pinnae dividing a second time. It was an exceptionally beautiful and delicate variety, but appears to have been lost to cultivation. The plant now in cultivation under this name, originating from a different find, is not bipinnate, but has very large pinnae, up to 1.5 cm long, very deeply crenately lobed and with pronounced auricles. It is still an attractive and distinctive plant.

A.t. cristatum. This cristate form would appear to be a not uncommon variation, having been found separately on a number of occasions at stations widely separated from each other. The apex of the frond branches repeatedly into a delicate tracery of pinnae no larger than a pinhead, presented on thread-thin, wiry black stems. A real gem, and very rare. A good percentage will come true from spores, but these need to be grown on for three years before the cristate forms can be sorted from the type forms.

A.t. incisum. Another variety that has been found on several different occasions, and again from widely separated stations. It remains exceedingly rare, since it is completely sterile and can only be increased by division: it will be appreciated that anyone who has succeeded in growing a healthy clump would be most unwilling to disturb it. The pinnae are very finely incised.

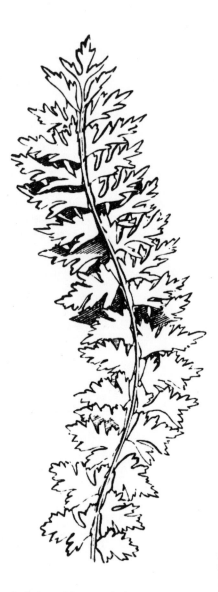

Asplenium trichomanes incisum

Asplenium viride
The green spleenwort

Another typically diminutive wall fern, easily mistaken by the un-initiated for *Asplenium trichomanes*, but really quite distinct from that species in its remarkably bright green fronds and in its bright green rachis. The pinnae segments are also deeply toothed, a characteristic not normally found in *Asplenium trichomanes*.

DESCRIPTION: dwarf, tufted, more or less wintergreen, monomorphic wall fern.
Stock: creeping, tufted, the younger parts clothed in dark brown scales.
Fronds: up to 15 cm long, linear in outline.
Stalks: from $\frac{1}{4}$ to $\frac{1}{2}$ as long as the blade, reddish brown to purplish black on the lower part only, rapidly becoming bright green.
Rachis: bright green.
Blade: pinnate.
Pinnae: up to 30 pairs, opposite at the base and apex, becoming sub-opposite in the centre, bright green, glabrous, less coriaceous than those of *Asplenium trichomanes*, ovate, crenately margined, the crenation being variable in the depth of the incision, persistent (i.e., not falling from the rachis as do the pinnae of *Asplenium trichomanes*), the whole frond decaying together.
Venation: Eupteridian.
Sori: occurring on the secondary veins and on the acroscopic forks.
Indusium: linear, entire, occasionally minutely toothed.

HABITAT: walls, rock crevices, particularly on basic rocks and only where there is a calcareous content in the rock.

GEOGRAPHICAL TYPE: Circumpolar.

DISTRIBUTION: Europe from the Arctic to the southern Alps and thence eastwards through Trans-caucasia into western Asia across the Himalayas to Siberia; North America from Newfoundland to Alaska and thence southwards to Oregon.

CULTIVATION: relatively easy in a rock crevice or in a pan, but succeeding only where there is some lime present, either in the rocks or in the growing media.

VARIETIES: *A.v. cristatum* 'Kaye' is a finely crested trifid form, apparently fertile, a small proportion coming more or less true from spores.

A.v. imbricatum 'Jackson', is a singularly distinct form with the pinnae overlapping.

A.v. incisum, a very deeply incised form, was recorded in Victorian times, lost, found again, and now believed lost again.

It is interesting that these three forms have all been discovered in the last decade. The plant is known to be variable, and it may well be that there are other interesting forms, but that little effort has been made to find them.

Cheilanthes alabamensis
The Alabama lip-fern
The smooth lip-fern

Though closely related to both the woolly and the hairy lip-ferns, *C. tomentosa* and *C. lanosa*, respectively, this plant is immediately distinguishable from either of those two species by its relative lack of either hair or wool. It is also distinguished by having the most lanceolate frond of the three, and by having a black, polished stalk.

DESCRIPTION: dwarf creeping monomorphic wintergreen wall and mountain fern.
Stock: slender, creeping, dark brown, branching periodically, scaly or where the stock appears above ground, slightly hairy, fronds produced in small tufts irregularly along the top of the stock.
Fronds: wintergreen, up to 20 cm.
Stalks: almost equal in length to the blade, sometimes a little shorter; thin, wiry, brittle, black, polished. slightly hairy only when young.
Rachis: black, polished, smooth, hairy only when young.
Blade: lanceolate in outline.
Branching: bipinnate to pinnate.

Pinnae: up to about 20 pairs, opposite, the lower ones fully pinnate, the upper ones pinnate-pinnatifid, narrowly lanceolate in outline, shallowly dentate.
Venation: not established.
Sori: continuous round the margins of the pinnules.
Indusium: absent, the sporangia protected by the incurled pinnule margins.

HABITAT: crevices in dry limestone rock or walls.
GEOGRAPHICAL TYPE: restricted.

DISTRIBUTION: U.S.A., limited to the Alabama area.

CULTIVATION: another calciphile fern, requiring an alkaline compost and perfect drainage. It is not really frost-hardy, especially if it is wet when frost strikes, and is probably best grown in a cold house in all but the mildest areas.

VARIETIES: none recorded.

Cheilanthes lanosa
The hairy lip-fern

Another typical little 'resurrection' fern, looking completely dead when dry, but springing into bright green life again once it has had a good soaking. It is not so easily confused with the woolly- lip-fern as might be expected, and differs from that species mainly in the more lanceolate outline of the frond and in the colour of the hairs, which are a greyish-brown rather than a tan brown.

DESCRIPTION: dwarf, monomorphic wintergreen mountain or wall fern.
Stock: short, creeping, slender, branching irregularly, rooting beneath, producing fronds above, the fronds produced in small tufts periodically along the stock, roots shallow, creeping, few almost black.
Fronds: very hairy, up to 20 cm long, wintergreen.

Stalks: very short, less than ¼ as long as the blade, usually even shorter than that, slender, wiry, brittle, dark purplish-brown, hairy.
Rachis: dark brown, lightly covered in hairs which are white when the fronds are young but become greyish as the fronds increase in age.
Blade: oblong-lanceolate in outline. The upper surface of the frond is deep green, the lower part paler green covered in thick greyish woolly hairs.

Branching: bipinnate.
Pinnae: narrowly triangular to ovate in outline.
Pinnules: deeply and crenately lobed, sometimes pinnate.
Venation: not established.
Sori: virtually continuous along the pinnule margins.
Indusium: absent but the sporan-

Cheilanthes lanosa

gia are protected by the pinnule margins.

HABITAT: crevices in dry rock ledges, mortared walls.

GEOGRAPHICAL TYPE: Circumpolar.

DISTRIBUTION: the U.S.A., from southern New York to Georgia.

CULTIVATION: reasonably frost-hardy, though in wet areas and in areas of severe frost best grown in a cold house. Needs perfect drainage and an alkaline compost.

VARIETIES: none recorded.

Cheilanthes tomentosa
The woolly lip-fern

This is another 'resurrection' fern, normally a rather furry bright green tufted little fern but becoming a curled mass of brown woolly, shrivelled matter when dried out— only to come fully to life again once wetted thoroughly.

DESCRIPTION: wintergreen, monomorphic tufted wall or mountain fern.
Stock: erect, stout, short, branched, densely covered with dark brown woolly hairs under which are partly concealed whitish scales, the older parts bearing the dark brown decayed frond bases.
Fronds: presented in a basket-like tuft, up to 20 cm long, wintergreen.
Stalks: very short, less than $\frac{1}{4}$ the length of the blade, densely covered, like the stock, with dark brown hairs beneath which are the partly concealed whitish scales.
Rachis: similarly hairy and scaly.
Blade: oblong-lanceolate.
Branching: bipinnate.
Pinnae: up to about 20 pairs, opposite, widely spaced becoming less widely spaced, ovate-oblong in outline with rounded tips.
Pinnules: opposite, up to 3 pairs plus a terminal segment, all obovate in outline. Pinnae and pinnules slightly hairy above, densely covered below with whitish, woolly hairs.
Venation: not established.
Sori: occurring on the margins of the pinnules, small.
Indusium: absent, but the pinnule margins curve over the sporangia, protecting them.

HABITAT: deep fissures in dry rock ledges, walls.

GEOGRAPHICAL TYPE: Circumpolar.

DISTRIBUTION: southern U.S.A., into Mexico.

CULTIVATION: tolerant of only slight frost, this is really a cold house plant needing an alkaline compost and perfect drainage.

VARIETIES: none recorded.

Cystopteris bulbifera
The North American
bladder fern

One of the most beautiful and graceful of mountain and wall ferns and also one of the most responsible of all ferns to its environment. While it will grow and grow well enough in crevices high up on dry rocky mountain slopes or in dry situations in walls, it is undoubtedly at its best in moister situations, really coming into its own when growing close to a waterfall, where its delicate fronds will form tufts of feathery greenery, shaping themselves to the shape of the rocks they grow on and reflecting in their flowing lines the fluidity of the waterfall. In such situations the fronds can be up to 90 cm long, whereas in drier situations they may be as little as 10 cm long. Notable for the production of bulblets.

DESCRIPTION: very variable delicate deciduous, apogamous monomorphic wall and mountain fern.
Stock: short, slender, varying

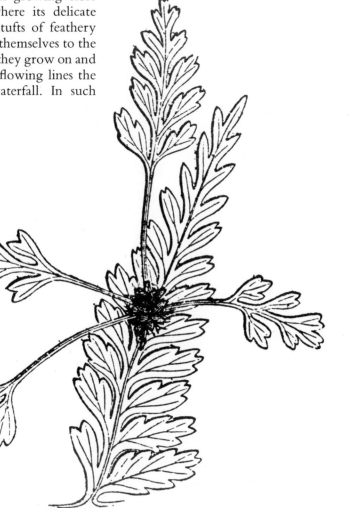

Cystopteris bulbifera

from horizontal to vertical, scaly, black.

Fronds: deciduous, varying from 10 to 90 cm, depending upon the amount of moisture available.

Stalks: $\frac{1}{5}$ the length of the blade, yellowish, with a swollen, blackish-purple base.

Rachis: yellow, shiny, very slender, very brittle.

Blade: narrowly triangular, of flimsy texture.

Branching: pinnate.

Pinnae: up to 5 cm long on large plants, becoming progressively and regularly smaller towards the apex, triangular-lanceolate in outline, acuminate, pinnate-pinnatifid, the segments rather blunt.

Venation: not established.

Sori: few, scattered, occurring on the acroscopic side of the secondary segment veins midway between the margin and the midrib.

Indusium: dome-shaped, inflated.

Bulblets: few, occurring on the rachis, usually about $\frac{2}{3}$ of the way up the fronds.

HABITAT: limestone formations, rocks, walls, mortared brick walls, in dry or damp situations.

GEOGRAPHICAL TYPE: Circumpolar: restricted.

DISTRIBUTION: North America, from Canada southwards as far as Tennessee.

CULTIVATION: forms variable in hardiness depending upon provenance, some forms fully frost-hardy. Does well in a crevice in a limestone rock garden, provided that the situation is well shaded.

VARIETIES: none recorded.

Cystopteris fragilis
The brittle bladder fern

Dainty, delicate-looking ferns that could easily be mistaken for weakly forms of *Dryopteris carthusiana* at first glance. The bladder ferns have acquired their name on account of the domed indusium which covers the sorus rather like an inflated hood, a characteristic which is somewhat unique among the ferns of the temperate regions.

DESCRIPTION: diminutive, monomorphic deciduous fern.

Stock: very short, usually horizontal, occasionally but not invariably branched, the older parts retaining the decaying stumps of the spirally arranged frond stalks, the younger parts covered with thin yellow lanceolate scales.

Fronds: up to 35 cm, but seldom more than 20 cm, presented spirally on the stock in rather shuttlecock fashion, seldom more than 5 or 6 fronds being produced in each season, dying down in early winter.

Stalks: usually about $\frac{1}{2}$ as long as the blade, but varying between $\frac{1}{3}$ and $\frac{2}{3}$ as long, dark brown and covered, especially at the base, in straw-yellow scales: very brittle, easily snapped.

Rachis: green.

Blade: generally very variable,

varying not only in size, but also in outline and in the amount of dissection; generally oblong-lanceolate to ovate-lanceolate in outline, acuminate or acute, of thin, delicate texture.

Cystopteris fragilis

Branching: bipinnate to tripinnate.

Pinnae: up to 15 on either side of the rachis, opposite towards the base becoming alternate towards the apex, shortly stalked, similar in outline to the blade as a whole, pinnate or almost bipinnate, especially about $\frac{1}{3}$ of the way up the blade.

Pinnules: ovate at the base of the pinna, oblong towards the apex of the pinna, the larger (lower) ones being deeply pinnatifid, the others pinnately toothed.

Venation: Pecopteridian.

Sori: in two rows, one on either side of the midrib of each pinnule.

Indusium: ovate-lanceolate, membraneous, inflated.

HABITAT: damp walls and moist crevices on mountains.

GEOGRAPHICAL TYPE: Cosmopolitan.

DISTRIBUTION: mountainous districts of arctic Europe and Asia, southwards through the Himalayas to Morocco, through Ethiopia, to South Africa: Arctic North America (including Greenland) thence southwards through the high mountains of Central America and down the Andes into Chile: thence through Hawaii to New Zealand and Tasmania.

CULTIVATION: easily cultivated in the rock garden or in a dry stone wall. It needs room to spread itself and, given conditions that suit it, will gradually spread into a pleasing mat.

VARIETIES: *C.f. alpina* differs from the type plant only in its more dwarf growth and somewhat more finely divided fronds. Not very distinct.

C.f. cristata is a slightly taller growing plant than the type, the tips of the fronds beautifully crested.

C.f. sempervirens is distinct only in that it will remain in leaf throughout the winter in mild localities, or in situations where it is protected from direct frost.

Dryopteris villarii
Dryopteris rigida
Lastrea rigida
The rigid buckler fern

Another relatively small wall fern distinct on account of its singularly rigid fronds. It is also unique among temperate ferns in emitting a pleasant, balsam-like fragrance when crushed.

DESCRIPTION: small, deciduous, tufted monomorphic wall fern.
Stock: ascending or horizontal, the older parts retaining the blackish decaying ends of the frond stalks, the younger parts covered in light brown lanceolate scales.
Fronds: numerous, tufted but variable in their presentation, either erect or spreading, often intermediate, densely covered in short, yellowish hairs.
Stalks: about $\frac{1}{2}$ as long as the blade but occasionally equal in length to the blade, and varying between these two extremes, distinctly swollen towards the base, at which part it is dark brown, but otherwise yellow to greenish yellow, covered in reddish-brown scales.
Rachis: yellowish-green to green.
Blade: lanceolate to narrowly triangular in outline, rather similar in colour to the blade of *Asplenium ceterach*, but paler below.
Branching: bipinnate.
Pinnae: up to 25 on either side of the rachis, sub-opposite at the base becoming alternate towards the apex, the lowest pair of pinna being the largest pair, the lower ones obovate-lanceolate in outline, becoming ovate-lanceolate in outline towards the apex, pinnate.
Pinnules: opposite becoming alternate towards the apex, very shortly stalked becoming first sessile and then decurrent, lobes rounded with acute teeth.
Venation: Pecopteridian.
Sori: arranged in 2 rows on each of the fertile pinnules, very large.
Indusium: reniform, crowded or overlapping.

HABITAT: old mortared walls, fissures in limestone faces.

GEOGRAPHICAL TYPE: Mediterranean.

DISTRIBUTION: the Mediterranean region, extending as far eastwards as Afghanistan and westwards through the Alps and the Pyrenees to the mountains of southern

Germany, into Britain: rare throughout its range.

CULTIVATION: too rare in the wild to be collected, it should be grown only from spores, from which it is easily raised. In spite of its rarity in the wild it is quite easy to cultivate, making a good plant for a crevice in the rock garden. There are both diploid and tetraploid forms of the type plant, but there appear to be no external characteristics by which these can be distinguished.

VARIETIES: a crested variety has been collected recently but not named.

Pellaea atropurpurea
The purple
rock-brake

This is one of that relatively small number of ferns which, when once seen, will be recognised instantly on all future occasions. Like the rest of its genus, it is a small-growing fern, but is quite distinct from all other ferns by reason of its conspicuous wiry purplish stalks, the leathery blue-green pinnae and in particular on account of its singularly bright brown sporangia, these being borne in marginal rows.

DESCRIPTION: low-growing, dimorphic wintergreen wall and mountain fern.
Stock: very short, erect, the younger parts densely covered in lustrous pointed brown scales, the older parts with the almost black decayed frond bases through which the numerous wiry black roots appear.
Fronds: up to 30 cm tall, rigid, leathery.
Stalks: about equal in length to the blade, sometimes less, never more, dark purplish-brown, dull or shiny, covered with light brown hairs.
Rachis: dark brown, smooth, covered with a few sparse light brown hairs.
Blade: lanceolate to linear in outline, coriaceous, blue-green.
Branching: bipinnate becoming pinnate.
Pinnae: the lower ones pinnate, often with two pairs of opposite pinnae and a long terminal segment: the middle ones with only a pair of pinnae, and also a long terminal segment, the apical pinna consisting really of only the terminal segment of the lower pinnae: the pinnae often covered with light coloured powder. On fertile fronds the pinnae are more lance-shaped than on barren fronds.
Venation: not established.
Sori: occurring along the margins of the fertile pinnae, forming a very conspicuous bright brown.
Indusium: formed by the reflexed frond margin.

HABITAT: inaccessible limestone cliffs and mortared walls, usually in positions where they receive some direct sun during the day.

GEOGRAPHICAL TYPE: Restricted.

DISTRIBUTION: eastern North America.

CULTIVATION: this is a calciphile fern and must be grown in an alkaline soil, preferably in a limestone rock garden. It requires perfect drainage; some direct sun during the day, and appears to be frost hardy.

VARIETIES: none recorded.

CHAPTER NINE

Succulent Ferns

The succulent ferns described in this chapter form a quite distinct group, both visually and botanically. This is not surprising, since they are by far the most primitive of all the ferns described in this book—so primitive, indeed, that many botanists would not even include them in the ferns, dismissing them merely as fern allies, along with the horsetails and quillworts, to which they are closely related.

A glance at the table showing the evolutionary relationships of the various groups within the plant kingdom in the introductory chapter of this book does much to clarify the position. The succulent ferns, along with the true ferns and the water ferns, all belong to the class Filicinae. The great majority—about 90 per cent—of the ferns in this book belong to the sub-class Leptosporangiatae, which embraces both the true ferns, the Eufilicales, and the water ferns, the Hydropteridales. The succulent ferns, on the other hand, belong to a different and more primitive subclass, the Ophioglossales.

The family Ophioglossales is represented in the cool temperate world by two genera, Ophioglossum and Botrychium, the adder's-tongue ferns and, respectively, the moonworts of the Old World and the grape-ferns of the New World. The family also includes two other genera, Helminthostachys, which occurs in Asia, and Rhizoglossum, which occurs in South Africa. There are only the four genera in the family—all that remains of what was probably a very large group in the relatively distant geological past.

The number of species in each genera is rather limited, there being only thirty-six species of Botrychium and fifty-four species of Ophioglossum world-wide—although different botanists give different numbers of species for each genus. This is not mere perversity: the difficulty in classifying the succulent ferns is that they are so very primitive that the distinctions between species are not always clear-cut. Intermediate or transitional forms are frequently encountered, and this makes the decision where to draw the line between one species and another remarkably difficult.

The succulent ferns differ from the true ferns in a number of notable ways. Firstly they do not produce their young fronds in the fashion known in Britain as a 'crozier', and in America as a 'fiddlehead', as is the case with the true ferns. With the true ferns the croziers gradually uncurl as they grow.

In the genus Botrychium the young shoots come through the soil straight, with the frond simply folded back over the stalk.

In the genus Ophioglossum the young shoot comes through straight and erect. Then, in both cases, the blade opens sideways. The succulent ferns grow from a succulent or almost tuberous rootstock, which is a quite substantial, fleshy body. Each season this subterranean stock will develop several buds, usually as many as three or four. It rarely happens that all these buds actually produce fronds in the following season: they may produce two or three, or occasionally none at all. This peculiarity is not known to occur in any of the true ferns. Their mode of life limits their field pattern. And because they grow from a perennial subterranean rootstock and are only able to produce a strictly limited number of fronds each year, they never grow into large plants: they seldom even form clumps, and they cannot spread into carpets as can some of the true ferns that have creeping stocks. They further differ from the true ferns in that each stock typically will produce only one fertile and one barren frond in each season—although in some species two barren fronds is the norm. Botanically the point of greatest distinction between the succulent ferns and the true ferns is their spore-cases. In the succulent ferns these are round, naked (that is, they are not protected by an indusium) and they lack an annulus or ring. When ripe they open by splitting transversely, a phenomenon not found in the true ferns.

A further peculiarity of the succulent ferns occurs in the sexual generation. This is not at all like the normal prothallus of the true ferns—which is a green, heart-shaped object which sits on the surface of the soil. Instead, it is a tuberous body, leading a subterranean existence, completely lacking in chlorophyll and obtaining its nourishment by association (probably of a symbiotic nature) with a fungus. It can lead this subterranean existence for as much as eight years in some species before producing the visible, non-sexual generation.

With the possible exception of the rattlesnake fern, the succulent ferns have little garden merit, but they are curious plants and deserve a place in any collection of ferns that has pretensions to being at all representative. They are perhaps more notable for their supposed magical properties than for anything else, and figure prominently in early herbal and old witches' tales.

Botrychium australe
The southern
parsley fern

The southern parsley fern is no relation whatsoever of the parsley fern of the northern hemisphere. The latter is a true fern, a member of the Eufilicales, whereas the fern we are dealing with here is a succulent fern, a member of the Ophioglossales, which, as already explained, should probably be regarded as fern-allies rather than as ferns. It has gained its common name, however, in precisely the same way as *Cryptogramma crispa* gained its common name: the barren frond does look almost exactly like a parsley leaf. It is generally unlikely to be confused with any of the other members of the genus Botrychium because there is no overlap with ranges of any of the other species described in this book, and in cultivation it is quite distinct on account of its parsley-like barren fronds.

DESCRIPTION: dwarf, deciduous, dimorphic succulent fern.
Stock: erect, short, somewhat stout; roots short, fleshy, branching, forming a tangled mass, occurring about 4 cm below the surface of the soil, and growing mainly in a horizontal plane.
Fronds: dimorphic, the taller fertile frond reaching as much as 45 cm in height.
Stalks: round, smooth, succulent, slender, fragile, the stalk of the fertile frond arising from within the stalks of the barren fronds, this species frequently produces two barren fronds, the fertile frond stalk emerging from the casing of the smaller of the two barren fronds, that in turn have emerged from the stalk of the larger of the two barren fronds.
Rachis: round, green, succulent, slender and rather fragile.
Blade: broadly triangular, somewhat variable, acuminate or truncate.
Branching: tri- to quadripinnate.
Pinnae: sub-opposite to alternate, there sometimes being a terminal segment resembling exactly the pinnae, but sometimes this is completely absent, creating a truncate frond.
Pinnules: long stalked, pinnate to bipinnate or even tripinnate, segments very fine, bright green.
Venation: not established.
Fertile fronds: small, usually consisting of two large branches and a terminal segment, densely covered in bright yellow sporangia.
Sori: conglomerate.
Indusium: absent.

HABITAT: deep, rich soils in woodlands.

GEOGRAPHICAL TYPE: Australasian.

DISTRIBUTION: Australia (including Tasmania); temperate South America; New Zealand.

CULTIVATION: rather less frosthardy than the other species described here. In its own area of distribution needs deep, rich, well-drained soil: in areas of severe frost it needs cool house treatment.

VARIETIES: none recorded.

Botrychium dissectum
The cut-leaved
grape-fern

Probably the most variable of the grape-ferns, growing from a few inches to as much as a foot high, and with a barren frond that is recognisably fern-like—which is decidedly not the case with the majority of grape-ferns. It is quite distinct from all other species in the genus in that the stalks carrying the barren and the fertile fronds branch very low down, and in that the barren frond has a long stalk completely separate from that of the fertile frond.

DESCRIPTION: dwarf, semi-wintergreen, dimorphic succulent fern.

Stock: erect; roots fleshy, numerous, the majority produced from the stock at a depth of about 5 cm, somewhat branched, usually growing in a more or less horizontal plane, one root however often growing vertically downwards in the manner of a taproot, but branched.

Fronds: variable in length from 7–35 cm long, broadly triangular in outline, leathery, of coarse texture, fleshy.

Stalks: varying in length with the vigour of the plant, but always proportionate, the stalk of the barren frond being approximately $\frac{1}{2}$ the length of that of the fertile frond, the two stalks diverging only just above soil level, the stalk of the fertile frond appearing from within the stalk of the barren frond.

Rachis: round, green, succulent.

Blade: broadly triangular in outline, more or less wintergreen, bent in relation to its stalk and held parallel to the ground.

Branching: into three quite distinct portions, each of which is pinnate.

Pinnae: narrowly oblong in outline, pointed, margins toothed.

Venation: not established.

Fertile frond: erect (it being the barren frond that inclines away from the vertical), the spore-bearing portion occupying only about $\frac{1}{8}$ the length of the frond, pinnate, some of the pinnae themselves pinnate, densely covered in sporangia.

Sori: conglomerate.

Indusium: absent.

HABITAT: pasturelands, heathlands, open woodlands, not fussy as to soil; growing in conditions varying from rather dry to quite boggy.

GEOGRAPHICAL TYPE: Circumpolar.

DISTRIBUTION: in North America from Nova Scotia to Florida; China; Japan.

CULTIVATION: deep rich soil, with some shade.

VARIETIES: none recorded.

Botrychium lanceolatum
The lance-leaved
grape-fern

This diminutive grape-fern is immediately distinguishable from all other grape-ferns by the way in which the barren blade is carried almost at the top of the stalk, with the fertile blade almost touching it.

DESCRIPTION: dwarf, deciduous, dimorphic succulent fern.
Stock: erect, roots smooth, numerous, fleshy, branching, growing outwards from a central point, but becoming a tangled mass.
Fronds: deciduous, up to about 7 cm tall.
Stalks: up to 6 cm tall, smooth, round, fragile, pale green.
Rachis: smooth, round, pale green, rather fragile.
Blade: up to 2.5 cm long, dark, green, thick, fleshy, succulent; triangular in outline.
Branching: into 3 distinct lobes, each lobe itself deeply lobed.
Venation: not established.
Fertile frond: appearing from within the stalk of the barren frond and immediately above the barren frond, again branching into 3 distinct segments, each densely covered with sporangia.
Sori: conglomerate, yellow.
Indusium: absent.

HABITAT: acid soils, often at the edges of woods, in marshy ground, often in association with *B. matricariifolium*, with which it sometimes hybridises.

GEOGRAPHICAL TYPE: Circumpolar.

DISTRIBUTION: North America from Nova Scotia to New Jersey.

CULTIVATION: seldom cultivated; needs deeper, richer soil than most succulent ferns, and also a more shaded position.

VARIETIES: none recorded.

Botrychium lunaria
Moonwort

A short, stout, terrestial perennial herb remarkable in that the fronds take three years to develop. According to the old folklore the fronds can be used to unlock doors, and also possess the power of removing the shoes from horses passing over them.

DESCRIPTION: short, deciduous dimorphic fern, normally producing only two fronds in each season, one fertile, the other infertile.
Stock: subterranean, erect, usually unbranched, very rarely branched, sheathed in the dry bases of the old fronds, cylindrical, terminating abruptly in a clump of thick, fleshy radiating roots.
Fronds: 5 to 25 cm, more commonly about 15 cm.
Stalks: ½ as long as the blade, sheathed in a membraneous covering derived from the base of the previous year's fronds, fleshy, cylindrical, hollow.
Rachis: round, hollow, light green.
Blade: oblong in outline.
Branching: pinnate.

Pinnae: opposite in pairs, fan-shaped, the margins slightly crenate.
Venation: Cyclopteridian.
Fertile fronds: normally taller than the sterile frond, its stalk sheathed in the stalk of the sterile frond; pinnately or bipinnately branched, covered in clusters of sporangia which are conspicuously golden brown when ripe. Sporangia are born on the margins of the segments of the fertile frond.
Sori: conglomerate, golden-brown.
Indusium: absent.

HABITAT: heaths, hillsides, pastures.

GEOGRAPHICAL TYPE: Bipolar.

DISTRIBUTION: Arctic and northern temperate zones: Antarctic and southern temperate zones. Europe generally, although absent from the coastal regions of the Mediterranean: Asia into Japan: New Zealand, Tasmania, southern Australia: North America (including Greenland) from Newfoundland to Alaska thence southwards as far as California: South America northwards to Chile and Patagonia.

CULTIVATION: generally difficult to establish in gardens, and not very successful in pans. Some success can be achieved with it on the rock garden, but it seldom persists for long.

VARIETIES: the plant is quite variable and aberrant forms with two fertile fronds are not infrequently encountered. The only variety named is *B.l. subincisa*; it differs from the type plant in that the pinnae are deeply crenate.

Botrychium lunaria

Botrychium matricariifolium
The daisy-leaf grape-fern

This is one of the larger of the succulent ferns, and it derives its specific name from the likeness of its fronds to the leaves of Matricaria: the resemblance is indeed very close.

DESCRIPTION: deciduous, dimorphic succulent fern.
Stock: erect, fleshy: roots, thick, fleshy, branching appearing from all over the stock, spreading, those nearest the surface usually being about 5 cm long.
Fronds: deciduous, up to 15 cm long.
Stalks: up to 10 cm long, erect, slender, fragile, smooth, pale green.
Blade: up to 3 cm long.
Branching: pinnate.
Pinnae: deeply cut, like the leaves of Matricaria.
Fertile fronds: appearing from within the stalk of the blade, close to the barren frond, often almost clasped by it, similar in form but densely covered with prominent yellow sporangia.

HABITAT: heathlands and the edges of moist woodlands.

GEOGRAPHICAL TYPE: Circumpolar.

DISTRIBUTION: North America from Nova Scotia to New Jersey. Recorded from Britain over a hundred years ago, and now presumed extinct there, though the original record is suspect anyway.

CULTIVATION: seldom cultivated. Needs moist conditions.

VARIETIES: none recorded.

Botrychium multifidum
The leathery grape-fern

Another very variable grape-fern, but distinct in being quite the most leathery and coarsest textured of all the grape ferns. The barren frond is truly fern-like. This species derives one of its distinguishing characteristics from its excessively leathery nature, and that is that the old year's frond is usually still present, though rather withered, when the new season's frond appears.

DESCRIPTION: small, wintergreen dimorphic succulent fern.
Stock: erect: roots thick, almost rhizomatous, few, coarse, sparsely branched, wide-spreading, occurring in a horizontal plane about 7 cm below the surface of the soil.
Fronds: dimorphic, up to 20 cm, usually less, fern-like.
Stalks: of both fertile and barren fronds branching only just above ground level, the stalk of the barren frond appearing to come from within the stalk of the fertile frond (rather than the other way about, as is more commonly the case in the genus), that of the barren frond being about ½ the length of the fertile frond, though when the blade is added the total length of each frond is about the same.
Rachis: smooth, round, pale green.

Blade: broadly triangular, coarsely leathery, fleshy, succulent.

Branching: bipinnate.

Pinnae: obovate in outline, the blade consisting of 2 distinct pairs of opposite pinnae and a large terminal segment which exactly resembles one of the upper pinna.

Pinnules: opposite, deeply pinnatifid to pinnate-pinnatifid, margins entire or toothed, lobes sometimes rounded, sometimes acute.

Fertile frond: exactly resembling the barren frond in its branching but much reduced in size, densely covered with sporangia, appearing later than the barren frond and not usually ripening until very late in the season.

Sori: conglomerate, golden-brown.

Indusium: absent.

HABITAT: meadows, heathlands, generally found in drier situations than most of the other species of the genus.

GEOGRAPHICAL TYPE: Circumpolar.

DISTRIBUTION: in North America through Canada to New York State.

CULTIVATION: deep, rich but rather sandy soil and a slightly shaded situation.

VARIETIES: none recorded.

Botrychium simplex
The little grape-fern

This is the most diminutive member of its genus and is, as its Latin name suggests, the simplest of its genus. Indeed, it is altogether rather a simple little plant: compared with the rest of its kind one feels if it were to reduce itself much further it would disappear altogether.

DESCRIPTION: dwarf, deciduous dimorphic succulent fern.

Stock: erect, simple, roots smooth, few, usually arranged in a star-fish pattern at the base of the rootstock, the shallowest roots being about 4 cm below the surface of the soil.

Fronds: up to 4 cm long at the most, often even shorter.

Stalks: up to 2 cm long, smooth, round, fragile, pale green.

Blade: up to 1.5 cm long, ovate in outline, simple, deeply lobed, the number of lobes varying between 3 and 7, smooth, fleshy, pale green.

Venation: not established.

Fertile frond: taller than barren frond and its stalk appearing from within the stalk of the barren frond, similar in shape but much reduced in all its parts, amounting to little more than 3 or 4 pairs of sporangia, spore-cases prominent, straw-yellow.

Sori: conglomerate, yellow becoming brown.

Indusium: absent.

HABITAT: pasturelands, heathlands and the edges of woods.

GEOGRAPHICAL TYPE: Circumpolar.

DISTRIBUTION: Canada southwards to Maryland.

CULTIVATION: seldom cultivated. Needs rich, damp soil in full sun.

VARIETIES: none recorded.

Botrychium virginianum
The rattlesnake fern

This is by far the largest species in its genus growing as much as 60 cm tall and probably the only one worthy of general cultivation. It is readily distinguished from all other species by its larger size (being twice the size of its nearest rival), by its very early appearance in the season, by its very ferny appearance, by its lacy-cut barren fronds and by the thin texture of the barren fronds.

DESCRIPTION: medium-sized, deciduous, dimorphic succulent fern.
Stock: erect, rather stout, very short: roots thick, fleshy, numerous, branching and forming a tangled mass, occurring about 5 cm below the soil surface. The roots have curious erect bud-like appendages whose purpose has never been satisfactorily explained: they are perhaps vestiges of a stoloniferous mode of reproduction.
Fronds: deciduous, up to 60 cm tall.
Stalks: both barren and fertile fronds share a single, erect stalk from which the stalk carrying the fertile portion departs at the point at which the blade branches, the main rib of the barren frond and the stalk carrying the fertile portion diverging at equal angles.
Rachis: pale green, smooth, round, fragile.

Blade: broadly triangular in outline, light green, thin-textured, not leathery.
Branching: bipinnate.
Pinnae: opposite, becoming alternate, well-spaced.
Pinnules: opposite, sub-opposite or alternate, deeply pinnatifid to pinnate-pinnatifid, the segments being toothed, either lightly or deeply.
Venation: not established.
Fertile frond: appearing on a stalk arising out of the axil of the stalk of the barren frond, its stalk being equal in length to the length of the stalk of the barren frond: the spore-bearing portion occupying less than $\frac{1}{4}$ that length and consisting of about 8 tapering, widely-spreading branches densely covered in bright yellow sporangia.
Sori: conglomerate, yellow becoming brown.
Indusium: absent.

HABITAT: rich, and usually moist acid or neutral soils, damp meadows, woodlands.

GEOGRAPHICAL TYPE: Circumpolar.

DISTRIBUTION: in North America from Nova Scotia to Florida.

CULTIVATION: this is the one species really worthy of cultivation, making a striking specimen when well suited. It needs deep, rich leafy soil and plenty of moisture. It does best given light shade. It is singu-larly attractive to slugs, both above and below ground, and precautions should be taken accordingly.

VARIETIES: none recorded.

Ophioglossum englemanii
The limestone adder's-tongue fern

This is another typical adder's-tongue fern with remarkably wide barren fronds. It is native only to North America, and prefers an alkaline soil. In most text books it is described as a rare plant, but botanists are increasingly coming to believe that it is possibly much more common than is realised: like the other adder's-tongues, it is probable that it is simply over-looked. It differs from *O. vulgatum* in its shorter stature, in its less erect habit and in its relatively broad barren frond.

DESCRIPTION: dwarf, deciduous dimorphic fern.
Stock: consists of a star-like cluster of thick, fleshy smooth roots, usually buried 4–5 cm under the surface of the soil, the fronds being produced from the centre of the root-cluster, often more than one frond appearing from the centre of each cluster, some of the roots being stoloniferous, new plants appearing at the tips of them and the plants spreading underground by this means: buds for the follow-ing season's fronds appear at the centre of the root cluster at the base of the frond stalk or, where two or more fronds are produced from a single root-cluster, in the midst of them.
Fronds: deciduous, up to 7.5 cm long.
Stalks: up to 5 cm long, fleshy, brittle, round, smooth, pale green, brownish at the base, the frond stalk containing the fertile frond stalk within it.
Blade: eliptical, entire, with a distinct point at the apex, the upper portion curving outwards and downwards, thick and succu-lent in texture, pale green, pro-duced late in summer and dying down again quickly.
Venation: not established.
Fertile frond: projecting above the barren frond, sometimes almost as much as twice as tall as it, the stem appearing from within the stalk of the barren frond, the blade area about 4 cm long, tightly incurled.
Sori: conglomerate, yellow be-coming light brown.
Indusium: absent.

HABITAT: limestone depressions, moist ground, pasturelands, lime-stone ledges.

GEOGRAPHICAL TYPE: Circumpo-lar.

DISTRIBUTION: western North America.

CULTIVATION: seldom cultivated, but as for other species.

VARIETIES: none recorded.

Ophioglossum lusitanicum
The dwarf or lesser adder's-tongue

Essentially a dwarf version of *O. vulgatum*, for which it could easily be mistaken.

DESCRIPTION: as for *O. vulgatum*, except that the frond is no more than 10 cm high at the most, often half that size, and that the blade of the sterile frond is lanceolate or even narrowly lanceolate (as opposed to more ovate in *O. vulgatum*). Its most obvious difference is, however, that the fronds appear in November, last through the winter and die down in April, whereas those of *O. vulgatum* appear in June and die down at first frost.

HABITAT: heaths, meadows.

GEOGRAPHICAL TYPE: Mediterranean.

DISTRIBUTION: throughout the Mediterranean islands and the Mediterranean coastal regions: the Channel Islands: the Scilly Isles.

CULTIVATION: seldom cultivated, but succeeds best in boggy soil in turf.

VARIETIES: none recorded.

Ophioglossum lusitanicum

Ophioglossum vulgatum
The adder's-tongue

The ophioglossums form a group of curiously unfern-like ferns around which a considerable amount of folklore and superstition has gathered, including the imbuing of the plants with various magical properties. The genus as a whole is made up of rather short terrestial perennial herbs, but is poorly (though typically) represented by this species and its subspecies. In some of the tropical species the barren frond is divided as in a viper's tongue: on the other hand on one saprophytic species the sterile frond is absent altogether. Some of the tropical members are epiphytic.

DESCRIPTION: short, perennial deciduous dimorphic herb.

Stock: subterranean, short, erect, clothed or even sheathed by the bases of the old fronds, terminating abruptly in a basal cluster of radiating roots: some of these roots elongate to form stolons, the tips swelling to produce buds from which new plants can arise.

Fronds: solitary, but occasionally 2 or 3 together, up to 30 cm tall, usually about $\frac{1}{2}$ that size, cylindrical, hollow with a sheath at the base in which the following year's frond bud may be found.

Stalks: usually about equal in length to the blade but deceptive, since approximately $\frac{1}{2}$ the stalk is subterranean.

Blade: variable, normally ovate or ovate-lanceolate, rarely narrowly lanceolate, apex obtuse, texture glabrous, very fleshy, rapidly becoming flaccid if severed.

Venation: irregular, reticulate, not conforming to any regular classification.

Fertile frond: sharing a common stalk with the sterile frond in which its own stalk is sheathed up to the

Ophioglossum vulgatum

12 *Athyrium filix-femina clarissima* (page 194).

13 (Right) *Athyrium filix-femina cristata minima* (page 195); the red flowers are those of *Tropaeolum speciosum*.

14 (Below) *Athyrium filix-femina frizelliae* (page 196).

point at which the frond diverges: visible spike stalk approximately equal in length to the fertile portion, usually taller than the barren frond. The outer edges of the upper part of the spike are closely set with 2 parallel rows of up to 40 pairs of large, sunken sporangia, the spike terminating in a sterile point.

Sori: round, yellow becoming brown.

Indusium: absent.

HABITAT: heaths, meadows, pastures.

GEOGRAPHICAL TYPE: Circumpolar.

DISTRIBUTION: Europe from Iceland in the north, southwards to Algeria and the Azores, eastwards into Asia including the Indian subcontinent; North America throughout Canada and southwards along the eastern coastal belt as far as Florida.

SUBSPECIES: *vulgatum* differs from the type mainly in that its barren frond is substantially broader at the base, in that the fertile spike has fewer sporangia and in its different chromosome count.

Subspecies *ambiguum* differs from the type in its always smaller growth, fronds only 4–10 cm long, and in that it usually produces only fertile fronds, seldom barren fronds. Barren blade when produced narrowed at the base: spike 1–2 times as long as the blade, bearing not more than 14 sporangia on each side.

CULTIVATION: difficult, seldom adapting and probably only succeeding in a rock garden where it can be grown among short, heath-type grasses.

VARIETIES: none recorded.

CHAPTER TEN

Ferns of Wet Places

The ferns of wet places form a distinct group only in that they are all in-habitants of places that are naturally extremely wet. As a group they lack the homogenity of such groups as the succulent ferns and wall ferns. Indeed, the ferns of wet places are a distinctively diverse group, both botanically and in appearance.

It is tempting, remembering that ferns are primitive plants, and that, since all plants came originally from the sea, to think that those ferns which have the greatest dependence on moisture are the most primitive ferns. Though this is true in some instances, it is not necessarily the case: many of the ferns in this group are simply species of genera that are common throughout the woodlands of the temperate world that have adapted themselves to growing in extremely wet conditions.

Cryptogramma stelleri
The slender cliffbrake

A tiny, delicate, very fragile-looking fern with almost trans-lucent fronds that is commoner than is generally supposed, but which is seldom seen, since apart from being overlooked because of its diminutive stature, it hides itself in the densest shade in wet, boggy patches in woodlands. A further reason for its seldom being seen is that, whereas with most ferns the fronds endure throughout most of the season, with this fern they en-dure only a few weeks, disappear-ing after their brief hour as though they had never been there at all.

DESCRIPTION: very dwarf, slender, creeping, dimorphic deciduous moisture-loving fern.

Stock: slender, creeping, pale brown, beset with a few scattered hairs and scales; roots very fine, thread-like, shallowly spreading.

Fronds: deciduous dimorphic, short-lived, the barren fronds appearing in late spring and dis-appearing in early summer, the fertile fronds appearing and dis-appearing just a little later, remain-ing a little while on the plant once the barren fronds have gone. Fertile fronds no more than 7.5 cm tall, barren fronds less than $\frac{1}{2}$ that height.

Stalks: of both barren and fertile fronds longer than the blades, smooth, fragile, pale green becom-ing pinkish-brown at the base.

Rachis: smooth, pale green.

Blade: eliptic-lanceolate in outline, flimsy, pale green.
Branching: pinnate.
Pinnae: usually about 6 opposite pairs, these being deeply lobed, the lobes round-ended, somewhat denate.
Venation: not established.
Fertile fronds: taller and narrower than the barren fronds, the pinnae lanceolate in outline, divided into clearly distinct lanceolate lobes, the pinna edges thickly beset with sporangia.
Sori: tiny.
Indusium: formed by the inrolled edges of the pinnules.

HABITAT: deep shade in boggy ground in woods, any cool, deeply shaded highly humid spot, caves, ravines.

GEOGRAPHICAL TYPE: Circumpolar.

DISTRIBUTION: in North America through Canada to New York.

CULTIVATION: extremely difficult out of doors, but makes an ideal subject for a bottle garden.

VARIETIES: none recorded.

Dryopteris cristata
Lastrea cristata
The crested buckler fern

This is a strong-growing fern with somewhat fleshy fronds, found growing only in bog conditions. Something of a mystery exists as to why its specific epithet is *cristata*, since it is not crested in any way.

DESCRIPTION: strong-growing deciduous dimorphic terrestrial fern.
Stock: creeping, rather stout, dark brown with many mid-brown scales.
Fronds: presented in a broad, open tuft composed of both fertile and barren fronds; fertile fronds erect up to 100 cm, barren fronds spreading up to 50 cm.
Stalks: approximately $\frac{1}{2}$ as long as the blade on barren fronds, up to the same length as the blade on fertile fronds: green above, brown beneath and towards the base, covered with many dull brown scales.

Rachis: green above, brown beneath, covered in a few scattered scales.
Blade: linear-lanceolate in outline, yellowish-green, smooth.
Branching: pinnate.
Pinnae: up to 20 pairs, opposite or sub-opposite, widely spaced, triangular-oblong in outline, shortly stalked, sometimes appearing almost sessile, deeply pinnatifid.
Venation: pecopteridian.
Fertile fronds: have their pinnae twisted so that the upper surfaces face the sky.
Sori: presented in 2 rows midway between the mid-vein and the margin of each segment of the pinnae.
Indusium: reniform.

HABITAT: bogs and wet heaths, usually of a slightly acidic nature, swampy ill-drained woodland.

Most frequently found growing amongst other lush vegetation.

GEOGRAPHICAL TYPE: Circumpolar.

DISTRIBUTION: northern and central Europe, rarer in north-western Europe including the British Isles, eastwards through the Caucasus into western Siberia thence discontinuously to Japan: eastern North America from Newfound-land westwards to Saskatchewan, and southwards as far as Arkansas.

CULTIVATION: successful only where it can be provided with a slightly acid, woodsy soil and a shaded position and where it will receive plenty of moisture. Most easily cultivated in the bog garden or in a stream-side position.

VARIETIES: none recorded.

Matteuccia struthiopteris
The ostrich fern

One of the largest and most distinct of temperate ferns. It is dimorphic in character, but differs from most dimorphic ferns in that the fertile fronds are much smaller than the barren ones. It is these that are its really spectacular feature, being produced in basket-like tufts, each frond of which somewhat resembles an ostrich feather.

DESCRIPTION: strong-growing, dimorphic tufted deciduous moisture-loving fern.
Stock: very stout, erect, covered with dark brown scales, the crown projecting above the soil surface: roots numerous, wiry, black forming a tangled mass, growing from the surface to a considerable depth in the soil: the stock also produces stout stolons and spreads by means of these into large clumps.
Fronds: barren, erect, slightly outspreading, deciduous, up to 150 cm in rich soils.
Stalks: short, less than $\frac{1}{16}$ the length of the frond, stout, rigid, dark brown, deeply grooved on the face, rounded at the back.
Rachis: dark brown becoming green, deeply grooved on the face, rounded at the back.
Blade: eliptic-lanceolate, broadest about $\frac{2}{3}$ of the way up, diminishing in width towards the base.
Branching: pinnate.
Pinnae: deeply pinnatifid, dentate, with blunt tips to the segments, acuminate.
Venation: not established.
Fertile fronds: about $\frac{1}{2}$ the length of the barren fronds, pinnate, contracted, erect, forming a smaller shuttlecock within the larger shuttlecock of the barren fronds, appearing later in the season than the barren fronds, the pinnae linear, densely crowded with dark brown sori.
Sori: dark brown, numerous.
Indusium: absent.

HABITAT: swamps, stream and

pond sides, low wet woodlands, generally preferring sunny situations.

GEOGRAPHICAL TYPE: Circumpolar.

DISTRIBUTION: native of North America from Nova Scotia to New Jersey: naturalised in parts of Great Britain and continental Europe.

CULTIVATION: any deep, rich, moist soil, very hardy. Very vigorous in situations that suit it, and care should be taken siting it: it can easily overgrow less robust neighbours. If damaged, for example, by slugs, dogs, or children, it is liable to produce fronds intermediate between the fertile and the barren fronds. The proud possessor should not immediately assume that his plant has given rise to some valuable new variety.

VARIETIES: none recorded.

Matteuccia struthopteris

Onoclea sensibilis
The sensitive fern
The bead fern
The American oak
fern

This delightful dimorphic fern is one of the commonest ferns of North America, where it is found growing in abundance on roadsides, in wet woodlands and meadows, streamsides and indeed almost anywhere where ferns will grow. Owing to its adaptability it is very variable in size, the barren fronds varying from a few inches to exceptionally as much as 90 cm, though it more typically produces barren fronds about 60 cm tall. Curiously enough, even the smallest mature plants, growing in situations where they receive little moisture and produce barren fronds only 2 or 3 in. high, will still produce perfect fertile fronds in miniature.

Onoclea sensibilis

DESCRIPTION: medium-sized dimorphic deciduous moisture-loving fern.

Stock: creeping, branching freely, brown, stout, smooth; roots numerous, shallow, black, forming a tangled mass.

Fronds: deciduous, very variable in size, from 5 to 90 cm, but probably more typically about 60 cm tall, pale green becoming yellow then brown at the end of the season, smooth, not leathery.

Stalks: as long as or longer than the blade, pale green, sometimes yellowish green, smooth, somewhat swollen at the base where it is brownish in colour and somewhat covered in lanceolate, light brown scales.

Rachis: smooth, pale green, shiny.

Blade: triangular-ovate to almost deltoid in outline, flimsy.

Branching: pinnate.

Pinnae: the lower ones entire, with rippled margins, well spaced becoming closer, the upper ones no longer pinnate but pinnatifid becoming ultimately decurrent.

Venation: not established.

Fertile fronds: about $\frac{1}{2}$ the height of the barren fronds, stalks about as long as on the barren fronds, fertile protion a much reduced pinnate section, the pinnae each curling round groups of sori to form bead-like appendages, green at first becoming mid-brown then dark brown when ripe. The fertile fronds remain on the plant long after the spores have been dispersed, often after the barren fronds have withered at first frost and may still be present when the new croziers unfurl themselves the following season.

Sori: round, green at first, becoming brown.

Indusium: absent.

HABITAT: wet places generally, in sun or shade.

GEOGRAPHICAL TYPE: Circumpolar.

DISTRIBUTION: in North America from Nova Scotia to New Jersey; naturalised in parts of Britain and continental Europe but not native there.

CULTIVATION: easily grown in any deep, rich moist preferably leafy soil. In situations which suit it, it will spread rapidly. Where there is adequate moisture it will grow well in full sun, but otherwise should be given some shade.

VARIETIES: only one variety has been recorded, *O.s. obtusilobata*, which form produces fronds intermediate in form between the fertile and the barren fronds. It is a curiosity, not beautiful.

Osmunda cinnamomea
The cinnamon fern

One of the commonest of the North American ferns, this close relative of the royal fern *Osmunda regalis* thrives in similarly boggy conditions, and bears generally a superficial resemblance to the royal fern. It is, however, quite distinct from the two other members of the genus Osmunda described in this book—firstly on account of the appearance of the fertile fronds before the barren fronds (it may in fact be more precise to say that they grow more rapidly than the barren fronds and therefore *seem* to appear before them) these being produced as early as May, whereas in the other species the fertile fronds do not appear until much later in the season; secondly on account of the colour of the fertile fronds, these being at first dark green and later cinnamon brown, whereas in the other species the colouring of the fertile fronds is much less red; and thirdly by the rusty wool that is to be found at the base of the fronds in mid-season, this being the remains of the white glistening wool that clothes the young fronds when they first emerge.

DESCRIPTION: strong-growing deciduous dimorphic moisture-loving fern.
Stock: remarkably stout, creeping, partly exposed above ground but mainly subterranean, the younger parts containing buds for the fronds of future years, densely clothed in bright brown hairs, the older parts thickly covered with a stubble of dark brown, dead frond stalks, the whole having a rather bristly appearance; roots wiry, very tough, sprouting from all over the stock and very firmly fixed in the soil.
Fronds: up to 150 cm tall, more often 90 to 100 cm tall, deciduous, leathery, dark green.
Stalks: about $\frac{1}{5}$ as long as the barren blade, but twice as long as

Osmunda cinnamomea

the fertile blades, smooth, round with a slightly grooved face, green, the lower parts covered in cinnamon wool, this being white when the fronds first uncurl, changing colour and gradually disappearing as the season advances.

Rachis: round, smooth, green, lightly scattered with cinnamon-coloured wool disappearing as the season advances.

Blade: broadly lanceolate.

Branching: pinnate.

Pinnae: pinnatifid, oblong, lanceolate in outline.

Venations: not established.

Fertile fronds: bearing no barren pinnae, bipinnate, narrowly ovate, the pinnules densely covered in sporangia which are at first dark green, becoming cinnamon brown on maturity.

Sori: large, short-stalked, in clusters.

Indusium: absent.

HABITAT: in wet places generally, especially in waterlogged localities where it often forms large luxuriant stands; streamsides, pondsides.

GEOGRAPHICAL TYPE: Circumpolar.

DISTRIBUTION: in North America from Nova Scotia to Florida.

CULTIVATION: needs a deep, rich, permanently moist, even waterlogged soil. Will grow in full sun where conditions are wet enough, but elsewhere should be grown in light shade. Fully frost-hardy.

VARIETIES: only one variety is recorded, but its status is somewhat dubious, since it generally only occurs in areas that have been burned over: the character appears after fire, and since it disappears with the passage of time, may arise only from fire damage to the stock. It, *O.c. frondosa*, differs from the type plant only in that it produces a few barren pinnae below the fertile pinnae on the fertile fronds.

Osmunda regalis
The royal fern

The common name of this fern does not belie its true characteristics: it is indeed a regal fern— probably the largest of the terrestial ferns of the temperate regions of the world. A mature specimen growing under optimum conditions may have fronds reaching a height of as much as 3.5 m, and a circumference of as much as 5 m, although its dimensions are usually about half those. Even at that size it is a remarkably handsome fern.

Handsome is indeed probably the word that best sums up the general aspect of this fern, for it does not possess the delicacy usually associated with ferns. It is also sometimes known as a flowering fern on account of the remarkable fertile fronds which do in many ways resemble the seedheads of the astilbes. It does not, of course, flower—no ferns do—but one can easily understand why people might call it a flowering fern.

DESCRIPTION: very large deciduous dimorphic fern with prominent, persistent supraterrestial stock. *Stock:* stout, erect or oblique, covered thickly with the persistent bases of the old fronds among and through which the tangled, much branched black roots wind their way down to the soil, the whole mass increasing in size with the age of the fern and building up as does the 'trunk' of a tree fern, in time forming a more or less ovoid ball up to about 30 cm in diameter.

Fronds: up to 3.5 m, usually only $\frac{1}{2}$ that length, tufted and set in a close spiral, the outer ones sterile and inclined to lean outwards, the inner ones fertile at tips, erect.

Stalks: smooth, round, channelled

Osmunda regalis

on the face, pale yellowish-brown, reddish at the base: on sterile fronds the stalk may be up to $\frac{1}{3}$ the length of the blade, in fertile fronds up to $\frac{1}{2}$ the length of the blade; densely covered with pale brown tomentum when young, becoming glabrous; winged.

Rachis: round, channelled on the face, green, reddish where growing in conditions of poor light.

Blade: lanceolate in outline, up to 140 cm long.

Branching: bipinnate, tripinnate in the fertile portion of fertile fronds.

Pinnae: up to 9 pairs on either side of the rachis, opposite or almost opposite, never alternate, individually up to 40 cm long, set very wide apart on the rachis and presented at an acute angle to the rachis: oblong in outline; stalks short.

Pinnules: narrowly oblong, acroscopic pinnules somewhat shorter than basoscopic pinnules: terminal pinnules longer than typical pinnules.

Venation: Neuropteridian.

Fertile fronds: have pinnules at the tips, contracted and entirely covered with sporangia, light brown, densely incurled.

Sporangia: not confined to sori, rather large, pear-shaped, entirely covering the tips of the fertile fronds. Spores remain viable for no more than 68 hours.

Sori: pear-shaped cluster, up to 2 mm long.

Indusium: absent.

HABITAT: neutral or acidic conditions in bogland, marshy ground, ill-drained woodlands and streamsides.

GEOGRAPHICAL TYPE: Cosmopolitan.

DISTRIBUTION: extensive but discontinuous, embracing the forest zone of Europe and Asia from the British Isles through to Kamchatka with outlying stations in Scandinavia: southern India: Ethiopia, central and southern Africa: the Azores, the Mascarene Islands: North America, in the north-east and central-western U.S.A., Florida, and from Mississippi southwards into South America; the West Indies.

CULTIVATION: a magnificent specimen for waterside planting, though also growing well in any good garden soil well enriched with peat or leaf-mould; preferring neutral or acid conditions. The fronds turn a delightful russet in autumn.

VARIETIES: *O.r. crispa* (syn. *undulata*) is a not very striking variety in which the pinnules are evenly undulate.

O.r. cristata is a very fine variety, which is not only cristate but percristate, the pinnules and pinnae as well as the apex being crested: usually smaller growing than the type plant. A fair proportion of plants come true from spores, but these need to be sown as soon as ripe.

O.r. purpurascens, a remarkable

and valuable garden plant, is especially beautiful in spring when the young fronds come through a bright coppery pink. The stalks and rachis remain purple throughout the season but the blade fades to green as the season advances. Comes 100 per cent true from spores, and this in itself casts some doubt on its varietal status: it may prove to be a species.

Polystichum acrostichoides
The North American
Christmas fern
The dagger fern

A delightful wintergreen North American native. It belongs to the same genus as the European holly fern. *Polystichum lonchitis*. Both are in good condition at Christmas time, and the North American species is much used for yuletide decoration—a practice which should not be followed when the fern is cultivated since repeated cutting of the fronds weakens the plant. It is unlikely to be confused with any other species.

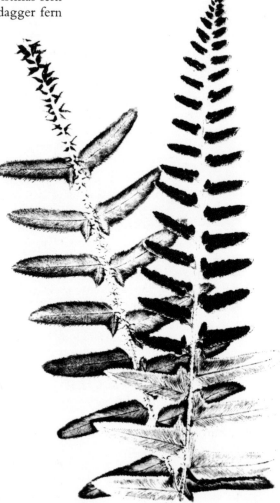

DESCRIPTION: low-growing, monomorphic tufted wintergreen moisture-loving fern.
Stock: horizontal or erect, short, pale brown, the younger parts densely clothed in pale brown scales, the older parts densely covered in the almost black dead stalk bases; roots rather short, numerous, forming a tangled mass around the stock.
Fronds: wintergreen, up to as much as 90 cm tall but more usually about 60 cm tall, very dark, glossy green, leathery.
Stalks: about ⅕ as long as the blade, very scaly, green, becoming brown towards the base, the base swollen, the face slightly grooved.
Rachis: green, very scaly, grooved on the face.

Polystichum acrostichoides

Blade: narrowly lanceolate.

Branching: pinnate.

Pinnae: oblong, finely serrate, auriculate on the acroscopic side, there being as many as 40 pairs of opposite or sub-opposite pinnae: the upper $\frac{1}{2}$ or $\frac{1}{3}$ of the frond bears the fertile pinnae, which are much reduced in size, clearly differentiated from the barren pinnae, lanceolate in outline.

Venation: not established.

Sori: numerous, becoming confluent on maturity, round, occurring at the ends of the veins on the fertile pinnae.

Indusium: circular, entire, toothed, attached at the centre.

HABITAT: rich, moist limy soil.

GEOGRAPHICAL TYPE: Circumpolar.

DISTRIBUTION: in North America throughout the north-eastern and central states, becoming rarer further south.

CULTIVATION: this is a fully frost-hardy species, revelling in deep, rich, leafy soil to which some chalk or old mortar has been added. It is a variable species and a number of varieties have been recorded.

VARIETIES: *P.a. crispum* is a form in which the pinnae are nicely crisped.

P.a. cristatum, a form in which all the pinnae are crested, and which has a fine terminal crest.

P.a. gravesii differs from the type only in that the fertile pinnae are abruptly truncate, the midrib projecting beyond the tip of the pinna.

P.a. incisum is the most charming form, in which the pinnae are deeply cut, pinnatifid, the segments overlapping.

Polystichum braunii
Braun's holly fern

Braun's holly fern is closely related to the European holly fern *Polystichum lonchitis*, being another species of the same genus. It differs from the European species in its much stronger growth and in its deciduous habit.

DESCRIPTION: medium-sized, deciduous tufted monomorphic moisture-loving fern.

Stock: erect, rather stout, mid-brown, the younger part consisting of about 8 light brown 'knuckles' which are present throughout the year; the knuckles become the fronds, but as each frond develops another knuckle replaces it; the older parts densely clothed with the almost black, dead stalk-stubs; roots black, wiry, far-reaching.

Fronds: deciduous, up to 90 cm tall, arranged in a basket-like fashion of no more than 8 on any one crown, the fronds deciduous, the previous season's fronds remaining attached to the stock for a large part of each season.

Stalks: short, about $\frac{1}{5}$ as long as the blade, green, densely clothed in mid-brown hairs and scales, flat on the face, rounded behind, often

scarred where scales have fallen off.
Rachis: pale brown, densely clothed in mid-brown hairs and scales, front flat, grooved, sides, flat, back rounded.
Blade: eliptic-lanceolate.
Branching: bipinnate.
Pinnae: oblong-lanceolate, up to about 20 pairs on either side of the rachis, opposite becoming sub-opposite.
Pinnules: obovate, slightly auriculate, with incurving teeth, terminating in a sharp bristle.
Venation: not established.
Sori: round, large, occurring in 2 rows on either side of the pinnule midribs, about mid-way between the mid-ribs and the margins, more sori occurring on the acroscopic side than on the basiscopic side on the midrib.
Indusium: circular-peltate, short-lived.

HABITAT: moist spots in woodlands, streamsides, ravines.

GEOGRAPHICAL TYPE: Circumpolar.

DISTRIBUTION: throughout the north-east and north central states of the U.S.A.

CULTIVATION: fully frost-hardy and requiring a deep rich soil in a shaded situation.

VARIETIES: none recorded.

Thelypteris noveboracensis
The New York fern

A delightful, delicate ferny-fern with yellow-green fronds appearing in pseudo-tufts of three or four together along a creeping rootstock. One of the ways in which it can be distinguished from the marsh fern, *Thelypteris palustris*, with which it was for long confused, is that the two grow in rather different habitats, the marsh fern growing in really wet, boggy ill-drained ground, this species tending to grow in rather drier situations, at the edges of swamps rather than right in them, and in moist sunny clearings in woodlands. The two species seldom occur together.

DESCRIPTION: medium-sized, deciduous monomorphic moisture-loving fern.

Stock: dark brown, slender, somewhat scaly, horizontal, creeping just below the surface of the soil, branching irregularly, rooting from beneath, producing fronds from the upper side in pseudo-tufts of 2 or 3; roots black, sparse, spreading, fine.
Fronds: yellow-green, erect and somewhat spreading, up to 45 cm tall, those bearing fertile pinna more erect than those without, not dimorphic.
Stalks: less than $\frac{1}{4}$ the length of the blade, often less, light green, smooth or slightly hairy on the face, brown and scaly at the base.
Rachis: green, smooth or only very slightly hairy.
Blade: ovate-lanceolate in outline, tapering at both ends.
Branching: pinnate.

Pinnae: alternate, never opposite, lanceolate in outline, up to about 20 pairs, deeply pinnatifid, the lobes rounded, the lowest lobes often tiny.
Venation: not established.
Sori: minute, numerous, occurring on the secondary veins of the pinna lobes, rather nearer the margin than the midrib.
Indusium: kidney-shaped, pale, slightly hairy.

HABITAT: wet places, on the edges of swamps and in damp, sunny clearings in woodlands.

GEOGRAPHICAL TYPE: Circumpolar.

DESCRIPTION: inaccurately known, owing to the former confusion of this species with *T. palustris:* northeastern and central North America.

CULTIVATION: requires a deep, rich moist soil: will withstand some sun.

VARIETIES: non recorded.

Thelypteris palustris
Dryopteris palustris
Lastrea thelypteris
The marsh fern

Probably the most vigorous of the Thelypteris species, yet as dainty as the others, particularly in the light, bright green of the fronds, growing up to 1.76 m. Sometimes confused with *Oreopteris limbosperma*, from which it may however readily be distinguished by the creeping stock and the irregular production of fronds, the invariably inrolled edges of the fertile segments and the longer stalks. It is a fern of very widespread distribution, in places common, and even in its rarer haunts locally abundant. In some of the moister meadows of North America it is almost as common as the grasses with which it co-exists.

DESCRIPTION: moderately large, dimorphic deciduous fern of delicate appearance.
Stock: rhizomatous, slender, up to 25 mm diameter; long, up to 1 m, branching normally alternately at irregular intervals, bearing, at the growing point and frond buds only, ephemeral small light brown hairs; creeping only just below the surface of the soil.
Fronds: dimorphic, the fertile ones up to 100 cm, stouter and stiffer than the barren fronds and produced approximately one month later; barren fronds up to 60 cm, softer-textured, somewhat outspreading.
Stalks: of barren fronds approximately equal to the blade but sometimes less than equal; of fertile fronds rather longer than the blade, never shorter; both rather brittle, yellow to greenish yellow, becoming black-brown at the base, rarely clothed in a few lanceolate scales.
Rachis: yellowish to greenish-yellow.
Blade: of both barren and fertile fronds lanceolate in outline, tapering at both ends, the apex occa-

sionally narrowing abruptly not gradually, yellowish-green to bluish-green depending upon the amount of sunlight to which they are exposed, soft in texture, lacking glands.
Branching: pinnate.
Pinnae: up to 27 on either side of the rachis, linear to lanceolate in outline, sessile or very shortly stalked, deeply pinnatifid to virtually pinnate.
Segments: those of fertile fronds are narrower than those of the barren fronds, the margins somewhat recurved and infolded.
Venation: Pecopteridian.
Sori: numerous, small, round, occurring just above the forks of the veins and forming 2 rows on either side of the midrib of the segment midway between it and the margin, and occurring in such abundance as to completely cover the undersurface of the fertile segments.
Indusium: small, reniform, the margin appearing torn but techni-

cally toothed.

HABITAT: in non-acid marshes, moist meadows, pond and stream-sides and fens, seldom in standing water.

GEOGRAPHICAL TYPE: Cosmopolitan.

DISTRIBUTION: Europe, becoming rarer in southern Europe, through Transcaucasia, eastwards to the Himalayas, thence southwards into southern India and eastwards across the Altai range into China; Japan; Algeria, central and southern Africa; north-eastern North America as far south as Texas in the west and Florida in the east.

CULTIVATION: Generally easy provided there is an adequate supply of moisture; avoid extreme acidity or alkalinity; likes a little lime in soil; tends to be invasive.

VARIETIES: none recorded.

Thelypteris simulata
The Massachusetts fern

Another Thelypteris species that has been much confused with its generic relatives in the past, again, like *T. noveboracensis*, with the marsh fern, *T. palustris*, and with *T. noveboracensis* itself. Its habitat forms one of its main distinguishing features, it usually being found growing in sphagnum swamps or in boggy conditions in coniferous forests, particularly larch, spruce and cedar forests. It prefers shadier conditions than either of the two

species with which it is mainly confused.

DESCRIPTION: medium-sized, deciduous dimorphic moisture-loving fern.
Stock: slender, black, clothed in a few minute dark scales, creeping, freely branching and both wide-spreading and rapidly spreading; roots sparse, wiry, black, small, growing downwards (whereas with the species with which it is usually

confused, the roots tend to grow in a horizontal plane).

Fronds: up to 60 cm tall, erect, thin, yellow-green in colour, not coriaceous.

Stalks: up to ½ the length of the blade, green, somewhat hairy above, smooth beneath. Brownish at the base and beset with a few brown scales.

Rachis: green, slightly hairy above, smooth beneath.

Blade: oblong in outline, tapering more towards the tip than towards the base, widest in the middle.

Branching: pinnate.

Pinnae: deeply pinnatifid, lanceolate in outline but narrowed towards the rachis (this being one of its distinguishing features), up to about 20 pairs but more often less, opposite to sub-opposite, never alternate, the lowest pairs of pinnae tipping downwards, segments rounded.

Venation: not established.

Sori: small, numerous, occurring on the secondary veins of the pinna segments closer to the margin than to the midrib.

Indusium: kidney-shaped, pale, not persistent.

HABITAT: moist, even boggy woodlands, on acid soils.

GEOGRAPHICAL TYPE: Circumpolar.

DISTRIBUTION: inaccurately known owing to former confusion with other related species: through north-eastern and central North America; recorded as not common, but possibly more common than thought.

CULTIVATION: requires a deep, moist, rich soil with plenty of peat or leaf-mould and a shaded situation. Given these conditions it will spread rapidly.

VARIETIES: none recorded.

Woodwardia areolata
The netted chain-fern

This charming deciduous swamp fern is very much like a smaller version of the sensitive fern. Indeed, so great is its superficial resemblance that it was for a long time considered to be the same plant, and even today many people overlook it. It is, however, quite distinct from the sensitive fern in the reddish colouring of its young fronds in spring, in its more glossy, darker green and more translucent barren fronds, and in the shape of its fertile fronds, which more nearly resemble its barren fronds than is the case with the sensitive fern.

DESCRIPTION: dwarf, deciduous dimorphic moisture-loving fern.

Stock: creeping, forking, frequently, slender, deep brown, the younger parts densely clothed in pale brown hairs, the older parts with occasional pale brown scales; roots occurring in clusters from the underside of the stock, the fronds occurring on the upper side of the stock in the intervals between the points from which roots grow: the roots are rather sparse, slender and mid-brown.

Fronds: up to 60 cm tall, deciduous, pale green, translucent, flimsy.

Stalks: the same length as the blade, or longer; stout, yellowish-green becoming brown and slightly thickened towards the base which bears a few scattered brown scales, the face flattened and slightly grooved.

Rachis: yellowish-green, rather stout.

Blades: triangular-ovate in outline.

Branching: pinnate.

Pinnae: only the lower lobes are truly pinnae, these being well spaced, the spacing decreasing further up the frond where the lobes are no longer truly innate but merely deeply pinnatifid, becoming decurrent; eliptic-lanceolate in outline, finely serrate.

Venation: not established.

Fertile fronds: slightly taller than the barren fronds, slightly narrower in outline, the pinnae linear in outline, the undersides of each of the pinnae being thickly covered by the chains of sori.

Sori: linear.

Indusium: continuous along each pinna.

HABITAT: bogs, swamps, even on the edge of water, on acid formations, especially frequent in coastal localities.

GEOGRAPHICAL TYPE: Circumpolar.

DISTRIBUTION: in North America throughout the north-eastern and north-central states.

CULTIVATION: a fully frost-hardy species revelling in boggy conditions. It is more demanding in its cultivation than the sensitive fern, and will really only thrive in really wet situations. Planted in deep, rich leafy soil, it will be a poor thing by comparison with specimens grown where there is constant water at the roots.

VARIETIES: none recorded.

Woodwardia radicans
The European chain
fern

Although called the European chain fern, this plant is also native to western North America and to various other parts of the temperate world. It is one of the strongest-growing and most exotic-looking of all the ferns that could be considered hardy in the temperate world, throwing up luxurious fronds as much as 2 m tall, with individual pinna over 30 cm long, of a rather tropical green colour. As with the other chain ferns, fertile and barren pinna are borne on the same fronds, but are clearly distinguished from one another, the fertile pinna being much reduced in size. Unlikely to be confused with any other chain fern on account of its much greater stature.

DESCRIPTION: very strong-growing deciduous monomorphic moisture-loving fern.

Stock: erect, stout, the younger parts densely clothed in mid-brown hairs and scales, the older parts thickly beset with the dead frond bases; roots coarse, thick, seldom branching, far reaching, firmly embedded in the soil.

Fronds: deciduous, 2 m tall, produced in basket-like fashion, arching somewhat outwards, brilliant green.

Stalks: round, bearing large brown scales, lustrous brown.

Rachis: green; bearing occasionally, in the axils of the pinnae, very scaly buds which fall off to form new plants.

Woodwardia radicans

Blade: broadly ovate.
Branching: pinnate.
Pinnae: as much as 30 cm long, deeply pinnatifid, oblong-lanceolate in outline, the pinna segments linear-lanceolate with serrate margins. Only the upper quarter are fertile: these are simple, not pinnatifid, coarsely toothed.
Venation: not established.
Sori: elongated, arranged in a chain-like fashion along each side of the midribs of the fertile pinna.
Indusium: sausage-shaped.

HABITAT: swamps and boggy woodlands, always on acid formations.

GEOGRAPHICAL TYPE: Circumpolar.

DISTRIBUTION: in North America recorded from Pennsylvania, Florida and from several of the western states; southern Europe.

CULTIVATION: requires a deep, rich soil with plenty of peat and leaf-mould, and a shaded position. Only tolerant of light frost, and best grown in a cold house in areas where severe frosts are experienced.

VARIETIES: none recorded.

Woodwardia virginica
The Virginian chain-fern

This, as might be suspected from both its botanical and its common names, is a close relative of the netted chain fern *Woodwardia areolata*. What is perhaps surprising is that it is not with that species, nor with the sensitive fern *Onoclea sensibilis* which looks somewhat like the netted chain fern, that this species is confused, but with a totally different plant—the cinnamon fern, *Osmunda cinnaommea*. It is easily distinguished from that species by the fact that whereas that species grows in a single, basket-like tuft or group of tufts, this is a creeping fern, forming large masses of greenery. It is an attractive and eye-catching species, with very long dark purple stalks and rachises, and glossy leaves, reddish in spring.

DESCRIPTION: strong-growing creeping monomorphic deciduous moisture-loving fern.
Stock: creeping, very stout, up to 1.5 cm thick, the younger parts densely covered with brown scales, the older parts having a few scattered scales; branching freely; roots few, scattered, threadlike, occurring all round the stock though less often from the top of it than from the sides and bottom.
Fronds: deciduous, up to 120 cm tall, leathery, dark green.
Stalks: very long, up to twice as long as the blade, dark, shining purple-brown, the face deeply grooved, somewhat thickened at the base becoming almost tuberous just above the stock where the tissue becomes spongy.
Rachises: dark purple-brown becoming green towards the apex, the face grooved.

Blade: ovate lanceolate.
Branching: pinnate.
Pinnae: deeply pinnatifid, lanceolate in outline, lobes rounded at the tips, pinnae alternate or sub-opposite.
Venation: not established.
Sori: occurring in prominent chains alongside the pinna and segment midribs, becoming confluent as they ripen.
Indusium: flimsy, disappearing as the spores ripen.

HABITAT: very wet places, oozing mud, swamps, bogs, often growing with its feet in up to a foot of water: always in acid conditions.

GEOGRAPHICAL TYPE: Circumpolar.

DISTRIBUTION: in North America from Maine to Florida.

CULTIVATION: is a very unspectacular plant under the conditions under which ferns are ordinarily grown, needing really wet, acid ground to show its true paces. An ideal plant for the bog garden. Not suitable for pot culture: its roots need plenty of room to spread themselves.

VARIETIES: none recorded.

CHAPTER ELEVEN

Water Ferns

The water ferns known properly as Hydropteridales, form a very small and distinct group. Like the succulent ferns, they are not true ferns—not members of the Eufilicales, the group which embraces about 90 per cent of the plants described in this book. And like the succulent ferns they should strictly be regarded as fern allies rather than as ferns. However, whereas the succulent ferns are more primitive than the true ferns, the water ferns are evolutionarily more advanced. They are however more closely related to the true ferns than are the succulent ferns, being members of the Leptosporangiate group, while the succulent ferns belong to the Eusporangiate group.

The water ferns are represented in the cool temperate regions by only three genera—Azolla, Marsilea and Pilularia. Both Marsilea and Pilularia belong to the family Marsileaceae, while the Azollas belong to the family Salvinaceae. The group as a whole is essentially a tropical one and, apart from *Pilularia globulifera* which is a native of Great Britain and the other cooler parts of Europe, none of the other species is endemic to the cool temperate world. *Marsilea quadrifolia*, though widely naturalised in the U.S.A. as far north as Massachusetts, is a native of southern Europe, while the Azollas are essentially tropical species that have been spread into cooler regions by man.

The water ferns differ from the true ferns firstly and most obviously in that they are mainly free-floating, truly aquatic plants, but botanically and more importantly in that they produce two type of spores—male and female —whereas all true ferns produce spores of only one type. The female spores are known as megaspores, the male ones as microspores. The spores are borne in special bodies known as sporocarps, produced on short stalks. In the genera Marsilea and Pilularia both megaspores and microspores are borne in the same sporocarps, whereas in the genus Azolla they are borne in separate sporocarps.

Much of the normal terminology does not apply to water ferns: they have no stalks, rachises, blades, pinnae or pinnules in the normal sense, and there are no varieties.

Azolla caroliniana
The Carolinian pond fern
The water fern
The mosquito fern

A minute, free-floating, genuinely aquatic fern which, when growing well, forms great sheets across even quite large expanses of still waters. It gets one of its common names from its supposed ability to smother the larvae of mosquitoes. As with *Azolla filiculoides*, the colour of the fronds changes according to whether the plant is growing in sun or shade. Where it is growing in sun the colour turns from green in the spring to a glowing bright red as the season advances: indeed, it could be said to be one of the few ferns to give brilliant autumn colour. It differs from *Azolla filiculoides* in the smoother surface of the fronds, in the more rounded outline of the leaflets and in the swelling of the parts of the stem upon which the sporocarps are borne.

DESCRIPTION: minute, deciduous, free-floating truly aquatic fern. Differs from *A. filiculoides* in the wider spacing of the leaflets and in their generally larger size, in their pointed as opposed to obliquely ovate outline and in their smoother surface texture.

Sporocarps: megaspores, acorn-shaped; microsporangia, globular.

HABITAT: abundant in still waters, occasionally at the edges of slow-moving waters.

GEOGRAPHICAL TYPE: Circumpolar.

DISTRIBUTION: throughout the southern states of the U.S.A.

CULTIVATION: this is a rather tender fern, being killed by anything more than the slightest touch of frost. It is easily established in ponds in mild areas, where it may, however, become a nuisance because it spreads so fast. The mass of vegetation can be scraped off the surface of the pond at the end of each season and used to make compost—which it does very well. A fresh crop will grow the following year, the new plants coming from spores which have rested on the pond bottom over-winter. In colder areas needs cool greenhouse treatment.

Azolla filiculoides
The water fern
Azolla

A very small free-floating aquatic fern bearing a very close resemblance to a liverwort, both in its general appearance and in its mode of growth. One curious fact about the azollas recently discovered is that one of the two lobes of the fronds contains a chamber in which are found threads of the blue-green

algae *Anabaena*. The presence of this blue-green algae has not been fully investigated or explained, but it seems likely that a symbiotic relationship may exist between the fern and the algae.

DESCRIPTION: very small floating aquatic fern, in time forming large mats on pond surfaces which turn a brilliant russet colour if exposed to full sun.

Stem: about 1 mm diameter, growing horizontally on the water, much branched, bearing both roots and fronds, roots below, fronds above, almost entirely concealed, at least from above, by the fronds.

Roots: solitary, white, numerous, occurring on the underside of the stem at each point of branching.

Fronds: occurring on the upper sides of the stems in 2 rows, alternate obliquely angled away from each other: each frond deeply cut into 2 lobes, the upper one the larger of the two, a green, assimilating organ, the lower one thinner, smaller submerged, usually white. The upper lobes measure about 1 mm across and have numerous minute hairs on their upper surface, and are distinctly margined. These upper lobes are so tightly packed on the stem that they overlap like tiles on a roof: a similar pattern is found among the lower lobes but these, being smaller, do not produce the same effect, leaving the stem partially visible from beneath.

Sporocarps: borne in pairs, either one or two pairs, never more, on the lower lobe of the first frond of each lateral branch, the cluster of sporocarps being covered by a cowl-like flange arising from the upper lobe of the same frond. Each individual sorus is protected by its own indusium (a somewhat unusual feature). The indusium is translucent, and the sorus contained in it can clearly be seen under magnification. On maturity the sporocarp may either be a rounded, ball-like organ consisting of numerous microsporangia, or an acorn-shaped organ consisting of a single megasporangia. The sori in each pair may be either of the same or of differing sexes. The microsporangium is long-stalked containing numerous minute clumps of microspores, called massulae. The massulae are released by the decay of the indusium and the sporagnium wall, and some of the massulae then become attached by means of the minute hairs with which they are barbed to the megaspores: fertilisation follows.

HABITAT: free-floating in standing water: less often on damp ground or mud at the edges of lakes and ponds.

GEOGRAPHICAL TYPE: Pantropical.

DISTRIBUTION: native of tropical America but now widely distributed as an aquarium escape throughout much of the North American continent and in north-western and southern Europe. Recorded as a fossil in interglacial deposits in Suffolk, England and from Germany, Holland and Russia.

CULTIVATION: easily established in standing water: moderately frost-tolerant, but probably best grown in a pond under glass in regions of severe winter frost.

15 *Athyrium filix-femina glomeratum* (page 198).

16 *Athyrium filix-femina plumosum-divisilobum* (page 200).

Azolla rubra
The New Zealand
water fern

Differs from *A. filiculoides* only in its habitat, this extending from New Zealand into Australia including Tasmania.

Marsilea quadrifolia
The water shamrock
The water clover
Pepperwort

An aquatic fern of shallow waters with leaves floating, growing from a creeping rootstock embedded in the mud. The leaves are made up of four segments and very closely resemble those of a 'lucky' four-leafed shamrock. It is often overlooked because it tends to grow together with other marginal plants.

DESCRIPTION: deciduous, creeping, marginal–aquatic fern.
Stock: slender, creeping, seldom branched, running along the surface of or just below the surface of mud in still or slowly moving waters; roots emerging from joints in the stock, short, fleshy, branching, growing almost vertically down into the mud.
Fronds: up to 1.5 cm across composed of 4 equal segments like the leaves of a shamrock, the leaves being slightly convex on maturity, with pockets of air held between the raised surface and the water, the 4 segments somewhat overlapping.
Stalks: thin, green, long, up to 10 times the length of the width of the fronds, often twining around the stems of other marginals.
Sporocarps: occurring singly or in pairs on short stalks arising from the base of the frond stalks, bean-like, hard shelled, covered with yellowish hairs.

HABITAT: the edges of ponds, lakes and slow-moving waters.

GEOGRAPHICAL TYPE: Circumpolar.

DISTRIBUTION: temperate North America.

CULTIVATION: easily established in ponds. Not very frost-hardy and better grown in a cold house in areas of severe frost.

Pilularia americana
American pillwort

Very similar in all respects to the foregoing species, and most easily distinguished from it by the way in which the fronds are produced in tufts, not singly or in pairs.

DESCRIPTION: wintergreen aquatic or marginal fern, smaller in all its parts than *P. globulifera*.
Stock: up to 1 mm diameter, extending up to 30 cm, seldom branching.
Fronds: simple, cylindrical, up to 7.5 cm long, fresh green, glabrous, crozier-like as they unfurl, more or less equidistant on the stock, produced in tufts, not singly, 3 cm apart.
Sporocarps: sessile, up to 2 mm diameter.

H

HABITAT: still waters and the mud at the edges of still waters, usually where the waters occur on slightly acidic formations.

GEOGRAPHICAL TYPE: North American.

DISTRIBUTION: confined to North America: Georgia, Washington County, Piedmont, Arkansas and California.

CULTIVATION: as for *Pilularia globulifera*.

Pilularia globulifera
Pillwort

There are only six species of pillworts in all, distributed through Europe, Australasia and America, and all are very similar in general appearance, differing only in details. They are true aquatic or marginal plants, occasionally but seldom free-floating, and unique among ferns in their appearance. The fronds consist simply of single, rush-like spikes without pinna. At the base of each frond or cluster of fronds there is a single, spherical sporocarp, and it is from these that the genus derives its name. The general mode of the reproductive organs is very similar to that of the azollas (*q.v.*). In general appearance they do not look at all like ferns, being easily dismissed merely as

Pilularia globulifera

grass-like water weeds. Though rare in all their haunts, they are probably more common than is realised. Most easily recognised by the crozier-like manner in which the fronds unfurl.

DESCRIPTION: diminutive aquatic or marginal wintergreen fern.

Stock: cylindrical, seldom more than 1 mm in diameter extending to as much as 50 cm in length, up-curved at the growing point, producing fronds above and roots below, the roots occurring either immediately below the fronds or slightly behind them, much branched.

Fronds: simple, entire, up to 10 cm long, cylindrical, bright green, glabrous, coiled in crozier-like fashion as they unfurl: fronds produced on alternate sides of the stock, very variably spaced, the distance between fronds varying from 4 mm to 20 mm. At the point at which roots and frond unite on the stock a bud appears which extends into a new shoot.

Sporocarps: spherical, up to 3.5 mm diameter, often less, thickly covered in hairs which are at first yellowish green but which change through light brown to dark brown and finally to almost black when ripe, produced singly at the base of each frond on a very short stalk no more than 1 mm long: internally constructed of 4 vertical compartments each containing a single sorus. Each sorus consists of a swollen receptable containing microsporangia, in the upper por-

tion and megasporangia in the lower portion; the sporangia are sessile.

Megasporangia: ovoid.

Microsporangia: club-shaped. As with Azolla the internal tissues of the sporangia become mucilaginous when ripe. Splitting of the sporangia is achieved by swelling rather than by dehiscence: the husk breaks into quarters, releasing the spores.

HABITAT: ponds, lakes, still water generally or the mud at the edges of still waters.

GEOGRAPHICAL TYPE: Circumpolar, but restricted to Europe.

DISTRIBUTION: western Europe from Scandinavia in the north to Portugal in the south, from Ireland in the west through scattered stations across central Europe into southern Russia. Absent from North America.

CULTIVATION: of little intrinsic beauty and grown only for its curiosity value. Can only be grown in bog conditions and is difficult to establish in ponds, although it may spread there once established in the mud at the edge of a pond. Easy in a Wardian case or bottle garden, though requiring a damper and less well-drained compost than is usually needed.

Pilularia
novae-zelandiae
The New Zealand
pillwort

This fern is very similar to the two foregoing pillworts but even more diminutive in all its parts. It is confined to New Zealand, and has only been found on a very few occasions. Because of its generally unfernlike appearance it may well be underrecorded and more common than is thought at the present time.

DESCRIPTION: diminutive freefloating (or rarely marginal) wintergreen fern.
Stock: very slender, threadlike, less than 1 mm diameter.

Fronds: simply, cylindrical, bright green, up to 3 cm.
Sporocarps: spherical, hairy, up to 2.5 mm diameter.

HABITAT: mountain areas.

GEOGRAPHICAL TYPE: Australasian.

DISTRIBUTION: endemic to New Zealand.

CULTIVATION: not recorded as having ever been cultivated.

CHAPTER TWELVE

Filmy Ferns

The filmy ferns form another quite distinct and yet homogenous group. Unlike the two other distinct groups, the succulent ferns and the water ferns, they differ in degree rather than in kind. They are true ferns, members of the Eufilicales, and they bear spores of only one type.

Where they differ from other true ferns is in their structure, their membraneous fronds being usually only a single cell thick. Because of this they can only survive in places where the atmospheric humidity is above dewpoint. Taken away from such an atmosphere they will dry out and die rapidly. This extreme dependence on a very high degree of atmospheric humidity suggests that they are among the most primitive of living ferns. Botanically they are notable for bearing their spore cases on vein endings at the margins of the fronds. The spore cases are quite large and easily spotted.

As a group the filmy ferns are highly desirable garden plants, but virtually impossible to cultivate in the open garden. They can, however, be ideally suited in a Wardian case or bottle garden, but there they should not be mixed with other ferns, which they will tend to swamp; for, although delicate in growth, their thread-like stock increases rapidly underground, forming dense masses.

Hymenophyllum tunbrigense
The Tunbridge filmy fern

The filmy ferns are diminutive plants of singularly delicate appearance. The delicacy of their appearance does not belie the reality. In general appearance they could easily be mistaken for leafy liverworts or for mosses. There are a further approximately 25 species which are confined in the main, as might be expected, to tropical rain forests.

DESCRIPTION: dwarf, delicate, monomorphic, creeping, wintergreen fern.

Stock: very slender, almost thread-like, creeping.

Fronds: up to 11 cm long, of thin, flimsy texture, light, bright green.

Stalks: normally about $\frac{1}{3}$ as long as the blade, often less, seldom more, bright green, scales and hairs absent.

Rachis: winged.

Blade: up to 8 cm long, very flimsy, blue-green, almost translucent.

Branching: pinnate.

Pinnae: alternate (though the basal ones may be sub-opposite or even occasionally truly opposite), up to 14 in number, rhomboid in outline: segments flat, spreading, toothed towards the apex; each segment containing a single, clearly defined vein, ending short of the tip of the segment.

Venation: midribs only, the fronds appearing to be wings to the veins.

Sori: occurring only on the upper portion of the frond, situated at the vein endings.

Indusium: round, 2-valved, sharply tooth-edged.

HABITAT: acidic rocks, occasionally epiphytic on trees, only in areas of very high humidity or conditions of perpetual mist, such as might be found beside a waterfall.

GEOGRAPHICAL TYPE: Cosmopolitan.

DISTRIBUTION: decidedly discontinuous: the Atlantic seaboard of Europe including the British Isles: isolated stations in Germany, Italy and Corsica and Transcaucasia: Madeira, the Canary Islands, the Azores, Mauritius, South Africa, New Zealand, temperate Australia (including Tasmania), Jamaica, Brazil, Chile and Venezuela. Absent from North America.

CULTIVATION: an ideal subject for a Wardian case or bottle garden. Virtually impossible out of doors.

VARIETIES: none recorded.

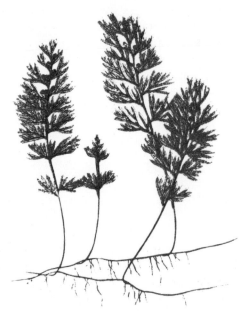

Hymenopyhllum tunbrigense

Hymenophyllum
wilsonii
Hymenophyllum
peltatum
Wilson's filmy fern

Wilson's filmy fern is in general very similar to the Tunbridge filmy fern, though somewhat more robust in general appearance: the arrangement of the divisions of the fronds is also somewhat more regular than in *Hymenophyllum tunbrigense*.

DESCRIPTION: dwarf, monomorphic creeping evergreen fern.
Stock: creeping, thread-like, producing fronds at irregular internals and rooting at those points at which fronds are produced; branching irregularly.
Fronds: up to 11 cm, more rigid than those of *H. tunbrigense*, more regular in form, more rigid and dark olive green rather than blue-green; somewhat recurved at the tip and margin.
Stalks: up to $\frac{1}{4}$ the length of the blade, often less, dark olive green.
Rachis: winged.
Blade: more rigid than *H. tunbrigense*, dark olive green.
Branching: pinnate.
Pinnae: always alternate, broadly lobed, the segments usually 3–5 in number, never more, toothed.
Venation: extending to the tips of the segments.
Sori: occurring only on the upper portion of the frond, on distinct vein-endings branching off the acroscopic side of the pinna midribs and situated in the angle formed between the segments and the rachis.
Indusium: oval not round, not toothed, projecting beyond the wing of the segments.

HABITAT: acidic rocks, occasionally epiphytic on trees, found only in areas of very high humidity, such as moist crevices in rock overhangs and close to waterfalls.

GEOGRAPHICAL TYPE: Cosmopolitan.

DISTRIBUTION: north-western Europe including stations as far north as western Norway and the Faroes: the Azores, the Canary Islands, Madeira, South Africa, New Zealand, Tasmania, Reunion, Chile, Tierra del Fuego.

CULTIVATION: ideal for a Wardian case or bottle garden: virtually impossible under normal garden conditions.

VARIETIES: none recorded.

Mecodium demissum
Hymenophyllum
demissum

The New Zealand filmy ferns, of which two are included in this book, were originally included in the genus Hymenophyllum, to which they are plainly very closely related. However minute botanical differences have led to their being separated into a genus of their own.

DESCRIPTION: wintergreen creeping monomorphic terrestial epiphytic filmy fern.

Stock: rather stout, creeping,

much branched, smooth, wiry; roots short, sparse.

Fronds: up to 40 cm long, usually about ½ that height, wintergreen, monomorphic. Erect or pendulous.

Stalks: equal in length to the blade, black, winged.

Rachis: also black, winged.

Blade: narrowly triangular in outline, flimsy, usually only one cell thick.

Branching: tri- to quadripinnate, the segments very narrow, almost translucent.

Pinnae: bi- to tripinnate.

Pinnules: simple or pinnate, winged.

Venation: midribs only noticeable, the pinnules appearing to be wings to the veins.

Sori: very small, borne at the tips of the terminal segments.

HABITAT: moist, deeply shaded situations of very high humidity, truly terrestrial or epiphytic on trees, fallen logs, rocks.

GEOGRAPHICAL TYPE: Southern circumpolar.

DISTRIBUTION: New Zealand, Java, Polynesia, the Philippines.

CULTIVATION: difficult in the open garden. Can be kept happy in a frost-free house in a pan plunged three-quarters of the way into live sphagnum moss, or in a bottle garden or Wardian case.

VARIETIES: none recorded.

Mecodium sanguinolentum
Hymenophyllum sanguinolentum

A strong-growing terrestrial or more often epiphytic filmy fern with beautiful, finely divided, olive-green fronds.

DESCRIPTION: wintergreen monomorphic terrestrial or epiphytic filmy fern.

Stock: stout, creeping, freely branching, pale brown, smooth; roots, few, shallow, persistent.

Fronds: wintergreen, up to 25 cm tall, erect or pendulous, somewhat undulate, notably olive-green, not translucent.

Stalks: up to ½ the length of the blade, not winged.

Rachis: olive green, winged.

Blade: broadly triangular in outline.

Branching: tri- to quadripinnate, the segments very narrow.

Pinnae: bi- to tripinnate, winged.

Pinnules: olive green, winged, pinnate or bipinnate.

Venation: simple, midribs only, the pinnules appearing to be wings on the veins.

Sori: numerous, large, occurring in the axils of the pinnules on the upper ½–⅓ of the fronds, notable for germinating while still in the sorus.

HABITAT: moist, deeply shaded, highly humid situations, on tree trunks, fallen logs, mossy rocks, wet crevices.

GEOGRAPHICAL TYPE: Pantropical.

DISTRIBUTION: New Zealand, Australia, Java, the Phillipines.

CULTIVATION: needs frost-free conditions. Cultivate as for *M. demissum.*

VARIETIES: none recorded.

Trichomanes boschianum
The bristle fern

North America's most delightfully finely divided fern, this is a true filmy fern, living only in caves and grottoes, well away from direct sunlight and in places of very high humidity. It might be mistaken for moss by the uninitiated.

DESCRIPTION: dwarf, creeping wintergreen monomorphic filmy fern.
Stock: creeping, thick, black, wiry, much branched, densely covered in tiny hair-like roots.
Fronds: wintergreen, up to 15 cm tall, erect or pendulous.
Stalks: about half as long as the blade, winged.
Rachis: similarly winged.
Blade: lanceolate in outline, light green, translucent.
Branching: tri- to quadripinnate, the segments somewhat truncate.
Pinnae: bi- to tripinnate.

Pinnules: pinnate to bipinnate.
Sori: occurring on pinnule margins in the axis between the pinnules on veins which extend through the fruit dots.
Indusium: cup-like.

HABITAT: caves and grottoes on acid formations.

GEOGRAPHICAL TYPE: Circumpolar.

DISTRIBUTION: in North America through Ohio, Illinois, Kentucky, Tennessee, Wisconsin, Virginia. Rare, especially in the northern part of its range.

CULTIVATION: as for the other filmy ferns.

VARIETIES: none recorded.

Trichomanes speciosum
Trichomanes radicans
The Killarney fern
The bristle fern

Another of the filmy ferns, with fronds whose structure and texture is so flimsy that they can grow only in places where the atmospheric humidity is perpetually above dew-point. It is, as might be expected, essentially a tropical fern and only occurs in outlying stations in the

temperate regions of the world, where it is generally rather rare. It is, like the other filmy ferns, a dwarf plant with very bright green ferns, in this case arising from a black stock.

DESCRIPTION: dwarf, monomorphic wintergreen creeping fern of an exceptionally delicate nature.

Stock: very thin, up to 1 mm diameter, creeping on the surface of soil or more usually rock, much branched, usually alternately black, more or less densely covered with almost black hairs.

Fronds: arising alternately from the creeping stock at intervals of 4 cm up to 20 cm, usually about ½ that size.

Stalks: as long as the blade, never longer, usually slightly shorter, black, wiry, winged.

Rachis: black, wiry, also winged.

Blade: ovate-lanceolate in outline, bright deep green, firmer in texture than its delicate appearance would lead one to believe: the blades persist for 3 years.

Branching: pinnate.

Pinnae: lanceolate in outline, doubly or trebly pinnatifid, irregularly presented on the rachis, varying from alternate to almost opposite.

Venation: not established.

Sori: occurring only on the margins of the upper pinnae, usually on the acroscopic side, small.

Indusium: cup-shaped.

Receptacle: bristly, projecting as much as 5 mm or more from the margin, giving the fern one of its popular names.

HABITAT: in conditions of extreme humidity, in the mist-spray areas of waterfalls, often epiphytic on rocks or trees: occasionally by streamsides, especially in rain forests.

GEOGRAPHICAL TYPE: Pantropical.

DISTRIBUTION: north-western Europe including Great Britain and France, western Spain, Portugal, the Azores, the Canary Islands, Madeira: the Himalayas, Burma, China, Japan: western Africa including the off-shore islands: Polynesia, the Hawaiian Islands; North America, (confined to Mexico and Alabama); the West Indies; Brazil, Equador.

CULTIVATION: an ideal and delightful plant for a Wardian case or bottle garden: virtually impossible out of doors.

VARIETIES: none recorded.

CHAPTER THIRTEEN

Woodland Ferns

More of the ferns that occur in the cool temperate regions of the world will be found growing in woodland than in any other type of habitat. There are two reasons for this. The first is that those regions of the temperate world in which ferns are found are basically heavily wooded and were, certainly until the beginnings of agriculture, in about 5000 B.C., almost entirely covered by forest. The other is an evolutionary reason. The ferns evolved in a world of high-humidity forests, those great primaeval forests of giant clubmosses and horsetails of which the ferns themselves, including the great tree ferns, were an element and which laid down the great coal seams of today. The forest is historically their natural environment. Those ferns, such as the mountain ferns and wall ferns, have evolved away from the norm in being able to survive under their special conditions. Possibly in the days when the pteridophytes were the dominant vegetations of the world, they were the pioneer plants, much like the ephemerals of the world of today—plants that produce many generations in each growing season, and colonise newly bared earth—and in which the angiosperms are dominant.

Although the ferns in this chapter are mainly woodland ferns, that does not necessarily mean that they will invariably and without exception be found growing in woodland, although they are most likely to be found growing in woodland. Some of the species are decidedly more adaptable than others: the hart's-tongue fern *Asplenium scolopendrium*, and the polypodies *Polypodium spp.*, will be found growing fairly frequently in other situations, particularly on walls, although their growth in those situations will usually be somewhat stunted if compared with specimens growing in woodland. The fronds, too, will almost invariably be yellower where the fern is growing on a wall, where it is more exposed to sunlight and to the winds, than it would be if it were growing in true woodland.

Adiantum pedatum
The North American
maidenhair fern

Though commonly known as the North American maidenhair fern, its range extends far beyond the U.S.A., running through the Aleutian Islands to Kamchatka and Japan. It is probably the most charming, as well as the best-known of North American ferns, and probably also the one fern that the majority of non-pteridophiles could be relied upon to recognise.

DESCRIPTION: low-growing deciduous monomorphic woodland fern.

Stock: slender, creeping, freely branching, dark brown, the younger parts densely clothed in light brown scales, the older parts becoming smooth except for the stumps of the old stalks; roots, slender, dark brown, short, mostly occurring near the growing tip, decaying quickly once their usefulness is past.

Fronds: deciduous; up to about 30 cm tall, sometimes a little more.

Stalks: up to about 30 cm tall, slender, brittle, shining dark blackish brown, smooth except for a very small number of scales at the base.

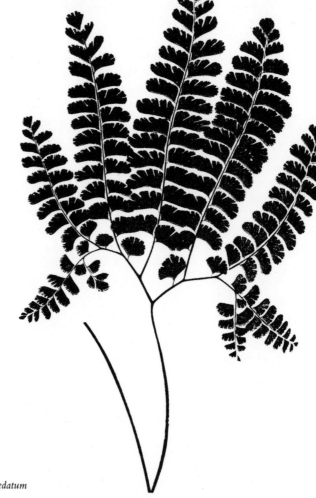

Adiantum pedatum

Rachis: dark brown to dark green, shiny, smooth.

Blade: bent abruptly back from the stalk and carried parallel with the ground, roughly circular in outline.

Branching: technically pedate—that is branching like a bird's foot, each branch being regarded as a pinna. There may be up to as many as 12 pinnae on each frond, though 8 or 9 are more normal.

Pinnae: lanceolate in outline, up to 12 cm long, pinnate.

Pinnules: oblong with cuneate bases, the margin deeply cleft, the midrib running close to the basiscopic edge.

Venation: not established.

Sori: occurring on the acroscopic pinnule margins.

Indusium: formed by the incurling of the pinnule margins.

HABITAT: deep rich soils in shaded woodland situations.

GEOGRAPHICAL TYPE: Circumpolar.

DISTRIBUTION: in North America from Nova Scotia to British Columbia, thence southwards to Georgia and Arkansas; the Aleutian Islands; Kamchatka; Japan.

CULTIVATION: fully frost-hardy and easily grown in any good leafy soil in a shaded border.

VARIETIES: *A.p. aleuticum* is a form from the Aleutian Islands differing from the type only in that it is rather dwarf, growing only 10 or 15 cm tall.

A.p. laciniatum is an entirely new break, recently raised by Reginald Kaye, one of Great Britain's leading pteridologists and fern nurserymen, in which the pinnules are very finely incised. A remarkably beautiful form.

A.p. japonicum differs from the type plant only in that the young fronds are a delicate rose-pink in the spring. It is very attractive.

Asplenium platyneuron
The ebony spleenwort

One of the commonest of the North American spleenworts, attaining a height of 45 cm in the warmer southern states. A striking plant in its season.

DESCRIPTION: small deciduous or semi-wintergreen tufted dimorphic woodland fern.

Stock: erect, thick, covered with a few scales and bearing the black stumps of the old stalks; roots numerous, wiry, wide-spreading.

Fronds: deciduous to semi-wintergreen, up to 45 cm tall, often less than $\frac{1}{2}$ that height. Fertile fronds erect, barren fronds shorter, spreading—both presented in a basket-like tuft.

Stalks: dark blackish-brown, shiny, smooth, stiff, erect, brittle.

Rachis: dark brown, shiny, smooth.

Blade: linear-lanceolate in outline.

Branching: pinnate.

Pinnae: up to 20 pairs, alternate to sub-opposite, sessile, narrowly oblong, pointed, lobed on the acroscopic side; fertile pinna narrower than barren pinna.

Venation: not established.

Sori: numerous, confluent, arranged in herringbone fashion on the undersides of the fertile pinna.

Indusium: silvery when young, soon disappearing.

HABITAT: woodlands, hedgebanks.

GEOGRAPHICAL TYPE: Circumpolar.

DISTRIBUTION: in North America from Nova Scotia to Florida.

CULTIVATION: does best in a gritty soil in a shaded situation. If grown in a pan is very sensitive to overwatering.

VARIETIES: *A.p. incisum* differs from the type in having the pinnae deeply incised. A striking variety.

A.p. proliferum is of little garden merit, and differs from the type only in that it has occasional proliferous buds on the stems, and these sometimes produce small fronds which can be used to propagate new plants.

Asplenium resiliens
The black-stemmed
spleenwort

This North American species is very closely related to the ebony spleenwort being, in effect, its southern counterpart. However, while the range of the ebony spleenwort overlaps that of the black-stemmed spleenwort, the black-stemmed spleenwort does not reach into the more northerly ranges of the ebony spleenwort. *A. resiliens* may be distinguished by its almost black stem and rachis, by the opposite as opposed to alternate to sub-opposite arrangement of the pinnae, and by the fact that with this species the fertile and barren fronds are both the same length and form.

DESCRIPTION: low-growing tufted dimorphic (though not obviously so) wintergreen woodland fern.

Stock: short, creeping, sometimes somewhat erect, the younger parts covered in stiff black scales, the older parts thickly beset with the persistent stalk bases; roots numerous, fine, wiry, branching, forming a tangled mass.

Fronds: dimorphic, wintergreen, up to 20 cm tall, erect.

Stalks: very short, less than $\frac{1}{16}$ the length of the blade, stiff, brittle, dark black-brown, shiny, erect.

Rachis: dark brown-black, smooth, shiny.

Blade: lanceolate in outline, erect.

Branching: pinnate.

Pinnae: narrowly oblong, somewhat lobed on the acroscopic side, sessile, always opposite. Blunt-tipped, tooth-edged, the lower pairs reflexed.

Venation: not established.

Sori: oblong.
Indusium: whitish when young, short-lived.

HABITAT: woodlands and hedge-banks.

GEOGRAPHICAL TYPE: Circumpolar.

DISTRIBUTION: in North America from New York southwards.

CULTIVATION: easily grown in any gritty medium, ideal for a shaded corner of the rock garden. Not particularly frost-hardy, and if grown in a pan in a cold house will prove very sensitive to overwatering.

VARIETIES: none recorded.

Asplenium scolopendrium
Phyllitis scolopendrium
Scolopendrium vulgare
The hart's-tongue fern

Tufted wintergreen fern so variable that a wander through a woodland colony of it will scarcely reveal a single, true, text-book example. On the other hand, it is so distinct in its general appearance that there is little chance of confusion arising. Even its multiplicity of variations contain nothing that could be confused with plants of any other genera.

The hart's-tongue was known to generations of gardeners under the generic name *Scolopendrium*, and even now is often referred to by fern enthusiasts affectionately as 'scolly'. The derivation of the name is interesting. It is taken from the name of a centipede, *Scolopendra*, because of the fancied resemblance of the sori to the legs of a centipede—which is, perhaps, not as far-fetched as some derivations.

DESCRIPTION: low-growing tufted monomorphic wintergreen fern.
Stock: short, upright, much branched, almost hidden by the almost vertical frond-stalks, light brown, the younger parts very densely clothed with light brown lanceolate scales with heart-shaped bases; roots black, wiry, sparse, shallowly creeping.
Fronds: very variable in size, 10–65 cm long, up to 12 cm wide, arising erect and then strongly curved outwards and downwards.
Stalks: very variable in length, anything from $\frac{1}{4}$–$\frac{1}{2}$ as long as the blade, green to brown becoming almost black towards the base, semicylindrical with a flat or shallowly convex face; the base swollen and covered with scales similar to those of the stock.
Blade: very variable, 5–50 cm long, up to 12 cm wide, more typically about 25–30 cm long and no more than 5 cm wide, typically simple, strap-shaped (technically linear-lanceolate) in outline, base typically heart-shaped, apex typically pointed, occasionally more or less digitate or crested, margin typically slightly wavy, occasionally pronouncedly wavy, normally entire, rarely serrated, bright green: midrib stout, covered when young

with soft, white hairs becoming light brown or reddish brown.

Venation: Taenopteridian.

Sori: linear, occurring in pairs on either side of a vein, often running together to form a cigar-shaped mass, variable in length, frequently running from midrib to margin: occurring more frequently on the upper part of the blade and often covering most of the upper $\frac{2}{3}$.

Indusium: membraneous, transparent at first, changing to dark brown when ripe, opening inwards.

HABITAT: wood, forests, hedgebanks, less commonly on walls. Most common on limestone formations, less common elsewhere.

GEOGRAPHICAL TYPE: Circumpolar.

DISTRIBUTION: throughout Europe, where it is one of the commonest ferns; north Africa, the Azores, Madeira; Asia Minor into Persia; Japan; eastern North America where it is uncommon (originally recorded from New Brunswick and Ontario, New York State and Tennessee); possibly now extinct in some of its original haunts, but becoming more widely distributed as a garden escape.

CULTIVATION: one of the easiest ferns to grow provided that the soil is not too acid: an excellent rock plant or plant for a border at the foot of a north wall. The plant is so variable that literally hundreds of varieties have been named in the past, many almost indistinguishable from each other. Any ramble through a colony will reveal forms that deviate to a greater or lesser degree from the normal, and many of these are worth cultivating. The majority of really fine forms do, however, remain in cultivation, and many of them come true from spores. The hart's-tongue is one of the few ferns that can be increased by cuttings of the old frond bases, which will form bulbils when pegged down into sandy compost, which will ultimately grow into mature plants identical to the parent: some forms are sterile and this is the only method of propagating these, especially since few growers would be prepared to divide a healthy, thriving specimen plant.

VARIETIES: *A.s. capitatum:* fronds terminate in a heavy crest.

A.s. cervi-cornu: frond narrow, margin finely and sharply toothed and lobed with a curious, warty, raised ridge running along the back parallel with the midrib but close to the margin; apex branched, ridged.

A.s. conglomeratum: frond normal, apical crest very large and twisted in relation to the axis of the blade.

A.s. cornutum abruptum: the frond apex abruptly truncated, the midrib becoming winged towards the apex. Now very rare.

A.s. coronatum: indistinguishable from *A.s. capitatum.*

A.s. crispum: frond margin deeply and sharply frilled like an Elizabethan ruff. A very beautiful plant

Asplenium scolopendrium capitatum

Asplenium scolopendrium cornutum abruptum

at its best, but there are many forms in cultivation and they are not distinguished by name. The best forms are invariably sterile and can only be propagated vegetatively. Some of the less fine forms occasionally produce spores, and a proportion of the sporelings will prove as good or better than their parents.

A.s. crispum cristatum: similar to the above, except that the apex of the frond is additionally crested; again, there are several forms in cultivation and they are not distinguished by names.

A.s. crispum fertile: a fertile frilled form, the frilling somewhat spoiled by the presence of the sporangia. However, since it is fertile it is readily increased by spores, which come largely true. It is ideal where a large number of plants are required for a mass planting.

A.s. crispum fimbriatum Drummondiae: fronds rather narrow, frilled and fimbriate, the apex dividing into a fine digitate crest. The tips may be layered to produce young plants that will be identical with the parent.

A.s. crispum 'Golden Queen': variegated hart's-tongues crop up from time to time, but most of them prove inconstant in cultivation: it is thought that the variegation may often be due to soil conditions which no longer obtain once the plant is removed from its wild station. In this case, however, the golden-green leaves remain pretty constant in colour, varying slightly from year to year, but on the whole remaining true. The fronds are well-frilled.

A.s. crispum 'Moly': a distinct form from the others in that the apex tapers to a rather abrupt point.

A.s. crispum muricatum: another frilled hart's-tongue, but with the surface of the frond erupting into elongated, warty projections, forming a rough surface. Quite distinct, with its rather greyish colouring.

A.s. crispum nobile: undoubtedly the finest of the frilled varieties, with dark green fronds reaching as much as 60 cm long and 10 cm wide, very deeply frilled.

A.s. cristatum: this is an aggregate rather than a variety, for many forms differing quite substantially from one another have been collected over the years, yet are all lumped together under the one name. Typically the frond divides about $\frac{2}{3}$ of the way up its length, the divisions dividing again, and occasionally yet again, each division terminating in a crest. In some cases the divisions are arranged in fan-fashion, in others they are corymbose. Some of the best are sterile, but many of the better ones are fertile, and a sowing of spores may produce some really outstanding plants. The sterile forms will come true from frond-base methods of propagation.

A.s. digitatum: basically a cristate form of the fan-type in which the fanning is so pronounced as to have assumed the characteristics of fingers, so that the crests are spread flat in the same plane as the blade, well spaced like the fingers of an opened hand.

A.s. laceratum: the edges of the frond are deeply and irregularly toothed, somewhat lobed, with the apex round and toothed rather than pointed.

A.s. laceratum 'Kaye's Variety': is superior to the above, the frond being very broadly ovate (as much as 10 cm wide in proportion to a length of no more than 30 cm), the margins very deeply cleft, the tips of the lobes tending to form minute crests.

A.s. marginato-multifidum: curious, possibly not beautiful, but never fails to attract attention, this is one of the varieties with rather greyish-green fronds with distinct, warty ridges on the upper surfaces

Asplenium scolopendrium digitatum

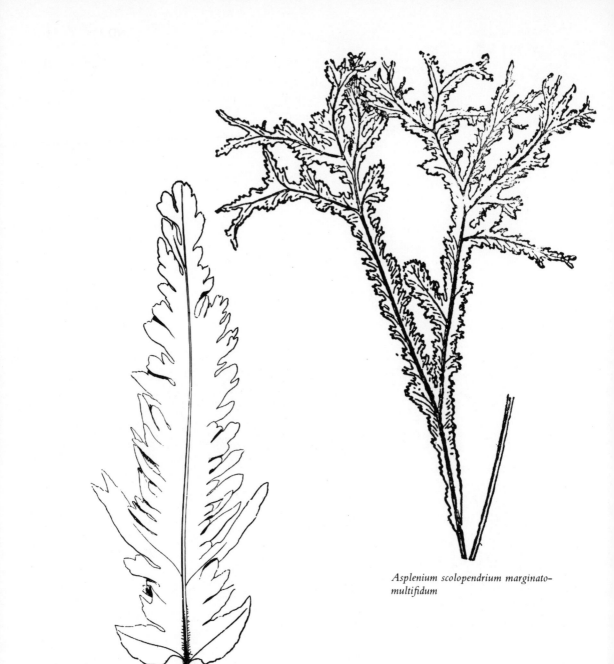

Asplenium scolopendrium marginato-
multifidum

Asplenium scolopendrium laceratum

of the fronds: the frond is deeply cleft into 2, 3 or occasionally more lobes, the lobes themselves being lacerated, the forking frequently occurring as low down as the stalk as well as in the blade.

A.s. marginatum: another of the grey-green varieties, the frond narrow, the margin deeply lobed with a raised ridge running close to and parallel with the margin. Again, curious rather than beautiful.

A.s. marginatum irregulare: the frond is somewhat broader than in the above variety, the margin less pronouncedly frilled.

A.s. muricatum: the whole upper surface of the frond is covered with irregularly placed warty wrinkles and ridges. Another of the grey-green varieties.

A.s. ramo-cristatum: a form with narrow fronds which branch repeatedly from the base, each section terminating in a fine crest.

A.s. ramo-marginatum: even finer than the above, with very narrow fronds with deeply frilled margins, branching repeatedly from the base, and terminating in exceptionally fine crests. One of the best.

A.s. sagittatum: very different from the other varieties, the variation being confined mainly to the

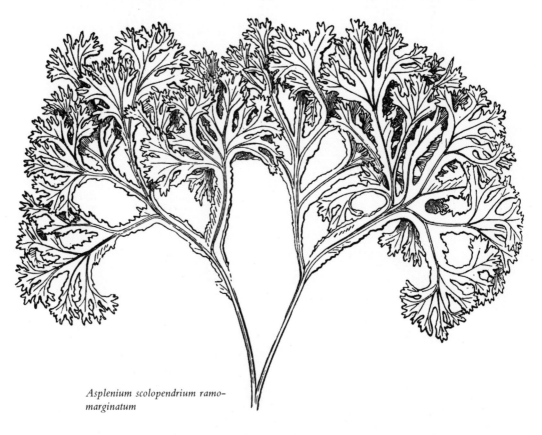

Asplenium scolopendrium ramo-marginatum

lobes at the bases of the frond. These are greatly elongated, giving the whole blade an arrow-head appearance.

A.s. sagittatum cristatum: similar to the above but remarkably crested, not only at the apex of the frond but also at the tips of the lobes at the base of each frond.

A.s. transverso-multifidum: a form with huge capitate crests, the branches of the heads crossing and recrossing each other.

A.s. undulatum: a variety with wavy edges to the fronds. It is not so deeply frilled as *A.s. crispum.* The name embraces two forms, one of which grows to normal hart's-tongue proportions, the other being dwarf, growing no more than 10 cm or so. The two are not distinguished by name.

Asplenium scolopendrium sagittatum-cristatum

Asplenium scolopendrium undulatum

Athyrium filix-femina
The lady fern

This is probably the commonest of all the ferns found in the temperate regions of the northern hemisphere. It is a typical ferny fern and indeed it is probably this fern that most people have in mind when they think of a fern. Having said that, and by implication having given the impression that the lady fern is a stable species, it must at once be pointed out that it is not necessarily the easiest of species to recognise in the field, though this comes fairly easily with a little practice. It is, on the contrary, probably one of the most unstable ferns of the temperate world, and, even within a single colony in a small copse or woodland, it will be difficult to find two plants absolutely identical in all respects. So pronounced is this genetic instability that the lady fern has probably given rise to more recorded varieties than any other fern of the temperate world, including what is probably the most extraordinary variation ever found in the wild, *A.f-f. victoriae.* Over 300 varieties have been named over the years, though it is doubtful whether even as many as one third of these remain in cultivation today.

DESCRIPTION: vigorous clump-forming deciduous monomorphic woodland fern.
Stock: stout, erect, simple but becoming branching with age: in young plants firmly set in the ground, but growing out of the ground with age and in time forming a short trunk-like caudex, up to about 10 cm high, densely beset with the decaying stubs of the old leaf-stalks through which the coarse, black, sparsely branched roots have to find their way down to the soil; the stock is clothed with lanceolate scales varying in colour

Athyrium filix-femina

from very dark brown to almost black.

Fronds: lanceolate in outline, bright green, sometimes yellowish-green, rather soft-textured and somewhat limp.

Stalks: varying from $\frac{1}{4}$–$\frac{1}{3}$ as long as the blade, the base swollen and broadened, blackish-purple, becoming green as it tapers upwards, lightly covered in brown lanceolate scales.

Rachis: pale green, slightly grooved or flattened on the face, lightly covered with hairs or lanceolate scales.

Blade: up to 70 cm long and as much as 25 cm wide.

Branching: bipinnate, becoming tripinnate in the lower $\frac{1}{3}$.

Pinnae: linear-lanceolate to linear-oblong in outline, up to about 30 on either side of the rachis, normally alternate but with a tendency towards becoming sub-opposite, this tendency becoming more pronounced with the lower pinnae; sessile or at most very shortly stalked, set very close together on the rachis.

Pinnules: again alternate but with a tendency towards the sub-opposite, this tendency becoming more pronounced in the pinnules nearest the rachis; oblong or oblong-lanceolate in outline, the upper segments pinnately lobed, the lower segments pinnately toothed.

Venation: Pecopteridian.

Sori: occurring on the lowest acroscopic veinlets and forming a conspicuous row on either side of the pinnule midrib; oblong or even linear in shape, seldom straight, usually hooked or curved, horse-shoe shaped, or kidney-shaped.

Indusium: also hooked, horse-shoe shaped or kidney-shaped, persistent, attached on one side only, the free margin usually irregularly toothed, the whole somewhat inflated.

HABITAT: woodland, hedgerows, less often damp meadows.

GEOGRAPHICAL TYPE: Cosmopolitan.

DISTRIBUTION: Europe; Asia into northern India and thence to China; Japan; Java; North Africa to the Azores, the Canary Islands, Madeira; temperate northern and north-eastern North America from British Columbia to Newfoundland, southwards to California and across to Florida; Central America from Mexico southwards into South America as far south as Peru.

CULTIVATION: easy in any soil rich in humus, particularly leaf-mould or peat. To do really well it also needs shelter from wind and shade, at least during the heat of the day. The numerous and often outstanding varieties, together with its ease of culture, make this one of the most desirable of all ferns for the garden.

VARIETIES: numerous varieties have been recorded, the great majority collected from the wild during the heyday of the Victorian fern craze. Perhaps no more than a third of these are still in cultivation today, but many varieties thought lost may still be found growing, their value completely unrealised, in cottage gardens, especially in the Old World. Owing to the genetic instability of this fern, others may be rediscovered: the majority were wild finds in the first place. Examples follow.

A.f-f. acrocladon: one of the rarest and most prized of all the varieties of the lady fern, this is an extra-ordinary plant whose fronds branch and rebranch continually through-out the growing season until in late summer. The plant is simply a ball-like mass of beautifully interwoven ferny verdure: 20–30 cm. It seldom produces spores, but when it does

Athyrium filix-femina acrocladon

J

these are well worth growing on. A proportion of the sporelings will closely resemble the parent, and many will be even more extraordinary. *A. f-f. unco-glomeratum* (*q.v.*) was raised in this way.

A. f-f. angusto-cristatum: an aggregate rather than a variety, the very finest forms are, alas, to be found only in the history books. The characteristics are very narrow arching fronds no more than 45 cm long by 3.5 cm wide, the apex branched to a greater or lesser degree. The really striking part of the frond is the pinnae, which are reduced to pairs of cruciate pinnules of very regular form—the more symmetrical the pinnae the finer the form. Fertile. Some excellent plants can be raised from spores.

A. f-f. caput-medusae: an extraordinary and yet very beautiful variety, also rather rare. In some ways it does not look at all like a fern, and it has been known for it to be mistaken for parsley! Rather difficult to identify as a variety of *A. f-f.*, since it lacks what are normally recognised as pinnae: what is visible above ground is simply a cluster of bare stems topped by a congested mass of very dense cresting. Fertile, but only a minute proportion come true from spores, which explains why these should be grown on for at least three years before any sort of selection is made, as the true characteristics do not reveal themselves until the plant is reaching its full size. The spores that do not

come true will still produce a large number of very interesting varieties, either cristate or tasselled. Seldom exceeds 15 cm.

A. f-f. clarissima: one of the rarest *A. f-f.* varieties, but not perhaps as beautiful as some of the others. Fronds up to 120 cm long and as much as 60 cm wide—very wide in proportion to the length, the pinnae and pinnules very slender and very finely divided into narrow segments, giving this fern a quite exceptionally elegant appearance. It is very slow to increase naturally, taking many years for the stock to branch. Although sori are present they do not produce fertile spores. On the other hand, it was with this variety that the phenomenon of spospory was first discovered, although this has proved an unreliable method of reproducing this variety, the young plants seldom being as fine as the parent.

A. f-f. clarissima cristatum: similar to the above but differing in having beautifully crested pinnae. It is light green or even golden-green in colour, and seldom grows more than 60 cm. Though aposporous, really only comes true if plants are increased by division.

A. f-f. congestum: again an aggregate name embracing, as the name suggests, several congested varieties. Characteristic plants have a drastically reduced rachis and densely imbricated pinnae. Seldom above 15 cm.

A. f-f. congestum cristatum: a dwarf congested form similar to the above, but having the added charm of a fine crest. About 20 cm.

A. f-f. congestum grandiceps: a form with a very large apical crest and crested pinnae. About 20 cm.

A. f-f. congestum minus: the smallest of the congested forms and a very pretty plant. The pinnae overlap and the frond apex is sharply pointed. Not above 15 cm.

A. f-f. coronatum: this 'crowned' variety has a heavy apical crest, but the pinnae are not crested. To 20 cm. A very handsome variety. Though fertile, only a very small proportion of sporelings come even remotely true. Division is the only means of perpetuating the form itself. Sporelings, although interesting and often well crested, are invariably inferior.

A. f-f. corymbiferum: again an aggregate name and, since this is a relatively common variation on the filix-femina theme, there are, as might be expected, better and worse forms. The characteristics are very heavy apical cresting, the crests dividing again and again to give a bunched, tassellated effect. The pinnae are similarly crested, though to a lesser degree.

A. f-f. craigii cristatum: a rather mediocre crested form, made more attractive by the comparatively narrow frond and the irregularly placed pinnae, the lower ones being spaced more widely apart than the upper ones. Fertile, 30 cm.

A. f-f. crispatum: a dwarf variety with fronds up to 15 cm, the fronds overlapping and very deeply dissected. Fertile.

A. f-f. crispum: probably the most dwarf of all the varieties of the lady fern, growing no more than 10 cm, and distinct on account of its slowly spreading, mat-forming habit. Fronds ramose, cristate. Very pretty, very rare. Division.

A. f-f. crispum coronans: similar to the above but slightly larger growing, up to 10 to 15 cm high, and with very large terminal crests. Very rare. Division.

A. f-f. cristatum: an aggregate name embracing a number of forms of varying merit, some worthless, some really rather good. In the past many of these had varietal names, but now only a very small number of exceptionally fine forms are named separately. The characteristics of this aggregate are flat, fan-like crests at the apex and on the pinnae. 20–50 cm. Fertile, sporelings usually more or less good.

A. f-f. cristulatum: a dwarf variety 20–30 cm tall with a terminal crest that is huge in proportion to the frond.

A. f-f. cruciatum congestum: a fascinating dwarf form which is both cruciate (i.e. the pinnae criss-cross) and congested, the fronds being no more than 30 cm long and a mere 2–2.5 cm wide, very stiff, and very dark green. Gradually forms small clumps. Division.

A. f-f. curtum: a dwarf up to 30 cm, smaller in all its parts than the type form, but differing little otherwise. Fertile.

A. f-f. curtum cristatum: similar to

the above, differing only in the neatly crested pinnae.

A. f-f. depauperatum edelsteinii: a misleadingly named variety which is not depauperate at all. It is a rather neat, singularly bright green variety with curiously twisted terminal and pinnae crests, the twisting being more pronounced in the terminal crest. 30 cm or a little more.

A. f-f. diadematum: this variety almost but not quite qualifies as a grandiceps. It has a very large dense corymbose terminal crest. Frond size normal. Fertile, sporelings very variable.

A. f-f. fieldiae: one of the stronger-growing varieties, reaching as much as 90 cm with good cultivation; it has long, very narrow fronds and bold, cruciate pinnae.

A. f-f. flabellipinnulum: a dwarf variety to 30 cm, with narrow fronds and deeply toothed pinnules.

A. f-f. foliosum grandiceps: unique among the lady fern varieties in being foliose, the pinnules being extraordinarily wide and leafy, overlapping, the frond terminating in a huge, handsome crest. One of the most remarkable varieties. 30–45 cm.

A. f-f. frizelliae: quite unlike any other variety of this or any other fern, it is so striking that it has even gained for itself a common name—something rather rare among fern varieties: it is known as the 'tatting fern', and for anyone familiar with the old-fashioned knotted lace edging work of tatting, that is an excellent description. The pinnae have been reduced to tiny congested balls of greenery, and the effect is dramatic. Up to 50 cm. Fertile. The two original finds, both in Ireland and each miles

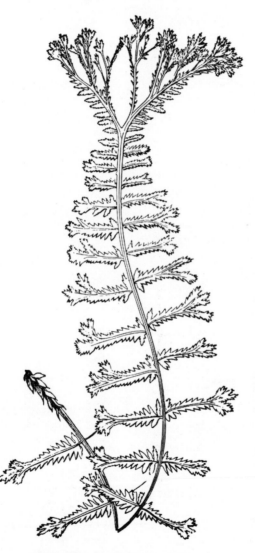

Athyrium filix-femina depauperatum edelsteinii

from the other, were not crested, but sowings of spores have produced a small proportion of crested forms, and from these a number of good crested forms have been produced. Botanists, of course, regard any deviation from the type plant as a monstrosity, and in a similar way the purists among pteridophiles claim that cresting spoils the lines of the frond, and in this case the claim is somewhat justified: by and large the cresting detracts from the tatting.

Athyrium filix-femina fieldiae

Athyrium filix-femina frizelliae

A. f-f. frizelliae capitatum: a tatting fern with a many-branched apical crest. 45 cm.

A. f-f. frizelliae cristatum: another crested tatting fern, but with a densely branched crest of such huge proportions that it would qualify

Athyrium filix-femina frizelliae capitatum

for the gradiceps classification: however, the tatting is regarded as the more important characteristic. The weight of the crest is such that it causes the frond to bend gracefully outwards. 30 cm.

A. f-f. frizelliae multifidum: (syn. *ramo-cristatum*) A ramose tatting fern, the fronds branching about $\frac{2}{3}$–$\frac{3}{4}$ of the way up and thence repeatedly forming a loose, broadly spreading crest.

A. f-f. frizelliae nanum: a dwarf, non-crested tatting fern, possibly now lost.

A. f-f. frizelliae ramosissimum: another dwarf form up to 15 cm, the fronds branching repeatedly from the base. Also possibly lost.

A. f-f. gemmatum: a remarkable variety with very dense corymbose crests on the pinnae and frond apices. There are two forms: 'Bolton's' with a reddish rachis, and 'Barnes's' with a green rachis. Fertile, but sporelings are invariably inferior. Division.

A. f-f. glomeratum: a form in which the crests on the pinnae are broader than the pinnae themselves, with a fine terminal crest. 60 cm.

A. f-f. grandiceps: a typical grandiceps variety with really huge terminal crests to the fronds. Some of the finest forms have been given separate names, and the varietal name should perhaps be regarded as an aggregate. The majority of plants come more or less true from spores, but a few are barren and can be increased by division only. Sporelings should not be selected until their third year, since they do not show their true characteristics when younger than that.

A. f-f. howardii: a very rare variety, generally barren and therefore increased only by division. The fronds are exceedingly finely divided, giving a delightful lacy effect and lightly crested. The pinnules are incredibly narrow.

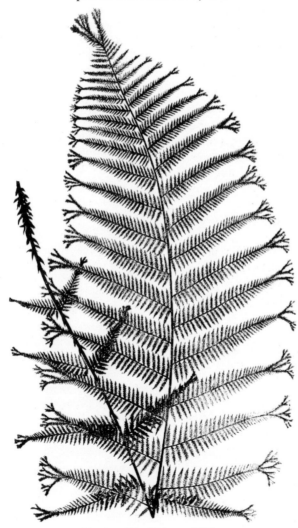

Athyrium filix-femina multifidum

A. f-f. kalothrix: a very beautiful variety, now believed lost, but mentioned here in case someone somewhere has a plant of it and does not realise its value: also because, apart from a wild find made in Ireland, it was also raised at the Oxford Botanic Gardens from a sowing of spores from a plumose variety, and this just might occur again. It is a plumose variety with what are probably the most finely divided fronds of all the lady ferns.

A. f-f. mediodeficiens polydactylum: one of the depauperate varieties, and exceptional in that it is a really effective garden plant. Many depauperate varieties merely look moth-eaten, but not this one. The depauperation is symmetrical, with the pinnae greatly reduced but branching into many-fingered crests. A vigorous variety up to 45 cm, the stock branching freely. A high proportion of sporelings come more or less true.

A. f-f. minutissimum: often described or classified as a congested form, but incorrectly. It is, in fact, nothing more nor less than a miniature lady fern, perfect in all details and perfectly proportioned. It grows to about 7 cm in sun, up to about 12 cm in shade, gradually forming a clump of small crowns.

A. f-f. multifidum: a cristate variety with the whole frond finely cut: the crests are slender and highly refined. 30 cm.

A. f-f. nudicaule cristatum: a strange variety with a long rachis from which most or rarely all the pinnae are missing, terminating in a huge crest; really a grandiceps variety, and also technically depauperate. 30 cm.

A. f-f. percristatum: a heavily crested form with the pinnae well crested as well as the apex. Strong-growing, up to 90 cm.

A. f-f. plumosum: decidedly an aggregate, many forms having been found in the wild, and many more raised in cultivation. Typically the fronds are of a light, almost translucent yellowish bright green, tripinnate or even quadripinnate, giving them a delightful feathery effect. Some of the most beautiful of the lady ferns belong to this section. In general the plumose character comes true from spores, but many forms are infertile. Sporelings often combine the plumose character with other variations, particularly the cristate, but usually at the expense of the plumose character. Again, sporelings should not be selected until at least their third year, since they are unlikely to show their true character much before then.

A. f-f. p. barnesii: a typical plumose variety, except that the stem is red.

A. f-f. p. cristatum: the name given to crested plumose varieties. Again, an aggregate; the plants varying in their decorative quality.

A. f-f. p. 'Druery': this is the finest of all the true plumose varieties, and was raised by C. T. Druery, one of the great Victorian fern hunters, growers and popularisers of pteridomania, after whom it is named. Each pinna is like a miniature frond.

A. f-f. p. furcillans: a lightly but delightfully crested plumose lady fern.

A. f-f. p. 'Penny': probably the most robust of the plumose varieties, reaching as much as 120 cm with good cultivation.

A. f-f. p. percristatum: a delicately crested plumose variety, the cresting occurring on pinnules and pinnae as well as at the frond apices.

A. f-f. p. superbum: an outstanding variety raised from spores of *A. f-f. p.* 'Druery'. Division. Very rare.

A. f-f. prichardii: a cruciate form closely resembling *A. f-f. fieldiae* but more vigorous. Up to 120 cm.

A. f-f. ramo-cristatum: typically the fronds branch from about half way up the rachis, the tips of each division being crested.

A. f-f. regale: this variety is both plumose and cristate, combining the best of both characteristics. Distinct, strong growing, to 120 cm, and certainly regal.

A. f-f. revolvens: a curious form with the ends of the fronds spirally twisted and congested. Comes pretty well true from spores.

A. f-f. semicruciatum: fronds cristate on the lower half of the frond, suddenly becoming cruciate, but terminating in a fine crest.

A. f-f. setigerum: another aggregate name with, as might be expected, plants of greater or lesser decorative value. The best have been named. Typically the plant has a setigerous character—i.e. it is bristly: both the pinnae and the pinnules are divided into bristly segments. 60 cm.

Athyrium filix-femina victoriae

A. f-f. unco-glomeratum: strictly speaking, this should probably be referred to *A. f-f. acrocladon*, from spores of which it was originally raised, and of which it is really only a superior form. Like that plant it forms a spherical mass of soft greenery. 15 cm. Possibly now lost to cultivation.

A. f-f. vernoniae: an unmistakable form with broadly triangular pinnae, strongly crisped. Comes true. 120 cm.

A. f-f. victoriae: anyone who dismisses fern varieties as mere monstrosities should have a look at this one. It is probably the most beautiful 'monstrosity' ever found. It is a robust grower, exceeding 120 cm with good cultivation, perfectly symmetrical, perfectly cruciate, and perfectly crested, the crests being in perfect balance with the proportions of the fronds, pinnae and pinnules. It comes true from spores, but the sporelings somehow never quite seem to have the quality of the original wild find. Two sporelings have been named: *A. f-f. v. foliosum,* which is a very vigorous form, larger growing than the type plant, up to 150 cm, the refinement of the type plant being rather obscured by the broad pinnae; and *A. f-f. v. gracile,* in which the pinnae are more finely cut.

A. f-f. victoriae × setigerum: a man-made hybrid which combines the best of both parents.

Athyrium pycnocarpum
Asplenium
pycnocarpum
Asplenium
angustifolium
The narrow-leaved
spleenwort

A rather slender, graceful, North American woodland fern with narrow deciduous fronds that usually grow in almost circular clusters of five or six. Though dimorphic, this characteristic is not particularly noticeable.

DESCRIPTION: deciduous, dimorphic, woodland fern.
Stock: up to 1 cm thick, creeping, rarely branching, the younger parts densely clothed in dark brown scales, the older parts bearing the remains of the persistent stalks; roots wiry, black, numerous, forming large tangled masses.
Fronds: dimorphic, the fertile fronds being fractionally taller and more erect than the barren ones, deciduous, up to 90 cm tall.
Stalks: about ¼ as long as the blades, stout, green, becoming darker to almost brown towards the base where they also become slightly scaly.
Rachis: green, slightly hairy on the underside.
Blade: lanceolate in outline, coriaceous.
Branching: pinnate.
Pinnae: simple, lanceolate in outline, opposite, well spaced, particularly on the fertile fronds, the lower ones somewhat deflexed.
Venation: not established.
Fertile fronds: differing from barren fronds in the wider spacing of the pinnae.
Sori: long, slightly curving, running from the pinnae midribs almost to the margins, arranged in parallel rows pointing outwards towards the tip of the pinnae.
Indusium: long, narrow, curved.

HABITAT: open sunny glades in woodland, hedgebanks.

GEOGRAPHICAL TYPE: Circumpolar.

DISTRIBUTION: in North America from Newfoundland to Alaska and southwards to Florida.

CULTIVATION: easily grown in any deep, rich, well drained leafy soil, preferably in a sunny spot but sheltered from cold winds. Fully frost-hardy.

VARIETIES: none recorded.

Athyrium
thelypteroides
The silvery
spleenwort

A reasonably strong-growing North American deciduous woodland fern, deriving its common name from its silvery indusia. Though dimorphic, this is not as apparent as it is in many other species. Unlikely to be confused with other ferns because, in addition to the silvery indusia, the undersides of the fronds are covered in pale yellow hairs.

DESCRIPTION: medium-sized deciduous dimorphic woodland fern.
Stock: stout, creeping, very seldom but occasionally branching, the younger parts densely clothed in light brown scales, the older

parts in the blackish stumps of the old stalks; roots wiry, long, branched, forming a large tangled mass.

Fronds: up to about 90 cm, deciduous.

Stalks: much shorter than the blade, seldom more than ⅛ the length of the blade, stout, green, hairy, slightly scaly, somewhat thickened and darker in colour at the base.

Rachis: pale green, slightly scaly and very hairy, the hairs being pale yellowish-white.

Blade: lanceolate in outline.

Branching: pinnate.

Pinnae: up to 30 pairs, opposite or sub-opposite, the lowest pinnae deflexed, all deeply pinnatifid, oblong to oblong linear in outline, the lowest pinna very short.

Venation: not established.

Fertile fronds: almost identical, but narrower in outline, the pinnae somewhat further spaced than on the barren fronds.

Sori: large, glaucous, beset with silvery hairs.

Indusium: silvery, somewhat inflated.

HABITAT: rich, moist, well-drained woodland soils, damp hedgebanks.

GEOGRAPHICAL TYPE: Circumpolar.

DISTRIBUTION: in North America from Nova Scotia to Florida.

CULTIVATION: easy in any good rich garden soil. Fully frost-hardy.

VARIETIES: none recorded.

Blechnum discolor
The crown fern

A striking wintergreen woodland fern, in essence a larger version of the common hard fern, *Blechnum spicant*, but differing from that species in its much larger fronds, their more coriaceous nature, and in the fact that it produces a distinct caudex as much as 45 cm tall.

DESCRIPTION: larged tufted dimorphic wintergreen woodland fern forming a distinct caudex.

Stock: stout, erect, forming a caudex up to 50 cm high, the younger parts densely clothed in bright brown hairs and scales, the older parts in the old leaf stumps among which is a mass of fibrous brown material.

Fronds: presented in a tuft or crown, polished dark green, wintergreen, dimorphic, the barren fronds spreading, the fertile ones more erect and taller, fronds measuring up to 120 cm long.

Stalks: very short, almost non-existent.

Rachis: dark shining green above, hairy below.

Blade: narrowly lanceolate in outline, dark shining green above, paler below and covered in a cinnamon-coloured tomentium.

Branching: pinnate.

Pinnae: oblong, acute, alternate, close set like the teeth of a comb.
Venation: not established.
Fertile fronds: narrower in outline, the pinnae reduced and linear rather than lanceolate, entirely covered with sori.
Sori: occurring on almost every pinna of the fertile fronds and practically covering the whole underside of each.
Indusium: absent.

HABITAT: moist woodlands.

GEOGRAPHICAL TYPE: Australasian.

DISTRIBUTION: Australia (including Tasmania), Norfolk Island, New Zealand.

CULTIVATION: not particularly frost-hardy, though it will succeed out of doors in areas where frost is not too severe; otherwise it needs to be grown in the greenhouse. A beautiful plant well worth growing, requiring deep rich soil and plenty of shade.

VARIETIES: none recorded.

Blechnum spicant
The hard fern
The ladder fern

A delightful little low-growing fern of great character, and unlikely to be mistaken for any other fern, certainly in the Old World. It owes much of its charm to the production of both fertile and barren fronds, each quite distinct, although obviously conforming to a basic plan.

DESCRIPTION: dwarf, tufted, dimorphic, wintergreen fern.
Stock: upright, tufted, the younger parts clothed with dark brown lanceolate scales.
Fronds: of two types, fertile and barren, the barren ones being produced earlier in the season than the fertile ones, and immediately distinguishable from the fertile ones in their broader segments and their spreading habit.
Barren fronds: up to 15 cm long.
Stalks: dark brown, becoming almost black-brown at the base,

deeply furrowed on the face.
Rachis: rich green, becoming brown at the lower end; deeply furrowed on the face.
Blade: lanceolate in outline, dark green, shiny above, paler green and not shiny below, leathery in texture.
Branching: pinnate in mature plants, but merely pinnatifid in young plants.
Pinnae: up to 60 on each side, usually less, set close together, very regularly spaced, about the space of a pinna between each pair of pinnae, the pinnae linear-oblong in outline but curved slightly or very slightly toothed; the lowest pinnae become smaller than the others, pinnatifid rather than truly pinnate, and more widely spaced.
Fertile fronds: taller than the barren fronds and more erect, up to 75 cm long, occurring as a clump in the centre of each tuft of barren

fronds; deciduous, not wintergreen like the barren fronds.

Stalks: up to ½ as long as the blade, dark purple-brown.

Rachis: dark purple-brown, deeply furrowed.

Blade: linear-lanceolate in outline dark green, leathery.

Branching: pinnate.

Pinnae: linear, much narrower than those of the barren fronds, and more closely set on the rachis: like the pinnae of the barren fronds, the pinnae are curved upwards towards the apex of the frond, but it is a far more acute curve than with the pinnae of the barren frond. Again, the lowest pinnae are pinnatifid rather than truly pinnate, and increasingly widely spaced towards the base.

Venation: not established.

Sori: linear, forming a continuous line on either side of the midrib, produced on almost every pinna of the fertile fronds, except for the very lowest ones.

Indusium: whitish becoming brown, swollen.

HABITAT: acid soils in woods, at streamsides, hedgebanks and heathlands.

GEOGRAPHICAL TYPE: Circumpolar.

DISTRIBUTION: markedly discontinuous. Throughout Europe from Iceland to Spain, westwards to Ireland and eastwards through the Mediterranean basin into Asia Minor, the Caucasus; Madeira: Kamchatka southwards to Japan; western North America continuously from Alaska to California.

CULTIVATION: easy in any humus-rich acid soil. Lime in any form is lethal. Though doing best in shade it will grow well in full sun pro-

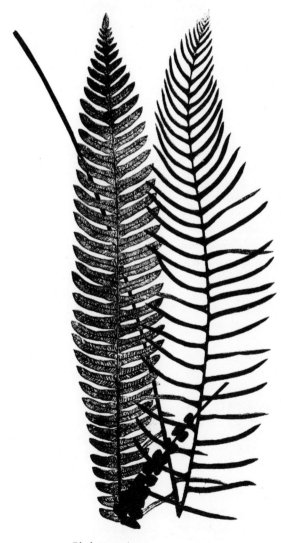

Blechnum spicant

vided that there is plenty of moisture in the soil. It is an excellent garden plant, making useful ground cover among rhododendrons, camellias, azaleas and other calcifuge subjects, and making an ideal companion for those lilies that like their heads in the sun but their roots in the shade. There are three varieties, but they are not perhaps as beautiful as the type plant.

VARIETIES: *B.s. anomalum* is anomalous in that it produces fronds of only one kind, all of which are fertile, and all of which are intermediate between the two normal types of fronds.

B.s. cristatum is a neatly crested variety. In *B.s. imbricatum* the rachis is congested so that the pinnae overlap like tiles on a roof. Both this and *B.s. anomalum* are not uncommon variants in the wild.

Dennstaedtia punctilobula
The North American hay-scented fern
The boulder fern

A vigorous though medium to small-sized North American woodland fern of great charm in the wild though somewhat invasive in the garden, forming large stands. It is deciduous, the fronds deteriorating appreciably by late summer. Though technically dimorphic there is little difference between the fertile and barren fronds.

DESCRIPTION: deciduous dimorphic creeping medium to small woodland fern.
Stock: slender, creeping, horizontal, the younger parts densely clothed with reddish-brown hairs, the older parts becoming dark brown and smooth except for the occasional decayed stalk stump; roots short, branched, brown, most numerous around the growing part of the stock, quickly decaying once their usefulness is past.
Fronds: deciduous, dimorphic, up to 45 cm tall, the tapering tip slightly curved.

Stalks: about ⅓ the length of the blade, black-brown at the base becoming reddish-brown above, smooth or with only a few scattered reddish hairs.
Rachis: slender, light brown to yellowish-red, bearing a few scattered reddish hairs.
Blade: lanceolate.
Branching: bipinnate. Pinnae opposite to sub-opposite, about 20 pairs, lanceolate in outline.
Pinnae: lanceolate in outline, pinnate.
Pinnules: obovate, deeply cut, lobes, rounded.
Venation: not established.
Fertile fronds: differing from barren fronds only in the greater spacing between the pinna and in their slightly greater height.
Sori: very small, occurring on vein endings at the edges of the pinnules.
Indusium: cup-shaped.

HABITAT: rather dry shade in

woodlands and hedgebanks.

GEOGRAPHICAL TYPE: Circumpolar.

DISTRIBUTION: in North America from Nova Scotia to Florida.

CULTIVATION: easy in almost any fertile soil, fully frost-hardy. Can be invasive with good cultivation, but hardly worth growing unless cultivated well.

VARIETIES: none recorded.

Dryopteris aemula
Lastrea aemula
Lastrea foenisecii
The hay-scented
buckler fern

A medium-sized buckler fern of great charm but rather rare throughout the whole of its rather limited range. It is one of those ferns that, though generally rare, is locally abundant.

DESCRIPTION: medium-sized, deciduous monomorphic woodland fern.
Stock: stout, erect, the younger parts clothed with lanceolate pale brown scales, the older parts covered with the bases of the dead fronds.
Fronds: tufted, recorded as growing up to 60 cm in length but more usually between 15 and 30 cm: scented, the smell resembling very closely that of new-mown hay, hence the common name.
Stalk: equal in length to the blade, brown-purple, very stiff bearing narrowly lanceolate rusty brown, sometimes lacerated scales —these being one of the features that distinguishes it from other ferns in the genus: the scales are often abundant on the reverse of the stalk, but lightly scattered on the face.
Rachis: dark green, flattened on the face, lightly covered in rusty-brown scales.

Blade: triangular in outline, bright green above, paler green beneath, both surfaces covered in minute sessile scales—these being another of its identifying features.
Branching: bipinnate to tripinnate.
Pinnae: up to 20 on either side of the rachis, borne on short but distinct stalks, opposite or sub-opposite, only those pairs nearest the apex becoming alternate; lanceolate to linear lanceolate in outline.
Pinnules: oblong in outline, alternate, the lower ones shortly stalked, the rest sessile becoming decurrent, the lowest ones pinnate, the remainder deeply and then less pinnatifid becoming merely toothed towards the tip, the ultimate segment oblong, pinnately toothed, the margins upturned.
Venation: Pecopteridian.
Sori: occurring in two rows on the ultimate segments, one row on either side of the midrib and nearer to it than to the margin, each sorus situated on the acroscopic fork of a secondary vein.
Indusium: reniform, the margin jagged.

HABITAT: rocky woodlands, by shaded streamsides.

GEOGRAPHICAL TYPE: Atlantic.

DISTRIBUTION: scattered through the British Isles including Ireland; north-western France, Galicia, the Azores, Madeira.

CULTIVATION: requires   a   very deep soil rich in leaf-mould or peat and a situation in fairly heavy shade. In spite of its rarity in the wild, it is quite easy to cultivate.

VARIETIES: none recorded.

Dryopteris austriaca
Dryopteris aristata
Lastrea dilatata
The broad buckler fern

A robust, strong-growing woodland fern with broader fronds than any other dryopteris species. Confusion could arise between this species and both *D. assimilis* and *D. carthusiana*. Its larger size, thicker texture, deeper colouring and smaller sori distinguish it from *D. assimilis*. Its dark-centred scales on the stalks distinguish it from *D. carthusiana*, which has uniformly pale scales.

DESCRIPTION: robust,   deciduous monomorphic woodland fern.
Stock: stout, upright, sometimes but not invariably branched, the younger parts densely clothed with scales light brown with a darker brown or almost black central stripe, the older parts covered with the almost black dead frond bases.
Fronds: up to 150 cm long, presented in a basket-like tuft.
Stalks: $\frac{2}{3}-\frac{1}{2}$ as long as the blade, dark, purplish-brown below, light brown or even green above, densely clothed towards the base and more lightly clothed higher up with light brown scales with a darker central stripe.
Rachis: green, covered with a few scattered light brown scales, with a less obvious darker central stripe.
Blade: triangular to lanceolate-ovate in outline, dark green above, paler beneath, with a few glandular swellings on the veins.
Branching: bipinnate to tripinnate.
Pinnae: stalked, up to 25 on either side of the rachis, opposite or sub-opposite on the lower part of the blade, becoming almost alternate towards the apex, the lower ones triangular in outline, the upper ones becoming more nearly lanceolate.
Pinnules: alternate, oblong to oblong-lanceolate in outline, pinnate or pinnatifid, the lower ones shortly stalked, becoming first sessile and then decurrent towards the tip. Final segments ovate to oblong, coarsely toothed.
Venation: Pecopteridian.
Sori: numerous, occurring in 2 rows, one on each side of the midrib of the pinnules, closer to the midrib than to the margin, each sorus situated on the acroscopic fork of a secondary vein.
Indusium: reniform, the margin usually toothed, occasionally glandular.

HABITAT: woodlands.

GEOGRAPHICAL TYPE: Circumpolar.

DISTRIBUTION: incompletely known, since this species was originally lumped together with *D. assimilis* and *D. carthusiana* as a single species. Certainly distributed throughout the whole of Europe including the British Isles, through Asia Minor and northern Asia; Japan; Greenland; Madeira; Cyprus; South Africa; North America from Newfoundland to Alaska and southwards to California.

CULTIVATION: easy, preferring a soil rich in leaf-mould and a situation providing some shade.

VARIETIES: *D.a. cristata:* an aggregate name, the best forms being neatly and symmetrically crested on both pinnae and apex.

D.a. crispa: a strong-growing crisped variety.

D.a. grandiceps: a form in which the pinnae are crested but in which the apixal crest is a vast, corymbose affair of great weight, bowing the frond. Comes true from spores.

D.a. hymenophylloides: a dwarf, congested variety of no particular charm.

D.a. lepidota: in this variety, which has exceptionally finely cut pinnules, the whole blade is more or less hairy, being covered with minute but conspicuous scales. There is also a crested form of this known as *D.a.l. cristata.*

D.a. succisa: a form in which the pinnae are abruptly truncated, creating a curiously narrow frond, only 10 cm across. About 60 cm.

Dryopteris carthusiana
Dryopteris spinulosa
Dryopteris lanceolatocristata
The narrow buckler fern

One of the most graceful in the dryopteris species, with light yellowish green fronds and an open habit. The only other species with which it could be confused is *D. austriaca* (q.v.) from which it is distinguished by the colouring of the scales of the stalk, these being a uniform pale brown in *D. carthusiana* and dark in the centre, but paler at the margins in *D. austriaca*. It is further distinguished by the absence of the fringed glands which are found on the margin of the indusium of *D. austriaca*.

DESCRIPTION: a normally deciduous, strong-growing monomorphic woodland fern.

Stock: stout, creeping, very scaly, the older parts covered in the bases of the dead fronds from among which the coarse black, widespreading roots appear.

Fronds: deciduous, rising singly, up to 120 cm in length.

Stalks: the same length at the blade, pale above, darker below, covered with evenly pale brown scales.

Rachis: pale green covered with a few scales of similar colouring to those of the stalk.

Blade: oblong-lanceolate to lanceolate in outline, light yellowish-green.

Branching: bipinnate.

Pinnae: up to 20 on either side, opposite becoming sub-opposite the uppermost ones being alternate: the lowest ones broadly triangular in outline and shorter than those immediately above them, the upper ones becoming lanceolate.

Pinnules: oblong-obovate, decurrent, deeply pinnatifid: ultimate segments pinnately toothed, the teeth somewhat incurved.

Venation: Pecopteridian.

Sori: numerous occurring in two rows one on either side of the pinnule midrib, situated on the acroscopic forks of the secondary veins.

Indusium: rounded, its margin entire, wavy.

HABITAT: damp woodlands.

GEOGRAPHICAL TYPE: Circumpolar.

DISTRIBUTION: abundant throughout the north temperate zone. The Mediterranean basin, northern and central Europe, through the Caucasus to northern Asia into Manchuria; North America from Labrador to Alaska and broadly southwards to approximately latitude 38°N.

CULTIVATION: easy, thriving in any soil rich in leaf-mould, and preferably in a situation affording it some shade.

VARIETIES: none recorded.

Drypteris filix-mas
Lastrea filix-mas
The male fern

This is one of the commonest ferns in the British Isles, and probably one of the most common throughout much of Europe. Though its distribution embraces North America it is relatively uncommon there. In Europe it is likely to be confused with *Dryopteris pseudomas* and with *Dryopteris abbreviata*: the points which distinguished those two species from this species are listed under those two. In North America it is only likely to be confused with *Dryopteris marginalis*, from which it differs chiefly in that the fronds of that species are of a blue-green colour, whereas in this species they are true green.

This fern, together with the lady fern, are the two commonest ferns of the English-speaking Old World and their common names go back to as early as Chaucer's time, probably even earlier. According to the ideas of natural history that were generally held in those times, in the plant world, as in the human world, everything was either male or female. It seemed apparent to these minds that the male fern and the lady fern were simply the male and the female of the same plant, and this is why they have come to be so named. The idea is a pretty one, but quite untrue, since ferns are neither male nor female, but if anything, neutral. Certainly the male fern is of more robust and virile habit than the delicate lady fern.

The plant is very variable in the wild and has given rise in the past to innumerable varieties, many of them very fine indeed, and certainly more effective for garden decoration than the wild form, attractive though that is. Relatively few of the varieties recorded in the past seem to be still in cultivation today.

DESCRIPTION: robust, deciduous monomorphic woodland fern.
Stock: stout, ascending, gradually branching to form a number of closely grouped crowns; the younger parts covered in light brown chaffy scales, the older parts

Dryopteris filix-mas

in the almost black dead frond-stalks, these being spirally arranged on the stock, the numerous black, wiry roots appearing from among these.

Fronds: deciduous, arranged in a basket-like tuft, up to 150 cm.

Stalks: $\frac{1}{5}$–$\frac{1}{3}$ the length of the blade, sparsely covered in pale brown lanceolate scales.

Rachis: green, lightly covered particularly on the lower part in light, brown scales.

Blade: lanceolate in outline, dark green above, paler beneath, soft in texture.

Branching: pinnate.

Pinnae: up to as many as 35 on each side of the rachis, sessile or only very shortly stalked, linear lanceolate in outline, deeply pinnatifid or rarely pinnate on the lower pinnae, arranged alternately on the rachis, the lower pinnae becoming sub-opposite but never truly opposite.

Venation: Pecopteridian.

Sori: numerous, occurring only on the pinnae of the upper half of the blade, situated on the acroscopic branches of the secondary veins and forming two lines on the pinnae, nearer the midrib than the margin.

Indusium: large, reniform, convex, with a noticeable deep notch.

HABITAT: woodlands, hedgerows.

GEOGRAPHICAL TYPE: Circumpolar.

DISTRIBUTION: throughout Europe to the Caucasus, the Himalayas, the Altai; Greenland; North America from Newfoundland westwards to Alaska, but confined southwards to the eastern states of the U.S.A., including Maine, Vermont, Michigan and New York State.

CULTIVATION: easily grown in any good garden soil well enriched with leaf-mould or peat, preferably in a situation giving it some shade from mid-day sun.

VARIETIES: *D. f-m. barnesii:* a form with very narrow fronds, no more than 12 cm in relation to a frond length of up to 90 cm: the narrowness is achieved by a reduction in the size of the pinnae, these being broadly triangular rather than lanceolate as in the type plant. Comes true from spores.

D. f-m. bollandiae: a fine plumose form that has the additional virtue of unexpected autumn colouring. The fronds are very finely dissected, giving a singularly light and airy appearance. This variety is normally barren, and spores, when produced, usually give rise to inferior forms. Increase by division.

D. f-m. crispa: this is a compact variety reaching no more than about 50 cm with well crisped pinnae. The crisping is not perhaps as attractive as it is on those ferns with simple fronds, such as *Asplenium scolopendrium.*

D. f-m. crispa cristata: a similarly low-growing form, the pinnae and apical segment terminating in neat crests. A delightful variety that comes virtually true from spores.

D. f-m. crispatissima cristata: similar to the above but with the pinnae even more pronouncedly crisped and crested, the terminal crest being very strongly developed. It would appear to be *D. f-m. crispa cristata* developed to absurdity.

D. f-m. cristata: an aggregate name embracing a large number of forms, some of them remarkably handsome. Typically every pinna and the terminal segment end in a crest. The form known as *D. f-m. cristata* 'Martindale' is probably the finest of all, the pinnae all being curved upwards towards the apex, those nearest the apex running together in fan-like form, all the pinna and the apical segment ending in fine crests. Comes virtually true from spores.

D. f-m. decomposita: this is a remarkable foliose form with exceptionally wide fronds, the pinnatifid pinnae having become truly pinnate, the segments of the pinnae deeply toothed. Division.

D. f-m. decomposita cristata: similar to the above, beautifully crested. Both reach about 45 cm.

D. f-m. depauperata: ferns that are depauperate (i.e. that have some of their parts missing) are roughly speaking attractive when the depauperation is symmetrical and rather less attractive when the depauperation is erratic. In this instance we have two quite distinct forms gathered together under the one aggregate name, but distinguished by further epithets, the one being symmetrical, the other erratic in the extreme. *D. f-m. depauperata* 'Padley' is a symmetrical depauperate form in which the pinnae are very narrow, the segments much reduced and confluent, creating rather the effect of rippling margins to a midrib than of segments at all. By contrast *D. f-m. depauperata* 'Staghorn' is an oddity of undoubted botanical but little garden interest: it is depauperate in all its parts, the fronds having been reduced to a tangle of branched rachises winged with a few irregularly occurring pinnae, the segments being nothing more than the occasional irregularly produced tooth. This form is sometimes not inappropriately known as 'Monstrosa'.

D. f-m. grandiceps one of the finest forms of the male fern, with a really huge terminal crest and fine neat crests on all the pinnae. To 60 cm, and forming a clump with many crowns.

D. f-m. 'Jervisii': a form in which the slender pinnae terminate in small crests. Not always symmetrical.

D. f-m. linearis: this is really a depauperate variety, some of its parts having been reduced almost to vanishing point, yet it is symmetrical and achieves a singular beauty. The pinnae have been reduced to the extent that they are little more than a wing along each side of the midrib. The effect is light and airy. Division. 90 cm.

D. f-m. linearis congesta: which grows to only 15 or 20 cm and makes a delightful rock garden plant is similar to the above. Division.

D. f-m. linearis polydactyla: again grows to about 90 cm, and in addition to the refinement of the pinnae has long-fingered crests on both pinnae and apical segments. Comes true from spores. A very pleasing garden plant.

D. f-m. lux-lunae polydactyla: this is one of the very few ferns that are variegated, the variegation remaining more or less constant. In addition to the variegation the pinnae and terminal segment are neatly crested. Highly desirable: very rare. Division.

D. f-m. polydactyla: a vigorous variety growing up to 90 cm with long slender crests of pinnae and terminal segments. Very elegant.

D. f-m. subcristata: in this form the pinnae are longer and appear narrower than in the type form, and terminate in rather small, neat crests.

Dryopteris goldiana
The giant woodfern

The largest growing of all the North American woodland ferns, almost matching in stature some of the large-growing, moisture-loving ferns. It is distinct from all other woodland ferns on account of the golden-green colour of the fronds, their backward tilt in relation to the stalk, and of course by its coarse growth.

DESCRIPTION: strong-growing monomorphic deciduous woodland fern.
Stock: short, stout, semi-erect to ascending, the younger parts densely covered in mid-brown scales, the older parts covered with the almost black old stalk bases.
Fronds: leathery, golden-green, deciduous, up to 120 cm tall.
Stalks: as much as $\frac{1}{3}$ of the length of the blade, very thick, straw-yellow, covered in large, pale tan scales, each with a darker centre, giving the whole stalk a shaggy appearance.
Rachis: green, with a few similarly coloured scales.
Blade: broadly ovate.
Branching: pinnate.
Pinnae: deeply pinnatifid, the margins bluntly serrate, the lowest pairs of pinnae pointing downwards, pinnae alternate.
Venation: not established.
Sori: occurring near the margins of the pinnules.
Indusium: kidney-shaped.

HABITAT: rich woodlands on any soil.

GEOGRAPHICAL TYPE: Circumpolar.

DISTRIBUTION: in North America throughout the north-eastern and north-central states.

CULTIVATION: fully frost-hardy and easily grown in any deep, rich leafy soil in a shaded situation.

VARIETIES: none recorded.

Dryopteris marginalis
The marginal shield fern
The marginal buckler fern

A graceful, leathery-fronded wintergreen fern growing in graceful clumps in woodlands. It derives its specific name from the way in which the sori are situated near the pinnule margins. It forms graceful clumps of erect, slightly outspreading fronds and, because it forms a distinct caudex in the manner of a tree-fern, it looks somewhat like a small palm tree. It is most conspicuous in winter, with its persistent green fronds showing boldly among the generally sere covering of the woodland floor.

DESCRIPTION: medium-sized wintergreen monomorphic woodland fern.
Stock: stout, ascending, caudescent, the younger parts densely covered in shaggy brown scales, the older parts clothed with the almost black dead stalks; roots, many, shallow-spreading, forming a dense, tangled mass.
Fronds: erect, somewhat outspreading, wintergreen, up to 45 cm.
Stalks: stout, rather brittle, grooved on the face, densely covered with large brown scales, giving it a shaggy appearance, green, becoming brown and swollen towards the base, about $\frac{1}{4}-\frac{1}{3}$ as long as the blade.
Rachis: green, stout, similarly covered with large brown scales and shaggy in appearance.
Blade: ovate-lanceolate.
Branching: bipinnate.
Pinnae: narrowly triangular, tapering.
Pinnules: crenate with rounded apex.
Venation: not established.
Sori: large, prominent, occurring on the margins of the pinnules.
Indusium: kidney-shaped.

HABITAT: woodlands, on any soil.

GEOGRAPHICAL TYPE: Circumpolar.

DISTRIBUTION: in North America throughout the north-eastern and north-central states.

CULTIVATION: any deep rich leafy soil in slight shade. Fully frost-hardy.

VARIETIES: none recorded.

Dryopteris pseudomas
Dryopteris borreri
Dryopteris filix-mas var. paleacea
Lastrea pseudomas
The scaly male fern

In general appearance this fern could easily be confused with the male fern, to which it has a great similarity. Its differences are, however, sufficiently marked to make recognition a not too difficult task. Many earlier writers regarded it merely as a form of the male fern, D. *filix-mas*, which rather confirms the general similarities between the two plants. The two most obvious differences—though one has to see the plants at the right time to observe these differences—are the bright golden-green of the croziers as they unfurl in spring, covered in coppery-gold scales, and the semi-wintergreen habit: *D. filix-mas* by contrast, looses its fronds at the first touch of frost. In cultivation under glass *D. pseudomas* is fully wintergreen.

DESCRIPTION: generally very similar to *D. filix-mas* but differs from that species in that the stalk and rachis are decidedly shaggy, being covered in linear-lanceolate to ovate-lanceolate acuminate scales which are bright orange-yellow when young, becoming golden or light brown on maturity, whereas those of *D. filix-mas* are less shaggy and of a less striking colour. It differs from *D. filix-mas* in the following ways:

Fronds: yellowish-green, leathery, semi-wintergreen as opposed to dark green and fully deciduous.
Pinnae: possessing a dark brown or even black patch near the base, this patch being absent on *D. filix-mas.*
Pinnules: (properly pinna lobes) with parallel sides and a sub-truncate apex instead of an acute apex.
Sori: 4–5 on each side of the pinnule midrib.
Indusium: with the margin incurred. Apogamous.

HABITAT: woodlands, woodland glades, on the banks of woodland streams.

GEOGRAPHICAL TYPE: north temperate regions of the Old World.

DISTRIBUTION: north-western Europe including Britain, western and southern Europe: southwest Asia northwards to the Caucasus.

CULTIVATION: easy, preferring a soil rich in leaf-mould and some shade, though this need only be light.

VARIETIES: *D. p-m. congesta cristata:* a very dwarf congested cristate form reaching only about 15 cm as opposed to 150 cm in the type plant. Quite pleasing.

D. p-m. cristata: an aggregate name containing two exceptionally fine named forms—viz:

D. p-m.c. 'The King': the finest cristate form, with a magnificent terminal crest causing the rather stiff fronds to arch gracefully. To 120 cm. Single crowns are generally more effective in the garden since once the plant builds itself up into a mass of crowns—as it tends to do—this crowds the fronds and prevents them from revealing the arching habit which gives the plant so much of its charm.

D. p-m.c. angustata: a form with very narrow fronds—no more than 5 cm wide in relation to a frond length of about 45 cm, neatly and symmetrically crested along its length as well as at the apex.

D.p-m. grandiceps: a form with a singularly large and heavy terminal crest: 60 cm.

D.p-m. polydactyla: in this form the frond divides to present two large terminal crests. Very effective. Up to 90–120 cm in optimum

17 (Above) *Polypodium australe cambricum* (page 221).

18 (Right) *Polypodium interjectum* (page 223).

19 (Right) *Polypodium vulgare longicaudatum* (page 226).

20 (Below) *Polypodium vulgare ramo-cristatum* (page 227).

conditions: very similar to 'The King' but with broader taller fronds and fewer fronds to each crown.

D.p-m. ramosissima: a very fine variety in which the fronds branch repeatedly, each branching terminating in a fine crest. 60 cm.

D.p-m. ramosa furcillans: a rather inconstant form, perpetually tending to revert to the type plant, but producing distinctive fronds each of which divides into two, the pinnae being lightly crested.

D.p-m. stableri: a form with very narrow fronds and short pinnae, of erect habit. 90 cm.

Oreopteris limbosperma
Thelypteris limbosperma
Thelypteris oreopteris
Dryopteris oreopteris
Lastrea oreopteris
Lastrea montana
The mountain fern

In spite of the nomenclatural nightmare that surrounds this fern, it does at last seem to have settled down into a genus of its own, where it is to be hoped it will remain. It is a strong-growing species with a tough rootstock that branches readily, forming dense clumps of a rather dark green.

DESCRIPTION: robust deciduous monomorphic fern with much-branched subterranean stock.

Stock: stout, much branched, the younger parts clothed densely with pale brown acuminate scales, the older parts with the dark brown stumps of the old frond stalks.

Fronds: up to 90 cm, usually about $\frac{3}{4}$ that height, tufted, with a balsam-like fragrance particularly noticeable when crushed.

Stalks: relatively short, not more than about $\frac{1}{5}$ the length of the blade, bearing a few pale brown, ovate-lanceolate scales.

Rachis: bearing a few white hairs intermixed with even fewer pale brown, lanceolate scales.

Blade: lanceolate in outline, narrowing at each end, bright yellowish-green.

Branching: pinnate.

Pinnae: up to as many as 30 on each side of the rachis, linear lanceolate in outline, alternate throughout most of the length of the blade, but becoming sub-opposite to opposite towards the base, sessile.

Pinnules: pinnatifid, oblong in outline, acute, the margins slightly toothed.

Venation: Pecopteridian.

Sori: small, situated on the ends of the secondary veins, nearer the margin than the midrib and forming two distinct rows.

Indusium: when present small, irregular in shape, the margin dentate, often absent and when present falling early.

HABITAT: woodlands, shady, folds in mountains.

GEOGRAPHICAL TYPE: Circumpolar.

DISTRIBUTION: throughout Europe including western Russia, southwards as far as northern Spain, eastwards to Italy and the Caucasus; Madeira; Asia Minor; Japan; western North America from

Alaska down the Rockies to Washington.

CULTIVATION: easy in any well-drained lime-free soil.

VARIETIES: a number of fine varieties have been recorded in the past, but none of these appears to be in cultivation any longer.

Osmunda claytoniana
The interrupted fern

The interrupted fern is well-named indeed. It is a dimorphic plant, and it is the fertile fronds which give it

Osmunda claytoniana

its common name. On these the flow of normal, barren pinnae is 'interrupted' in mid-sequence by the fertile pinnae, above which the pinnae again become barren. It is a remarkable fern to look at, quite unmistakable: there is simply nothing else like it.

DESCRIPTION: strong-growing dimorphic deciduous woodland fern. *Stock:* very stout, creeping, forming a large mass, covered with a veritable stubble of old frond bases; roots thickly matted, black, growing in all directions from the stock, anchoring the plant very securely to the ground.
Fronds: dimorphic, the fertile ones about twice as tall as the barren ones, fertile fronds erect, to 150 cm, barren fronds spreading, presented in basket-like fashion surrounding the fertile fronds.
Stalks: on barren fronds about $\frac{1}{2}$ as long as the blade, on fertile fronds about equal in length to the blade, stout, smooth, green, round but with the face slightly grooved.
Rachis: smooth, green, slightly grooved on the face.
Blade: oblong-lanceolate in outline.
Branching: pinnate. Pinnae narrowly lanceolate in outline, deeply pinnatifid, margins entire.

Fertile fronds: bearing about 3 or 4 well-spaced pairs of normal barren pinnae, followed by 3 or 4 pairs of fertile pinnae, the remainder of the frond being identical to the upper portion of the barren fronds: fertile pinnae much shorter than the barren ones, fully pinnate, each pinnule margin thickly covered in clusters of sporangia.
Venation: not established.
Sori: large, short-stalked, green at first, becoming brown.
Indusium: absent.

HABITAT: edges of woodlands, hedgerows.

GEOGRAPHICAL TYPE: Circumpolar.

DISTRIBUTION: in North America from Newfoundland to North Carolina.

CULTIVATION: perfectly frost-hardy and easily grown in any good leafy soil, preferably on the acid side, and in a shaded situation. The spores have a viability of only 2 or 3 days, so must be sown as soon as ready.

VARIETIES: non recorded.

Phegopteris connectilis
Thelypteris phegopteris
Polypodium phegopteris
Phegopteris polypodioides
Dryopteris phegopteris
The beech fern

A delightful, small-growing fern with rather light green fronds, found in shady woods on acid soils.

DESCRIPTION: low-growing, freely-branching, clump-forming deciduous monomorphic woodland fern.
Stock: slender, up to 2 mm thick, creeping, freely branching but sparsely rooted, blackish-brown in colour and clothed when young with tiny whitish woolly hairs and scattered golden-brown scales.
Fronds: deciduous, up to as much as 40 cm, usually rather less, arising singly, alternately, at irregular intervals along the stock.
Stalks: varying from as long as to twice as long as the blade, very brittle, the same shade of green as the blade except at the base, where it becomes blackish; clothed with minute reflexed hairs, the blackish basal portion clothed with light brown lanceolate scales.
Rachis: also clothed with scattered hairs and scales similar to those of the stalk.
Blade: triangular or triangular-ovate in outline, acute, thin and flimsy in texture, matt pale green.
Branching: pinnate.
Pinnae: up to as many as 20 on each side of the rachis, opposite or sub-opposite, occasionally becoming alternate towards the apex, fringed and scattered with minute hairs; deeply pinnatifid, the lowest pair spaced rather further apart from the next pair than succeeding pairs and deflected downwards, the other horizontal and attached by a broad leafy base, the higher pinnae deflected upwards, running together towards the tip.
Venation: Pecopteridian.
Sori: circular, situated close to the

margins of the segments.
Indusium: absent.

HABITAT: shaded woodlands on acidic formations.

GEOGRAPHICAL TYPE: Circumpolar.

DISTRIBUTION: throughout Europe from Iceland to the north of Spain,

eastwards to the Caucasus and into north-eastern Asia Minor and thence via the Himalayas to Japan; Greenland; Canada and the U.S.A. southwards as far as Virginia.

CULTIVATION: requires leafy soil, a shaded situation and acid conditions. Makes an ideal plant for a shaded situation in a shrubbery or in the rock garden.

Polypodium australe (formerly included in Polypodium vulgare) The southern polypody

The polypodiaceae is one of the most widespread of all the fern families, comprising some 200 genera and some 7,500 species, nearly all of tropical or subtropical distribution. All, including the genera which are represented in the temperate world, are fairly small, normally terrestial or epiphytic ferns with a creeping stock.

The British polypodies, which embrace those known in North America as *Polypodium vulgare*, have at different times been lumped together under the one heading of *Polypodium vulgare* or else split into three species known as *Polypodium vulgare, Polypodium interjectum* and *Polypodium australe*. It now seems certain that they should be separated into these three quite distinct species on cytological grounds. *Polypodium vulgare* is tetraploid, *Polypodium interjectum* hexaploid and *Polypodium australe* diploid. It has been suggested that the hexaploid *Polypodium interjectum* arose as a hybrid between the two other species and attained stability by a doubling of the chromosomes.

The differences between the three species are not stunningly obvious, and identification in the field can be difficult. The matter is further complicated by the existence of plants that are intermediate between the species which have probably resulted from further hybridisation. Thus the hybrid *Polypodium interjectum × vulgare* is not uncommon where the two species are found growing together. The occurrence of such hybrids can confuse even relatively experienced observers.

When it comes to the varieties of the polypodies these are usually listed under *Polypodium vulgare*, but this is largely a hangover from a period when the group was regarded as a single species, for it was during that period that the first serious attempts were made to list all the varieties. There is no doubt that a number of varieties originally listed under *Polypodium vulgare* do not in fact belong there, although the botanical basis for shifting them to other species is somewhat suspect, since many of the varieties are completely sterile.

The descriptions of both this species and *Polypodium interjectum* are confined to the ways in which they differ from *Polypodium vulgare*, for which a full description is given. All are low-growing monomorphic wintergreen ferns with a creeping rootstock. A hand lens is required for certain identification, though the outline of the fronds, together with the season at which the new fronds are produced, are a useful guide.

DESCRIPTION: low-growing creeping monomorphic wintergreen fern. Differs from *P. vulgare* in its generally broader fronds, these being broadly ovate to triangular as opposed to linear-lanceolate in outline, and in the texture of the fronds, these being of a softer texture than those of *P. vulgare*.

Pinnae: deeply toothed by comparison with *P. vulgare*, in which the teething is normally but not always virtually absent; the lowest pair or sometimes 2 pairs of pinnae inflexed. New fronds develop in the autumn.

Sori: oval with branched hairs known as paraphyses mixed with the sporangia. Annulus with 4–7 indurated cells, these being shorter and broader than in the other two species.

HABITAT: woodlands, often ephiphytic; dry stone walls, hedgebanks.

GEOGRAPHICAL TYPE: Circumpolar.

DISTRIBUTION: uncertain, since until recently plants of species would have been recorded under *P. vulgare*. Distribution for which accurate records exist include Great Britain, Ireland, south and southwest Europe, the Azores, the Canary Islands, Madeira and Aden.

CULTIVATION: an easy plant for garden or rock garden, preferring a light, leafy soil, but one which is well-drained though never dries out. In the wild it is found growing as an epiphyte or on very shallow, stony soil, never on rich deep soils, and the addition of plenty of grit to the soil will often be found beneficial where there is any doubt about the drainage of the soil. Will not endure waterlogged conditions.

VARIETIES: *P.a. cambricum:* originally found in Wales, hence the varietal name, it has subsequently been found in several other places and a number of named forms exist, some of them very fine. The typical form differs from the type plant in that the pinnae are very deeply pinnatifid, the segments of the pinnae overlapping. This form is foliose and completely barren. The following named forms are all outstanding garden plants.

P.a.c. barrowii: a form in which the equally deeply pinnatifid pinnae segments are even longer and more pointed, and the whole frond is even more foliose.

P.a.c. hadwinii: in this form the pinnae segments are blunter, and the whole frond narrower, the pinnae somewhat upcurved.

P.a.c. oakleyi: a dwarf form, reaching no more than 10 or 12 cm —as opposed to as much as 20 cm in most of the other forms.

P.a.c. 'Wilharris': a form in which the pinnae are not quite so deeply pinnatifid, but in which the tips are crisped and curled, making it perhaps the most delightful of all. Very rare.

P.a. semilacerum: in this variety the lower pinnae are deeply inflexed, and also deeply pinnatifid, but the upper part of the frond is normal. Fertile.

Polypodium australe cambricum

Polypodium interjectum (formerly included in *Polypodium vulgare*)

As already explained this species is a hybrid between *P. australe* and *P. vulgare*. It has stabilised itself by doubling its chromosomes and, as might be expected, it is therefore intermediate in most respects between its two parents.

DESCRIPTION: differs from *P. vulgare* in that its blade is ovate-lanceolate in outline, the lower pinnae somewhat inflexed.
Sori: pale brown, oval, indurated cells, 8–12, paraphyses absent. New fronds produced in late summer.

HABITAT: generally found growing in wetter conditions than *P. australe* or *P. vulgare:* woodland, hedgerows, beside streams.

GEOGRAPHICAL TYPE: Circumpolar.

DISTRIBUTION: uncertain, since this species was formerly included in *Polypodium vulgare*. Recorded throughout Britain and probably also occurring in Europe.

CULTIVATION: as for *P. vulgare*, except that it will tolerate wetter conditions.

VARIETIES: none recorded.

Polypodium vulgare The common polypody

For centuries this was regarded as the only species of polypody in Britain, and the other species were regarded merely as subspecies or varieties of it. It is only within the last decade or so that the other two British species have come to be recognised as species in their own right. The other two British species are described only in so far as they differ from this species, for which a full description is given.

DESCRIPTION: low-growing, creeping, monomorphic wintergreen terrestical or epiphytic woodland fern.
Stock: horizontal, creeping usually on, occasionally just beneath, the surface of the soil; branching occasionally but not frequently, the younger parts covered in cinnamon-coloured lanceolate scales which become dark brown on the older parts of the stock, the older parts commonly scarred where the fronds of previous seasons have broken off, somewhat flattened in cross-section; roots produced from the underside of the stock; dark brown, rooting shallowly, fronds produced from the upper side of the stock, alternately.
Fronds: up to 50 cm but usually about $\frac{1}{2}$ that length, wintergreen.
Stalks: varying from $\frac{1}{3}$ to equal the length of the blade, green, lacking scales.
Rachis: green, lightly covered with yellowish-brown hairs and scales.
Blade: lanceolate in outline, leathery in texture.
Branching: strictly pinnatifid but appearing almost pinnate, the segments alternately arranged on the

rachis, oblong, lanceolate or lanceolate in outline, the majority of segments of equal length, the lowest segments not inflexed, margins simple or occasionally toothed, sometimes quite deeply.
Venation: Eupteridian.

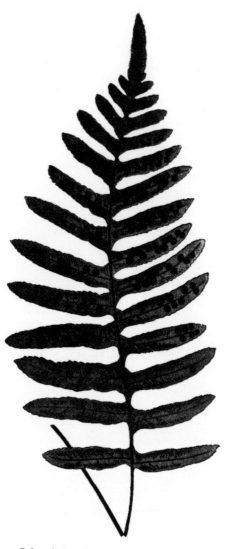

Polypodium vulgare

Sori: large, round, occurring in 2 rows on either side of the midrib and nearer to it than to the margins of the segments, each sorus situated on the lowest acroscopic branches of the secondary veins: paraphyses absent: annulus with 13–16 dark brown indurated cells. New fronds produced in early summer.
Indusium: absent.

HABITAT: woodlands, dry walls.

GEOGRAPHICAL TYPE: Circumpolar.

DISTRIBUTION: throughout Europe including the British Isles, Azores, the Canary Islands, Madeira, southern Europe, the Caucasus; South Africa; North America from Newfoundland to Alaska and thence southwards as far as Mexico, common in both the eastern and western states but absent from the Great Plains; the Aleutian Islands; Kamchatka.

CULTIVATION: easy in garden or rock garden, requiring a well-drained soil and preferably one to which both leaf-mould and grit have been added. Both the type plant itself and its varieties are most useful garden plants, providing excellent ground cover, especially among shrubs, and ideal amongst those shrubs which like their roots cooled by a mulch of leaves, since the fronds of the polypodies naturally collect any leaves blowing about—which benefits both the polypodies and the plant under which they are growing.

VARIETIES: *P.v. bifidum:* a not uncommon variety in which the lower pinnae divide into a fishtail fork at the tip. In some forms all the pinnae terminate in this way.

P.v.b. multifidum: a form with longer, narrower pinnae segments and in which all the segments including the terminal one end in fishtail crests.

P.v. congestum cristatum: a very dwarf form growing no more than about 10 cm high, the fronds deeply pinnatisect, overlapping,

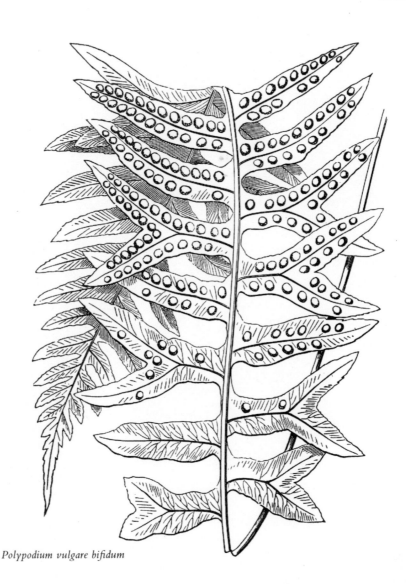

Polypodium vulgare bifidum

crested. Very beautiful, rather rare.

P.v. cornubiense: also to be found under the varietal names *P.v.*

Polypodium vulgare cristatum

elegantissimum and *P.v. whitei*, it would probably better be called *P.v. inconstans*, which at least describes it in a recognisable way. It produces normal fronds, fronds that are tripinnate and fronds that are quadripinnate, fronds that embrace all these varieties in one and fronds that are intermediate between any or all combinations. Kept in good shape it is certainly a charmer, but it is necessary to keep a watchful eye open for any normal fronds that may occur, and remove them when they do.

P.v.c. multifidum is a form in which the pinna segments and the apical segment terminate in neat, flat crests. It has less tendency to produce normal fronds.

P.v.c. trichomanoides is the most beautiful of the group, having remarkably finely dissected pinnae. It has the same tendency to revert as *P.v. cornubiense*, it is, unfortunately, extremely rare.

P.v. cristatum: a strong-growing form with many-fingered crests. Distinct and attractive: division.

P.v. grandiceps: a very fine form in which the pinnae terminate in many-fingered crests, and the terminal crest is huge. Division.

P.v. longicaudatum: differs from the type only in its extremely elongated, tail-like apical segment.

P.v. omnilacerum: a vigorous variety growing up to as much as 60 cm with good cultivation, the pinna segments are deeply pinnatifid, giving a delightful fringed effect: the segments are narrow and placed very close together.

P.v. pulcherrimum: superficially this form very closely resembles *P.a. cambricum:* it differs from it in its greater vigour, its more leathery fronds and in the fact that it is fully fertile, the majority of sporelings coming reasonably true to form.

P.v. ramo-cristatum: a form in which the otherwise normal fronds branch repeatedly at the tip, each branch bearing a neat crest. Fertile: sporelings rather variable.

P.v. ramosum: in this form the only divergence from the norm is that the fronds branch repeatedly from the base. A curiosity, of little beauty.

Polypodium vulgare pulcherrimum

Polystichum aculeatum
Polystichum lobatum
The hard shield fern

The inclusion of this species among the woodland ferns is perhaps dubious, since it is almost as frequently found growing in mountainous situations. It was for a long time regarded merely as a form of *Polystichum setiferum*, but modern cytology has defined its specific status—*P. aculeatum* being tetraploid, *P. setiferum* being diploid. It is now thought probably that *P. aculeatum* arose as a hybrid between *P. lonchitis* and *P. setiferum*, and achieved stability by doubling its chromosomes.

This species is easily confused with *P. setiferum*, which it closely resembles, but may be distinguished from that species by the very much more rigid fronds, by their more leathery texture, by the fact that the pinnules, which tend to run together, are sessile not stalked, and are acute, not obtuse, at the base; and further by the way in which the veins on which the sori occur run right past the sori to the margin of the pinnule, whereas in *P. setiferum* these veins terminate at the sori. Although it has produced only a relatively small number of varieties, one of these, *P.a. pulcherrimum gracillimum*, is considered to be the finest of all fern varieties.

DESCRIPTION: strong-growing, monomorphic wintergreen woodland fern.

Stock: erect, as much as 10 cm thick, pseudo-woody, the younger parts densely clothed with pale brown ovate-lanceolate scales, the older parts densely covered in the dead frond stalks, through which the coarse, black, wiry roots thrust their way down to the soil.

Fronds: up to 90 cm, usually about $\frac{1}{2}$ that length, arranged in a basket-like tuft, the inner ones erect, the outer ones more or less spreading, rigid in texture, wintergreen.

Stalks: $\frac{1}{5}$–$\frac{1}{4}$ as long as the blade, clothed particularly on the lower parts with a dense scurf of large, brown, ovate-lanceolate scales.

Rachis: green lightly clothed with scales similar to those on the stalk, these being mixed with a few hair-like scales.

Blade: lanceolate in outline, narrowing towards the tip and towards the base; leathery in texture, rather rigid; dark green to yellowish-green above, usually paler beneath, the undersurface covered in a few scales.

Branching: pinnate to bipinnate.

Pinnae: up to as many as 50 on each side of the rachis, mostly alternate but becoming sub-opposite or even opposite towards the tip and towards the base; very shortly stalked, in fact virtually sessile, linear to ovate-lanceolate in outline, pinnate in the lower half of the frond, becoming deeply pinnatifid and then less pinnatifid in the upper part, the apical segment being sickle-shaped and toothed, curved towards the apex of the frond.

Pinnules: sessile and decurrent, unequal at the base, almost truncate on the acroscopic side: the lowest acroscopic segment being greatly enlarged, as in the case of *P. lonchitis.*

Venation: Pecopteridian.

Sori: small, occurring only on the upper half of the frond, the veins on which the sori occur continuing past them to the pinna margin.

Indusium: circular, peltate.

HABITAT: woodlands, hedgerows and less frequently scrubby areas and shaded rock ledges in mountain districts.

GEOGRAPHICAL TYPE: European.

DISTRIBUTION: uncertain owing to its confusion in the past with other species, but specifically recorded throughout Europe except Scandinavia, and in Russia confined to the southern regions.

CULTIVATION: generally easy, requiring a soil enriched with leaf-mould or peat, and a situation affording some shade.

VARIETIES: *P.a. acutilobum:* a form in which the pinnules have become extremely narrow and rather delicate in appearance, the outer fronds being more spreading than in the type. Fertile.

P.a. cambricum lonchitioides: very difficult to recognise in the wild, where its occurrence is apparently not uncommon. The enlarged basal lobes of the pinnules are much exaggerated, rather after the manner of *P. lonchitis,* with which it is easily confused. It is also easily confused with young plants of *P.*

setiferum. It has no particular garden merit.

P.a. grandiceps: a magnificent form with a huge terminal crest. Very rare, but fertile, and comes virtually true from spores.

P.a. plumosum: a plumose form with very finely cut pinnules. 45 cm. Very rare.

P.a. pulcherrimum: a very lovely form of an extremely delicate appearance, the pinnules being finely divided and well-spaced on the pinnae midribs, the upper ones curving towards the apex to form a tail. It is normally barren, but spores are very occasionally produced and these have given rise to some of the finest fern varieties known. *P.a.p.* 'Druery' was raised in this way and is even more refined.

P.a.p. gracillimum was similarly raised, and is regarded by many experts, including Mr Reginald Kaye, who is probably the greatest living authority on British fern varieties, as the most beautiful of all varieties of British ferns. The fronds are exquisitely refined, the pinnules being very long and remarkably thin, no more than 2 mm at the widest, with tail-like terminal tassels. Strong-growing. Extremely rare.

Polystichum setiferum
Polystichum angulare
The soft shield fern

Common in the countryside of parts of south-west England and Ireland, and almost as common throughout Europe, this lovely fern has given rise to a greater number of varieties than any other. Well over 300 have been named in the past, and this in itself gives some idea of the variability of the species and, by implication, some idea of the difficulties that may be encountered when trying to identify it in the field. It could very easily be confused with *P. aculeatum*, and the differences between the two species are given under that one. It should be pointed out, however, that young plants are generally harder to identify than mature ones.

DESCRIPTION: moderately robust, monomorphic, semi-wintergreen woodland fern.

Stock: erect, up to 10 cm thick, pseudo-woody, the younger parts densely clothed in large, pale brown lanceolate scales, the older parts densely covered in the stumps of the decayed frond stalks, through which the black, wiry but rather sparse roots push their way to the ground.

Fronds: up to 120 cm, more usually about $\frac{1}{2}$ that length, arranged in a basket-like tuft, spreading outwards in an arching fashion, semi-wintergreen except in really sheltered situations, where it is fully wintergreen.

Stalk: $\frac{1}{4}-\frac{1}{2}$ as long as the blade, deeply grooved on its upper surface, green becoming dark brown towards the base and clothed in large, pale brown, lanceolate scales.

Rachis: lightly clothed in scales similar to those of the stalk, as well as with hair-like scales.

Blade: lanceolate in outline, relatively soft in texture, rather thin, not rigid, bright green above, paler green beneath, the under-surface often having a rather blue-green colouring and being covered with a few scattered hair-like scales.

Branching: bipinnate.

Pinnae: up to as many as 40 on each side of the rachis, linear-lanceolate in outline, arranged alternately on the rachis, becoming sub-opposite and then opposite towards the base, the lower pinnae pinnate, the middle ones deeply pinnatifid, the upper ones less pinnatifid, the apical ones deeply toothed, the terminal segment sickle-shaped.

Pinnules: shortly stalked, (not sessile as in *P. aculeatum*) except towards the apex where they become decurrent and sessile, somewhat crescent shaped, unequal at the base being broadly truncate with a somewhat enlarged lobe on the side nearest the pinna apex, the basal acroscopic pinnule usually being much enlarged.

Venation: Pecopteridian.

Sori: small, round, occurring normally on tertiary veins, and occurring on the ends of the veins (the veins not continuing past the sori as in the case of *P. aculeatum*).

Indusium: circular, peltate.

HABITAT: woodlands, hedgebanks.

GEOGRAPHICAL TYPE: European.

DISTRIBUTION: uncertain owing to former confusion with other species, but certainly throughout Europe into the Mediterranean region.

CULTIVATION: easy in any good garden soil well enriched with leaf-mould or peat, and in a situation affording some shade.

VARIETIES: numerous. E. J. Lowe, one of the early popularisers of pteridomania, described as many as 360 varieties in 1890, but doubtless many of these were in fact duplicates. Druery reduced the number to 173 in 1902, partly by rejecting duplicates and partly by rejecting those forms which were not sufficiently distinct to warrant names of their own or which were not at that time considered of sufficient garden merit to be retained. Mr J. W. Dyce revised Lowe's listing in 1963 to include only those varieties known to be still in cultivation, and Reginald Kaye further systematised Dyce's classification in 1968. It is this assessment that I have followed here.

P.s. acutilobum: an aggregate name embracing a number of forms of differing merit. Many of the forms recorded both by Lowe and by Druery have been lost, but nonetheless many good forms remain. The group is characterised by having fronds narrower than the type, the pinnules being undivided and acute, and further by the production of bulbils in the axils of the pinnae. Usually smaller growing than the type plant—to 60 cm. The following named forms still survive:

P.s.a. crawfordianum: fronds ovate-lanceolate in outline, the rachis less scaly than usual, the pinna teeth tipped with sharp, hair-like points.

P.s.a. 'Hartley': a very compact form with very narrow pinnules set very close together on the pinnae, the fronds not erect but markedly spreading almost to the horizontal.

P.s.a. 'Wollaston': this form is very similar to Hartley's form, but the pinnules are slightly broader, the rachis very scaly, the fronds again spreading, and numerous bulbils occurring in the pinnae axes.

Other varieties include:

P.s. confluens: a rather beautiful variety easily confused with *P.s. lineare*, under which name it might well be included. In this form the pinnules are confluent, very slender and much reduced in length, occasionally absent altogether towards the base of the pinna, though the acroscopic basal pinnule is invariably present and invariably of normal size. A useful garden form, creating a light, airy effect.

P.s. congestum: several congested forms have been recorded, none exceeding 15 cm. The fronds are upright and composed of very dense, overlapping pinnae. Comes absolutely true from spores.

P.s.c. cristatum: is similar to the above, differing from it only in the neat apical crest.

P.s.c. grandiceps: is again similar but differs in its almost ridiculously larger terminal crest.

P.s. conspicuilobum: in this form the deeply incised pinnules are raised and stand out conspicuously, this being particularly true of the basal lobes. Up to 60 cm. This is probably no more than a really good form of *P.s. decompositum*, which is itself a relatively frequently occurring intermediate between the type form and *P.s. divisilobum*.

P.s. cristato-gracile 'Moly': a variety with unusually dark green fronds and small, neat and very regular crests to the pinnae, the pinnules also being subcristate. 60 cm. Fertile.

P.s. cristato-pinnulum: a curious variety, somewhat but not greatly depauperate, those pinnules which are present appearing to have been fixed on the pinna upside down: they are broadly wedge-shaped, the pointed end being the end affixed to the pinnae midrib. Infertile and believed until very recently to be extinct.

P.s. cristatum: really an aggregate name, but typically having neatly crested pinnae. There are several forms in cultivation but they have not been distinguished by epithets.

P.s. cruciato-pinnulum: botanists tend to classify any fern that departs from the typical as 'monstrosities', and in this case most gardeners would probably agree with them. It is certainly 'different', but being different does not necessarily make ferns, any more than people, beautiful. The lower part of the frond bears markedly auriculate wedge-shaped pinnules, while the upper part of the frond is contracted to abnormal narrowness, the pinnae of this part being much reduced in size, and cruciate.

P.s. decompositum: a form in which the pinnae are more deeply incised than normal: intermediate between the type plant and the divisilobum section. Occurs quite frequently in the wild, and spores will often produce even better forms.

P.s. divisilobum: an aggregate, the best forms of which have been given specific epithets. Typically the aggregate is characterised by the finely divided fronds, which are tripinnate or even quadripinnate, the pinnules very slender—those on the basiscopic side usually being larger than those on the acroscopic side. The fronds are spreading, becoming horizontal during winter.

P.s.d. 'Bland': a compact form with the pinnae set close together, the frond being tripinnate at the base, bipinnate in the middle and pinnate towards the apex. Proliferous. 45 cm.

P.s.d. grandiceps: a dwarf form up to 30 cm, and a typical grandiceps with a huge terminal crest. Unlike most grandiceps, the pinnae are not crested.

P.s.d. iveryanum: a proliferous form with well-developed crests on each pinna and a large terminal crest. The fronds are finely divided and completely prostrate.

P.s.d. laxum: a feathery variety with broad fronds in which the finely divided pinnae are widely spaced on the rachis.

P.s. flabellipinnulum: a most unusual and rather lovely variety in which the pinnae are fan-shaped, creating a completely unique effect. A most desirable garden plant, but excessively rare. Probably infertile.

P.s. foliosum: simply a foliose variety, but effective for all that. The pinnules often overlap. Fertile.

P.s. gracile: close to *P.s. lineare*, but differing from that variety in that, although the pinnules are very finely cut indeed, they are not in any way reduced. Very graceful.

P.s. grandidens: a dwarf form to about 30 cm, with deep green fronds, the fronds rather truncate, the pinnules broader than in the type and deeply cut. Fertile.

P.s. latipes: strong-growing with broad fronds and also broad and deeply cut pinnules: dark green in colour. Generally barren, but when spores are produced they seem to breed true. Not particularly outstanding.

P.s. lineare: the most delicate and airy of all forms of *Polystichum setiferum*, and probably of all ferns, it appears at first glance to be a relatively small-growing plant which has been reduced to little more than stalk, rachis and pinna midribs: in fact the pinnae have been vastly reduced, as have the pinnules, which are confluent at the

tips, although as a rule the pinnules nearest the rachis are well developed—almost normal. Barren.

P.s. manica-infantis: this form derives its verietal name from the supposed likeness of the pinnules to the outline of a baby's glove. The pinnules are very small. Comes virtually true from spores.

P.s. multifidum: the apex of the frond is widely and repeatedly branched, giving a tasselled effect.

P.s. plumosom-divisilobum: an aggregate name, some forms of which are sufficiently distinct to have been given their own epithets. Typically the aggregate is characterised by its quadripinnate fronds, these being so finely divided that they create a delightful affect of feathery greenery, among which it is not easy to make out the particular parts of each frond.

P.s.p–d. 'Esplan': almost but not quite as good as *baldwinii*, below, but similarly difficult to reproduce.

P.s.p–d. baldwinii: one of the most beautiful individuals in the aggregate, being exceedingly finely cut. About as rare as it is beautiful. It is sterile, very seldom produces bulbils, and hardly ever divides.

P.s.p–d. spiralis: differs from the characteristic *plumoso-divisilobum* in that all the fronds curve in a clockwise direction, creating a quite distinct effect, the spiral becoming tighter towards the apex.

P.s. plumosum grande 'Moly': a now rather rare but magnificent form with fronds up to 150 cm long and quite exceptionally broad, the

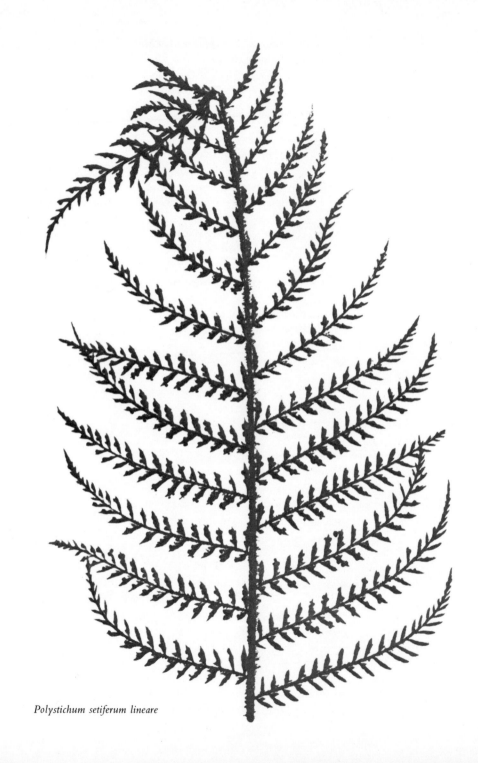

Polystichum setiferum lineare

pinnae themselves so large that they seem almost small fronds.

P.s. polydactylum: in this form the pinnae terminate in long, widely-fingered crests. Rather lovely.

P.s. pulcherrimum: this used to be an aggregate name, but alas only one line of this group remains, known as *P.s.p.* 'Moly's Green'. It is a vigorous grower, inconstant, but when in character the lower pinnules become long, sickle-shaped, and finely-divided to give a featheriness to the fronds. The pinnule tips are aposporous. The plant tends to divide into many crows, and really needs to be divided frequently and kept to a single crown if it is to show off its full grace.

P.s. rotundatum: a distinct form in which the pinnules are almost circular. Very striking. Though fertile, sporelings scarcely if ever come true.

P.s. rotundilobum: very similar to *rotundatum* except that the circular pinnules are decidedly hairy.

P.s. thompsoniae: a curious form in which the sporelings are ramose and densely crested, but in which the mature plants lose the ramose character and retain their fine crests. Comes true from spores.

P.s. tripinnatum: differs from the type only in its usually erect, soft green tripinnate fronds. Not outstanding.

P.s. wakeleyanum: a strong-growing, cruciate form in which the pinnae are arranged in pairs, each pair forming a pair of crosses with the opposite pair. Very delightful.

Pteridium aquilinum
Pteris aquilina
Bracken

The curious thing about bracken is that, although it is by far the commonest fern, both in Europe and in North America, the great majority of people who are not actually aware of the ferns as a distinct group within the flora, do not even realise that bracken is a fern. The chances are if you asked them to name a few common ferns they would not even mention bracken.

Bracken could properly be described as an invasive plant, forming dense undergrowth in woodlands, growing through hedges and even on open hillsides. In the wild, at any rate, it has considerable charm in spring when the soft green foliage first appears, and again in autumn when the dying fronds turn shades of white, yellow and russet.

Bracken is often described as being a nuisance to farmers on whose land it grows, and yet this is not perhaps entirely true. It has for long been regarded as poisonous to livestock, while apparently modern man has never even considered eating it. Yet there is strong archaeological evidence to suggest that the rhizomes were part of the winter diet of prehistoric man, and that the croziers formed part of their spring diet. Recent research suggests that the toxins are only present in the mature fronds, and experiments are being carried out in the West Country of Britain, using young bracken as a grazing crop for cattle.

DESCRIPTION: vigorous deciduous monomorphic, primarily woodland fern, with a deep-rooting, freely-branching rootstock.

Stock: far-reaching, much branched, somewhat flattened in section; up to 3 cm thick, black, roots black, coarse, spreading, produced sparsely along the stock; stock covered with short-jointed dark brown hairs.

Fronds: up to 3 cm, produced alternately along the rootstock; deciduous.

Stalks: erect, rigid, about equal in length to the blade, semi-circular in section, about 1 cm thick, chanelled on the face, swollen towards the base, where it is also black and hairy, becoming straw-coloured and then green.

Rachis: semi-circular in section, deeply channelled on the face, green.

Blade: very large, broadly triangular in outline, and more or less bent back from the vertical axis of the stalk.

Branching: bi- to tripinnate.

Pinnae: sub-opposite, the lowest ones being the largest and shortly stalked, ovate in outline, usually bipinnate, the middle ones sessile, oblong to lanceolate in outline, pinnate with pinnatifid pinnules, the upper pinnae linear-lanceolate in outline, pinnate.

Pinnules: alternate, lanceolate in outline, acuminate; ultimate segments sessile, close-set, confluent, sometimes lobed at the base, margins entire, leathery.

Venation: Neuropteridian.

Sori: linear, occurring all along the margins of the pinnules.

Indusium: following the course of the sorus, the inner one thin, the outer one thick, the outer one always present, the inner one only sometimes present, both fringed with hairs.

HABITAT: woodlands, hedges, hillsides, pastures, invariably on neutral to acid soils.

GEOGRAPHICAL TYPE: Cosmopolitan.

DISTRIBUTION: in the Old World from the Equator northwards into Arctic Europe, though not so far north in Asia, including the Altai mountains, into China, Kamchatka, Japan, the Indian subcontinent, Java, the Philippines, New Zealand: in the New World from sub-Arctic Canada southwards to Mexico.

CULTIVATION: owing to its very spreading and persistent habit, bracken has been little cultivated, although in the past some of its varieties have been grown in wild gardens. Its only requirement is a well-drained acid soil. Some of the varieties are decorative plants for larger gardens. Owing to its invasive character it is best confined within a concrete wall sunk in the ground or within a tough plastic cistern, the bottom of which has been knocked out. It resents transplanting and is not always easy to establish.

VARIETIES: *P.a. caudatum:* although listed as a variety the precise status of this plant is unclear. It is an attractive depauperate form, the pinnules normally being simple and only occasionally pinnate. It is widespread in tropical America,

and confined in the temperate regions to the Florida area.

P.a. crispum: a form with extra dark green, leathery crisped fronds.

P.a. cristatum: the most attractive variety, all the ultimate segments terminating in good crests.

P.a. polydactylum: in this variety some—but not all—of the pinnae terminate in many-fingered crests. Attractive, but inconstant. Fertile.

Thelypteris hexagonoptera
The broad beech fern

This is the larger and more erect-growing of the two beech ferns found in North America. It is distinct from the long beech fern, *Thelypteris phegopteris* (which is also native of the Old World), not only in its taller, narrower fronds but also in its habitat, in preferring sunny, open woodland glades and rather drier situations than the other species, which tend to grow only in very damp woodlands and at streamsides.

DESCRIPTION: medium-sized monomorphic deciduous woodland fern.

Stock: slender, creeping, freely branching, black, very scaly; roots numerous, black, scaly, creeping, branching and forming a very dense tangled mass.

Fronds: deciduous, mid-green, up to 60 cm tall.

Stalks: as long as or slightly longer than the blade, slender, straw-yellow, smooth, becoming darker coloured and slightly hairy and scaly towards the base.

Rachises: green, winged.

Blade: broadly triangular in outline.

Branching: pinnate.

Pinnae: usually about 12 pairs, opposite or sub-opposite, well-spaced, the rachis winged between each pair, the pinnae deeply pinnatifid, the segments lanceolate in outline, coarsely toothed.

Venation: not established.

Sori: small, round, occurring near the pinnular margins.

Indusium: absent.

HABITAT: dryish opening in woodlands and hedgebanks.

GEOGRAPHICAL TYPE: Circumpolar.

DISTRIBUTION: in North America from Nova Scotia to Florida.

CULTIVATION: easy in any woodsy soil in full sun. Fully frost-hardy.

VARIETIES: none recorded.

Woodsia obtusa
The blunt-lobed
woodsia

The commonest as well as the largest of the North American woodsias, it is evergreen in the more northerly reaches of its range, but deciduous further south—or at least semi-deciduous, the fertile fronds remaining green well into the winter, long after the barren fronds have withered. Though technically dimorphic, there is little obvious difference between the two types of frond.

DESCRIPTION: deciduous to winter-green medium-sized dimorphic woodland fern.
Stock: erect, short, stout, very dark brown, thickly beset with dark brown scales; roots coarse, rather sparse, much-branched, with finer roots departing from the main roots.
Fronds: dimorphic, the fertile ones being the taller, up to about 35 cm, and more erect than the barren ones, which are spreading and about ½ that height.
Stalks: orange at the base becoming yellow higher up, brittle, clothed in prominent scales with many white hairs when young.
Rachises: yellowish to brown, shining, slightly scaly, the face slightly grooved.

Blade: lanceolate in outline.
Branching: bipinnate.
Pinnae: opposite, widely spaced, sessile, usually about 12 pairs, triangular-ovate in outline.
Pinnules: irregularly lobed, blunt, decurrent.
Venation: not established.
Sori: produced on the ends of the tertiary veins of the pinnules, nearer the margins than the mid-rib.
Indusium: inflated, cup-shaped.

HABITAT: on limestone formations, in rocky woodland openings, occasionally on cliffs.

GEOGRAPHICAL TYPE: Circumpolar.

DISTRIBUTION: in North America from Canada to Georgia and Alabama and thence westwards to the Pacific.

CULTIVATION: a good plant for a limestone rock-garden where it needs a gritty soil and some direct sunlight. Intolerant of wet conditions. Makes a beautiful pan specimen.

VARIETIES: none recorded.

CHAPTER FOURTEEN

Tree Ferns

The tree ferns are among the most majestic and most beautiful of all ferns, yet none can really be considered truly native to the cool temperate regions of the world. Tree ferns are essentially tropical plants, and it is in the tropics, especially in the tropical rain forests, that they are most at home. They become rarer in the areas furthest away from the Equator, and the two species described here are probably the only two that will tolerate frost at all, and even they are natives of the warm temperate rather than the cool temperate regions of the world.

While the beauty of the tree ferns is probably best appreciated when they are grown as individual specimens, they are in a curious way most impressive when grown in bold groups. When one comes upon them growing like this, whether in the wild or in the garden, it is as though one had suddenly stumbled into the distant geological past. The tree ferns of today are but the diminutive relatives of those great tree ferns which, together with the giant clubmosses and giant horsetails, laid down those seams of coal upon which modern man is so dependent.

The majority of living tree ferns are tropical species, and live under conditions which approximate fairly closely to those of the coal age: they inhabit deep gorges and narrow ravines in the rain forests, forests where there is perpetual rain, where the humidity is constantly above dew-point and where the soil, although constantly wet, contains little nourishment—most of the nourishment having been leached away by the perpetual drainage of the rainwater. When one bears in mind that it is under such conditions that the majority of tree ferns are found, it is not surprising that there are few tree ferns in the cooler regions of the world, and none at all that is native to the cool temperate regions, with their clearly defined warm and cool seasons, and their unpredictable seasons of rain.

The two species described here can only be grown in areas where frost seldom occurs, where the rainfall is high, and where they will be sheltered from strong winds by surrounding trees.

Alsophila colensoi
Cyathea colensoi
The golden tree-fern
The mountain tree-
fern

Although included here as a tree-fern, and usually described as such, it gains entry to this chapter rather on account of its forming a true, vascular trunk than on account of a tree-like habit: although the trunk does occasionally grow erect to a height of one or one and a half metres, it more usually creeps just over the ground, or even sometimes rests right on the ground. It derives one of its common names from the curiously yellow-green colour of the fronds.

DESCRIPTION: wintergreen monomorphic tree-fern.
Stock: a woody, vascular trunk about 10 to 20 cm thick, greyish in colour, deeply scarred where the fronds have fallen from the stem.
Fronds: presented in a spreading, umbrella fashion, up to 150 cm long and as much as 50 cm wide.
Stalks: rachises and pinnae midribs densely clothed with rather soft yellowish or reddish hairs and scales.
Rachis: dark green, densely clothed with rather soft yellowish or reddish hairs and scales.
Blade: broadly triangular, tri-pinnate.
Branching: tripinnate.
Pinnae: bipinnate, up to 25 cm long.
Pinnules: pinnate, the pinnulets deeply incised.
Venation: not established.

HABITAT: shaded mountain gullies.

GEOGRAPHICAL TYPE: Antarctic alpine.

DISTRIBUTION: endemic to New Zealand.

CULTIVATION: not really frost-hardy, and needing cold house cultivation in all but the mildest areas. A highly desirable plant where conditions can be provided that will suit it.

VARIETIES: none recorded.

Dicksonia antarctica
The tree-fern

Probably the best-known and most widely cultivated of the tree-ferns, *Dicksonia antarctica* is, perhaps surprisingly, in some respects at any rate, not the easiest of tree-ferns to cultivate. It does not, like the group of tree ferns formerly known as Cyathea, form a true, vascular trunk. Instead it forms a grossly elongated stock, a caudex of ridiculous length; the 'trunk' in effect is nothing more than a cluster of dead roots, dead stock and dead frond bases, and the living roots have to find their way all the way down through this mass of dead material to the soil to derive nourishment—that at least is the case in cultivation. In the wild, where it grows in conditions of high humidity and the 'trunk' is thickly covered with ephiphytic plants, expecially epiphytic ferns, the roots can in fact feed off the humus collected by

21 *Polystichum setiferum* (page 230).

22 *Polystichum setiferum lineare* (page 233).

these other plants, and the living part of the plant is in effect an epiphytic fern sitting on the top of a constricted column of its own dead matter.

DESCRIPTION: evergreen, monomorphic tree fern.
Stock: stout, up to 30 cm thick, erect, caulescent, ultimately reaching a height of as much as 10 m in its native habitat, though usually less under cultivation. The younger parts are densely clothed with persistent reddish fibre which persists on the 'trunk', becoming darker in colour with age.
Fronds: up to 180 cm long, as many as 30 new fronds being produced each season.
Stalks: rigid, green, densely clothed with rather soft yellowish or reddish hairs and scales.
Rachis: green, rigid, densely clothed with reddish-brown hairs and scales.
Blade: broadly linear.
Branching: bipinnate.
Pinnae: as much as 45 cm long, linear.
Pinnules: deeply pinnatisect, fertile segments somewhat contracted.
Venations: not established.
Sori: numerous on the vein endings.
Indusium: bi-valved.

HABITAT: shaded gullies on high mountains.

GEOGRAPHICAL TYPE: Antarctic-alpine.

DISTRIBUTION: Australia, including Tasmania.

CULTIVATION: somewhat frost-tender and succeeding out of doors only in areas where frosts are light and infrequent. It demands a deep soil rich in humus, but its most important cultural consideration is that the 'trunk' should never dry out, which may mean daily watering, spray-lines being the ideal means of providing the right 'weight' of water. In colder areas it makes an excellent plant for a conservatory, providing that adequate attention is paid to watering.

VARIETIES: none recorded.

CHAPTER FIFTEEN

Epiphytic Ferns

Epiphytic ferns do not form a distinct and homogenous group by reason of any particular evolutionary advance or retardation as do the succulent ferns or the water ferns; nor do they form a distinct and homogenous group by reason of any particular feature of their growth, as do the tree ferns. They are distinct only on account of their habitat, as are wall ferns or mountain ferns. The only thing that is really remarkable about them is that they do not grow in the ground but, typically, on the branches of trees.

An epiphyte is a plant that lives upon another plant but does not derive any nourishment from its host (by contrast, a parasite does derive nourishment from the tissues of its host plant.) An epiphyte does not even penetrate the tissues of the plant upon which it lives: it perches there merely for support. And the fact that many epiphytic plants will grow as happily upon a mossy boulder as upon a tree is proof of this.

Epiphytic ferns will only be found growing in areas of high rainfall and relatively high humidity. They will be found growing on the trunks and branches of trees only in areas where those trunks and branches are well covered by mosses and lichens. The ferns will push their roots through and under the mosses and lichens, which shade them from the sun, and derive their nourishment from the humus that will have formed as a result of the decay of previous generations of the mosses and lichens.

Naturally such ferns are difficult to establish in cultivation in the same manner as they grow in the wild. Usually the only chance of establishing them in such a way is to attach them to the tree with raffia which must be frequently renewed, the roots pressed against the trunk or branch and then covered with a layer of living moss—and even this method is only likely to succeed if the tree is already well covered in mosses and lichens. Epiphytic ferns are generally more easily cultivated in pans, where it is essential that they are provided with extremely sharp drainage and a very open compost.

Asplenium falcatum   A medium-sized epiphytic fern endemic to New Zealand, making a delightful subject for cultivation in sub-tropical gardens in the U.S.A., or in a cold house in the U.K.

Venation: not established.
Sori: very long, reaching from the midrib almost to the pinnae margins.
Indusium: absent.

DESCRIPTION: medium-sized monomorphic wintergreen epiphytic fern.
Stock: slender, creeping, the younger parts clothed with bright brown hairs, the older parts with the stumps of the old fronds; roots very wiry.
Fronds: wintergreen, up to 100 cm long.
Stalks: $\frac{1}{3}$ the length of the blade.
Blade: oblong-lanceolate, dark green above, paler below; erect or decumbent.
Branching: pinnate. Pinnae narrowly triangular, cuneate at the base margins coarsely toothed, sessile.

HABITAT: epiphytic on living trees, fallen boughs, mossy rocks.

GEOGRAPHICAL TYPE: Antarctic alpine.

DISTRIBUTION: the Chatham Islands, New Zealand.

CULTIVATION: will only succeed out of doors in very mild areas, elsewhere needing cold house treatment. Needs a very open compost, and one composted largely of living sphagnum moss being ideal.

VARIETIES: none recorded.

Asplenium flaccidum
The hanging spleenwort

This very variable species can, when growing well, be one of the most dramatic of epiphytic ferns. In spite of its common name, the fronds are not invariably flaccid, but occasionally erect. It is, however, when the fronds are flaccid and pendulous, and the plant is growing on high branches, that it is at its most effective, the fronds of well-developed plants being as much as one metre long.

DESCRIPTION: epiphytic, monomorphic wintergreen fern.
Stock: short, stout, very hairy, with long wiry roots.

Fronds: wintergreen, flaccid and pendulous varying to rigid and erect, up to 90 cm long.
Stalks: about $\frac{1}{3}$ the length of the blade, smooth, dark green.
Rachis: dark green.
Blade: very narrowly lanceolate.
Branching: pinnate.
Pinnae: very narrowly lanceolate almost linear, acuminate, with truncate opposite lobes.
Venation: not established.
Sori: almost entirely covering the lower surfaces of the pinna, oblong.
Indusium: absent.

HABITAT: epiphytic on trees and

mossy rocks, also common in ravines. Both the rigid and the flaccid forms appear botanically identical except in that one feature, and both grow together in all their known habitats.

GEOGRAPHICAL TYPE: Pacific.

DISTRIBUTION: Australia (including Tasmania), several Pacific islands, New Zealand.

CULTIVATION: although plainly not frost-hardy to judge from its habitat, this delightful fern grows well in a cold greenhouse and might be worth experimenting with out of doors in the milder parts of the U.K. It grows well in a hanging basket in live sphagnum moss.

VARIETIES: none recorded.

Asplenium flaccidum

Cyclophorus serpens
Pyrrhosia serpens
The leather-leaf fern

A small-growing wintergreen epiphytic fern which looks like a very simple plant until it is put under a microscope, when it reveals some fascinating features.

DESCRIPTION: medium-sized, monomorphic, creeping epiphytic wintergreen fern.
Stock: slender, creeping, occasionally branching, densely clothed with pale brown scales; roots short, persistent.
Fronds: variable in size even on the same plant, fronds as little as 2 cm long being produced on the same stem and alongside fronds up to 10 cm long.
Stalks: jointed to the stock, running into the blade without differentiation.
Blade: simple, entire, oblong-linear with a rounded apex, grey-green above, thickly covered with a white tomentum underneath: when put under a microscope this tomentum is found to be composed of a myriad of little white star-headed hairs.
Venation: not established.
Sori: numerous, large, scattered in an apparently random manner and virtually hidden by the stellate hairs.
Indusium: absent.

HABITAT: epiphytic on trees, fallen logs, rocks, brickwork, even in quite dry situations.

GEOGRAPHICAL TYPE: Pacific.

DISTRIBUTION: eastern Australia, the Pacific Islands, New Zealand.

CULTIVATION: this is usually treated as a cold house subject in the U.K. but is in fact hardy in mild areas and situations where it can be sheltered from severe frosts. It makes an interesting specimen for a pan, but if the pan is kept on a capillary watering tray one is liable to find the fern rooting all along the tray as well. It also makes an interesting plant for a fern column. It is one of the few ferns that seems capable of recovering from periods of total drought—even in cultivation.

VARIETIES: none recorded.

CHAPTER SIXTEEN

Climbing Ferns

Climbing ferns, like tree ferns, have about them a delightful element of the unexpected. Unfortunately they share another characteristic with the tree ferns, and that is that they are essentially denizens of the warmer parts of the world. Of the two species described here, the Lygodium is the more spectacular, climbing to considerable heights: a similar species grows in Japan, but is perhaps slightly more tender. The other species described here climbs only to the extent that it curls its deciduous fronds around the vegetation among which it grows, and is an altogether rather diminutive plant.

Lygodium palmatum
The Hartford fern

A most unfern-like fern, not only in its climbing habit, but also in its fronds, which scarcely at all resemble the fronds of normal ferns and are much more like the leaves of a vine. Indeed, anyone unaware of the possibility of there being such a thing as a climbing fern, a first encounter with this plant could cause a severe strain on the powers of conjecture. It is an extremely beautiful fern, and has been much over-collected in its native haunts, indeed so much so that it is now protected by law from picking and removal from its habitat. It does, however, come readily from spores.

DESCRIPTION: deciduous or evergreen (depending on provenance) dimorphic climbing fern.
Stock: slender, creeping, cordlike, mainly subterranean, densely hairy, the younger parts clothed with reddish bristles; roots black, coarse, long, branching, anchoring the plant very securely to the ground.
Stem: twining, up to 1.5 m, sinuous, branching, brittle, wiry, smooth except towards the base where it is covered with a few reddish hairs; round, slightly flattened on the face.
Fronds: palmate, produced in pairs on short, dark green wiry stalks which fork about halfway along their length, each frond divided into 5–7 decurrent lobes, each lobe blunt-tipped; margins entire, texture thin, smooth, light green in colour.
Stalks: dark green, wiry.
Blade: simple, palmate.
Venation: not established.
Fertile fronds: borne at the tips of each season's growth, built on the same pattern as the barren fronds

but much reduced in size, the underside of each lobe completely covered in sporangia.

Sori: occurring in two rows on each side of the lobe midribs, there being 2–6 sporangia in each row.

Indusium: consist of overlapping scales.

HABITAT: moist thickets and woodlands.

GEOGRAPHICAL TYPE: Circumpolar.

DISTRIBUTION: endemic to North America from Massachusetts southwards.

CULTIVATION: can only be grown satisfactorily out of doors in frost-free areas or in areas where only the mildest frosts occur, though some forms reputedly more deciduous than others, may prove hardier than hitherto suspected. Needs deep, rich, acid soil and a shrub or trellis over which to climb. Alternatively it makes an ideal plant for the greenhouse border, given wires to climb.

VARIETIES: none recorded.

Lygodium palmatum

Schizaea pusilla
The curly grass fern

Although a climbing fern this is totally unlike the other climbing fern described in this book. In the first place it belongs not only to a different genus, but also to a different family: furthermore, it is totally different in appearance—even its climbing habit is different, this species climbing only perennial herbs. It is a very rare fern, though its rarity has probably been over-estimated since it is extremely difficult to find, even when you know where to look and what you are looking for. It is dimorphic, the barren fronds looking not in the least bit fern-like, and resembling nothing quite so much as blades of common pastureland grass. It is only the fertile fronds that reveal the fern's true nature to the seeking eye. It is probably easiest to find in winter, when its evergreen, sterile fronds are reasonably easy to find among the surrounding dead vegetation.

DESCRIPTION: diminutive winter-green dimorphic climbing fern.
Stock: erect, slender; roots coarse, unbranched but with forked tips.
Fronds: dimorphic, the sterile ones wintergreen, up to 5 cm long, the fertile ones deciduous, up to 8 cm long. Stalks absent, the fronds growing in tufts directly from the stock.

Blade: thread-like, slightly flattened, curled.
Venation: not established.
Fertile fronds: similar except that they are more erect, bent, but not curled, topped by a short, deeply pinnatifid segment consisting of about 5 minute, finger-like lobes on each side.
Sori: small, round, occurring in two parallel rows on each side of the segment midribs, entirely occupying the undersides of the segments.
Indusium: absent.

HABITAT: very wet, acid soils, swamps, bogs.

GEOGRAPHICAL TYPE: restricted.

DISTRIBUTION: also restricted, only a few stations recorded in North America including Newfoundland, Nova Scotia, Carolina and New York.

CULTIVATION: difficult, requiring sphagnum-swamp conditions difficult to reproduce artificially. Far too rare to be collected from the wild. Might succeed in a suitably acid compost in a bottle garden.

VARIETIES: none recorded.

CHAPTER SEVENTEEN

Hybrid Ferns

While the phenomenon of hybridity among flowering plants is familiar to most people, relatively few people are aware that ferns can hybridise, and that such hybrids occur naturally and quite frequently among related ferns, both inter-specific and inter-generic hybrids being known in the wild.

All that happens is that where the prothalli of two related species or genera grow side by side the sperm from one swims across to fertilise the archegonium of the other. The sporeling which then develops is likely to be intermediate between its parents.

Hybrid ferns are probably far more common than is generally supposed, and should be looked for wherever species known to be likely parents of crosses are found growing in close proximity.

No attempt is made here to describe any hybrid ferns, it being taken that they will be intermediate between their parents. The following are some of the hybrids commonly known to occur.

Asplenium × alternifolium	=	*A. septentrionale × A. trichomanes*
Asplenium × badense	=	*A. ruta-muraria × A. ceterach*
Asplenium × clermontiae	=	*A. ruta-muraria × A. trichomanes*
Asplenium × confluens	=	*A trichomanes × A. scolopendrium*
Asplenium × jacksonii	=	*A. adiantum-nigrum × A. scolopendrium*
Asplenium × microdon	=	*A. billotii × A. scolopendrium*
Asplenium × murbeckii	=	*A. ruta-muraria × A. septentrionale*
Asplenium × refractum	=	*A. billotii × A. trichomanes*
D. × pseudoabbreviata	=	*Dryopteris abbreviata × D. aemula*
D. × mantoniae	=	*D. abbreviata × Dryopteris filix-mas*
Dryopteris × dewereri	=	*D. austriaea × D. carthusiana*
Dryopteris × remota	=	*D. assimilis × D. pseudomas*
Dryopteris × subaustriaca	=	*D. austriaca × D. filix-mas*
Dryopteris × tavelii	=	*D. pseudomas × D. filix-mas*
Dryopteris × uliginosa	=	*D. cristatata × D. carthusiona*
Dryopteris × woynarii	=	*D. pseudomas × D. austriaca*
P. × mantoniae	=	*Polypodium interjectum × P. vulgare*
Polystichum × bicknellii	=	*P. aculeatum × P. setiferum*

Glossary

ACROSCOPIC	facing towards the apex of the frond
ACUMINATE	having a gradually diminishing point
ACUTE	sharp-pointed
ALTERNATE	(of pinnae or segments) arising alternately along the rachis, each one higher than the one before
ANNULUS	a group of thick-walled cells usually in the form of a ring; the annulus causes the sporangium to burst when it is ripe
ANTHERIDIUM	the male reproductive organ found on the prothallus
APEX	the tip of the frond, pinna or segment
APOGAMY	production of the fern direct from a bud on the prothallus instead of by sexual fertilisation. There is no meiotic division when the spores are formed so the prothallus contains the full complement of chromosomes and does not need the doubling-up of sexual fusion to produce the sporephyte
APOSPORY	production of prothalli by direct outgrowth of aborted spore capsules on the sites of spore maps (sorel apospory), or from frond, pinna or pinnule tips (apical apospory)
ARCHEGONIUM	the female reproductive organ found on the prothallus
AURICULATE	with ear-like appendages
AXILLARY	occurring in the axil of a frond
BASISCOPIC	facing towards the base of the frond
BIFID	dividing into two parts in fishtail fashion
BIPINNATE	a pinnate frond with pinnate pinnae
BIPINNATIFID	pinnatifid with the segments also pinnatifid
BULBIL	a small bulb-like growth from which young ferns may occasionally be grown
CAESPITOSE	growing in tufts
CONFLUENT	running together
CORDATE	heart-shaped

CORIACEOUS	leathery
CRENATE	(of a pinnae margin) with rounded teeth
CUNEATE	wedge-shaped
DECUMBENT	with the base resting on the ground but the tip upfacing
DECURRENT	(used of the base of a frond segment) running down the stalk below the point of union
DEHISCENCE	the bursting of the sporangium
DELTATE	shaped like an equilateral triangle
DENTATE	toothed
DIMORPHIC	producing both barren and fertile fronds
ENTIRE	a frond whose margin is simple—is not toothed
EPIPHYTIC	growing on another plant but deriving no nourishment from the host
FERTILE	(of fronds) capable of bearing spores
FLACCID	limp, flabby
FROND	that part of a fern (including the stalk) which is called the leaf in any other sort of plant
GLABROUS	free from hairs or glands
GLAUCOUS	covered with bloom
HASTATE	having two large out-turned lobes at the base
INDUSIUM	the membranes that covers the sorus when young
LANCEOLATE	lance-shaped
LINEAR	narrower than lanceolate, with sides parallel for much of their length
MEGASPORANGIUM	sporangium containing megaspores
MEGASPORE	the larger kind of spore found in water ferns
MICROSPORANGIUM	sporangium containing microspores
MICROSPORE	the smaller kind of spore found in the water ferns
MONOMORPHIC	having all fronds fertile
NODE	the joint on a stem from which one or several fronds arise
OBLANCEOLATE	lanceolate with the widest part above the middle
OBLONG	longer than broad, the sides more or less parallel
OBOVATE	inversely ovate with the widest part above the middle
OBTUSE	blunt
OPPOSITE	(of pinnae or segments) arising in matching pairs on each side of the rachis
ORBICULAR	circular in outline
OVATE	egg shaped, broadest towards the base
PALMATE	shaped like a hand, all the segments running together towards a central point

PELTATE	shield-like, with a central stalk
PINNA	the primary division of a compound blade
PINNATE	the segments forming distinct sections along either side of the rachis
PINNATIFID	used to describe a frond or segment that is so deeply cut as to be almost but not quite pinnate
PINNULES	the secondary pinnae
PINNULETS	the tertiary pinnae
PROTHALLUS	the sexual generation of the fern, arising from the germination of a spore
PUBESCENT	clothed with soft hairs
RACHIS	the central midrib of a compound frond excluding the stalk (which is that part below the blade)
RENIFORM	kidney-shaped
RHIZOID	a root-like organ doing little more than anchoring the plant to the ground and not serving the functions of a true root
RHIZOME	a usually fleshy, persistent root
SEGMENT	any division of the frond blade
SERRATE	toothed like a saw
SESSILE	stalkless
SIMPLE	undivided (as opposed to compound)
SINUATE	sinuous, wavy
SORUS	(plural sori) a cluster of sporangia
SPORANGIUM	(plural sporangia) a capsule containing spores
SPORE	dust-like particle produced on the fertile fronds of ferns which, when it germinates, gives rise to the prothallus (q.v.)
SPOROCARP	a ball-like body containing sporangia (occurring only in the Marsileaceae)
SPOROPHYTE	the spore-bearing, non-sexual generation of the ferns
STOCK	that section of the plant from which both roots and fronds arise
STOLON	an underground stem capable of producing a new plant at its tip
TERRESTIAL	a fern that grows in the ground (as opposed to an epiphyte)
TRUNCATE	terminating abruptly as if cut off square
ULTIMATE	(of segments) the apical segment
VENATION	the arrangement of the veins on a frond or part of a frond

Bibliography

N.B. The fullest possible information is given, but in some instances—especially with older books—it has not been possible to trace details of publisher, date of publication, etc.

ALLEN, D. E.	*The Victorian Fern Craze* Hutchinson 1969
BELLAIRS, N.	*Hardy Ferns: How I collected and Cultivated Them,* London, 1865
BOLTON, J.	*Filices Britannicae* 2 vols Leeds circa 1785 and Huddersfield 1790
BOWER, F. C.	*The Ferns* 3 vols Cambridge University Press 1923–28
CHANTER, C.	*Ferny Combes* London 1856
COBB, B.	*A Field Guide to the Ferns* The Riverside Press Cambridge Massachusetts 1956
DRUERY, C. T.	*British Ferns and their Varieties* London 1910
DURAND, H.	*Field Book of Common Ferns* Putnam New York and London 1928
FOSTER, F. G.	*The Gardener's Fern Book* van Nostrand 1964
FRYE, T. C.	*Ferns to Know and Grow* Hawthorn New York 1971 *Ferns of the Northwest* Binitfords and Mort Courtland Oregon 1934
HIBBERD, S.	*The Fern Garden* London 1860
HOOKER, W. J.	*The British Ferns* London 1861 *Species Filicum* 5 vols London 1846–64
HYDE, H. A., WADE, A. E., and HARRISON, S. G.	*Welsh Ferns* National Museum of Wales, 5th edition 1969
JOHNSON, C. and SOWERBY, J. E.	*The Ferns of Great Britain* J. E. Sowerby London 1855 and 1859
KAYE, R.	*Hardy Ferns* Faber and Faber 1968
LOWE, E. J.	*Fern Growing* London 1895 *Ferns, British and Exotic* 8 vols London 1867

	Our Native Ferns 2 vols London 1867–69
MACSELF, A. J.	*Ferns for Garden and Greenhouse* Collingridge 1952
MANTON, I.	*Problems of Cytology and Evolution in the Pteridophytat* Cambridge University Press 1950
MOORE, T.	*The Ferns of Great Britain and Ireland (Nature Printed)* London 1855
	Handbook of British Ferns (2nd ed.) London 1853
	The Octavo Nature Printed British Ferns 2 vols London 1859–60
	A Popular History of British Ferns London 1859
NEWMAN, E.	*A History of British Ferns and Allied Plants* London 1840 (later editions embrace ferns only).
PARSONS, F. T.	*How to Know the Ferns* New York 1899 Reprinted by Dover Books, 1961
SHAVER, J. M.	*The Ferns of Tennessee* George Peabody College for Teachers
SMITH, J.	*Ferns British and Foreign* London 1866
SOWERBY, J. and SMITH, J. E.	*English Botany* London 1891–92
TAYLOR, P. G.	*British Ferns and Mosses* Eyre and Spottiswood (in the Kew Series) 1960
VERDOORN, Fr. (Ed.)	*Manual of Pteridology* Nijhoff The Hague 1938
WHERRY, E. T.	*The Fern Guide* Doubleday 1961
	The Guide to Eastern Ferns The Science Press Lancaster PA 1937
WILLIAMS, B. S.	*Hints on the Cultivation of British and Exotic Ferns and Lycopodiums* London 1852
WILLIS, J. H.	*A Handbook to Plants in Victoria* Melbourne University Press 1962

APPENDIX

Fern Societies

Anyone with any real interest in ferns, whether in the wild or in cultivation, but particularly the latter, would benefit greatly by joining a fern society. These societies provide a common meeting ground for people with a common interest in ferns. Furthermore, for anyone keen on obtaining rarer varieties, it is only by swapping plants with other members of these societies that one is able to obtain many of the real treasures. They are simply not available in commerce. The societies help in many other ways. They organise fern hunting expeditions, often aimed either at establishing whether or not certain rare natives have survived in their recorded stations from earlier times, and often at hunting down rare natives or hybrids of which rumours have been heard but no positive identification made. At the same time no one should hesitate to join one of the fern societies merely because he feels that, although interested in ferns, he does not know enough to have a contribution to make to the society. The societies are there to help beginners and experts alike, and new members are always welcomed. They will benefit particularly from the advice and help of more senior members, especially when it comes to identifying ferns in the field, where an expert can show you in a moment the revealing detail between one species and another that you could spend hours poreing over a book trying to work out for yourself. If you have the slightest interest in ferns, *do* join a fern society.

The following are the main fern societies, and intending members should write to the following:

THE AMERICAN FERN SOCIETY	c/o Smithsonian Institution, Washington, D.C., U.S.A.
THE LOS ANGELES INTERNATIONAL FERN SOCIETY	Wilbur W. Olson, Membership Chairman, 2423 Burritt Avenue, Redondo Beach, California 90278, U.S.A.
THE BRITISH PTERIDOLOGICAL SOCIETY	Secretary J. W. Dyce, 46, Sedley Rise, Loughton, Essex.

THE JAPANESE PTERIDOLOGICAL SOCIETY	c/o Dr K. Iwatsuki, Dept. of Botany, Faculty of Science, Kyoto University, Kyoto, Japan.
THE NELSON NEW ZEALAND FERN SOCIETY	c/o Miss K. H. Stocker, Mapua, via Nelson, New Zealand.
THE NIPPON FERNIST CLUB	c/o Professor Satoru Kurata, Dept. of Forest Botany, Faculty of Agriculture, Tokyo University, Hongo, Bunkyo-ku, Tokyo, Japan 113.

(Names and addresses correct at the time of writing).

Index

Numbers in italics refer to illustrations